Excel for the CEO

P.K. Hari Hara Subramanian

Holy Macro! Books

Excel for the CEO
© 2006 Holy Macro! Books

Written by:
P.K. Hari Hara Subramanian

Edited by:
Linda DeLonais

On the Cover:
Design by Shannon Mattiza, 6'4 Productions.

Published by:
Holy Macro! Books
PO Box 82
Uniontown, Ohio, USA 44685

Distributed by:
Independent Publishers Group

First printing:
September 2006.
Printed in the United States of America

Library of Congress Data
Excel for the CEO / P.K. Hari Hara Subramanian
Library of Congress Control Number: 2006931382

ISBN: 1-932802-17-7

Table of Contents

Acknowledgements .... a

About the Author .... e

Starting off on the Right Foot 1

   Basic Terminology 2

      Title Bar 3

      Menu Bar 3

      Active Cell 3

      Toolbar Collections 3

      Toolbar Collections 4

      Help Bar 4

      Minimize / Maximize and Close Buttons 4

      Task Pane / Task Selector 4

      Task Pane / Task Selector 5

      Rows and Columns 5

      Formula Bar 5

      Name Box 6

      Scroll Bars 7

      Tab Scrollers 7

      Status Bar 8

   Creating, Saving, Opening, and Closing Workbooks and Worksheets ... 9

      Creating Workbooks 9

      Saving Workbooks 10

      Opening Workbooks 11

      Closing Workbooks 12

   Navigating in Excel – Within a Worksheet and Between Workbooks ... 12

   Selecting Cells, Rows and Columns, Non-adjacent Cells ... 13

   Editing, Updating, and Deleting Data – Ways Available ... 16

      Copying Data 16

      Moving Data 17

      Updating and Deleting Data 17

      Formatting Cells and Data 19

   Sheet Background, Name, Hiding, and Unhiding ... 21

      Entering Functions in Excel 21

   Entering Formulas in Excel 23

   Creating Charts – the Basics 24

Excel-lent Tips 27

   Activating the Menus 28

   Accessing the Toolbars with the Keyboard 29

Basic and Common Shortcut Keys..**29**
    Shortcuts with the Ctrl Key Combination 31
    Ctrl Key with Special Keys...34
    Ctrl Key with Function Keys 35
Shortcuts Using the Shift Key..**36**
    Shift Key with Numeric Pad Keys 36
    Shift Key with Function Keys and Other Keys......................................37
Shortcuts Using the Alt Key **38**
    Alt Key with Numeric Keys 39
    Alt Key with Alphabet keys 39
    Alt Key with Function Keys 40
    Special Shortcut Keys 40
Shortcuts Using the Function Keys...**44**
Twenty Terrific Excel Tips **45**
Links for More Tips...**51**
    Best Keyboard Shortcuts for Selecting Data 51
    Best Keyboard Shortcuts for Moving in a Workbook............................51
    Best Keyboard Shortcuts to Use with Functions and Formulas 51

Formulas, Functions, and More... .... **53**
What Is a Formula and How Does It Work?..**54**
    The Operator Precedence Rules...55
    Relative vs. Absolute Referencing..56
Introducing Array Formulas **57**
Common Error Messages in Formulas..**59**
How are Functions Different from Formulas? **59**
What are the Categories and Components of Functions?........................**60**
Financial Functions **61**
    Depreciation-related Functions 62
    Annuity-/Investment-related Functions..64
    Functions for Interest Computation 66
    Examples...66
Date and Time Functions **68**
    Examples of Time-related Functions 70
    Examples of Date-related Functions 71
Math, Trig, and Statistical Functions..**71**
    Math and Trig functions 72
    Statistical Functions..76
Lookup and Reference Functions..**78**
Database Functions **83**
Text Functions..**85**
    Examples of Text Functions 89
Logical Functions...**90**
    Practical Application of Logical Functions 91

Information Functions 91
    Practical Application of Information Functions..94
Nesting Functions...94
    Example of Multi-level Nesting 96
Troubleshooting and Evaluating Formulas and Functions................................97
Conclusion 101

Data Management in Excel 103
Database Management – the Basics...104
Data Management Functions Available in Excel...105
    Creating a Database 106
Sorting a Database 109
    Steps in Data Sorting 109
Filtering Data – AutoFilter and Advanced Filter 112
    AutoFilter...112
    Advanced Filter...116
Subtotals, Grouping and Outlining...120
    Grouping and Outlining 123
Data Validation Feature 125
Converting Text to Columns / Importing Text Data 130
Sound Interesting?...135

Advanced Data Management in Excel 137
Database Functions – the Concept 138
Detailed Listing of Database Functions..139
Using Database Functions 142
    DSUM Function...143
    DCOUNT Function..144
    Other Functions 144
Working with Data Tables..145
    Data Table Based on Two Variables 150
Creating and Managing Lists..152
    Advantages of Using a List..153
    Step-by-Step Process of Creating a List 154
Consolidation of Data 156
    Consolidation Using 3D Formulas 157
Importing External Data 159
Handling XML data..162
More Terrific Links...163
PivotTables, PivotCharts, and Reporting 165
Introducing PivotTables...166
When Should You Use a PivotTable? 166
Creating a PivotTable...167
Filtering and Modifying Fields within a PivotTable 174

Sorting Data and Listing Specific PivotTable Items...........................176
    Listing the Top / Bottom Items 178
    Drill Down Facilities 180
    Using Calculated Fields...183
PivotTable Report Formatting Options 188
PivotTable Field Settings..190
Things You Should Know When Using PivotTables 192
    Refreshing Data...192
    Changing the Range of Source Data 193
    Table Options...193
    Show Pages 195
Creating a PivotChart...196
Links for More Information 200

Auditing Tools.. **201**
Introducing Auditing Tools 202
Formula Auditing Toolbar 203
Error Checking Feature...203
    The Rules and What They Check for 206
    Other Buttons in the Error Checking Dialog Box................206
Tracing Precedents 207
Tracing Dependents..208
Removing Tracing Arrows 209
Trace Error Option 210
New Comment / Edit Comment Option.....................................210
Circling Invalid Data...211
Clearing Validation Circles..214
Showing Watch Window 215
Evaluate Formula Option 217
    Tips for Using Formula Evaluator 219
Tracking Changes Made to a Workbook 219
Viewing and Printing Formulas in Any Sheet............................221
    Example Using the Formulas Checkbox.............................222
Viewing and Printing Comments and Errors 223
    Controlling the Printing of Comments 225
    Controlling the Printing of Cell Errors 225
Related Links..226

Formatting and Printing Reports **227**
Print Preview Options and Zooming..228
Controlling Print Selection, Page, Cells, and Copies..................230
    Selecting Pages to Print...231
    Controlling Print Copies...231
    Printing to a File..232

Setting, Removing Page Breaks; Page Break Preview 232
Print Area – Setting, Clearing.. 235
Page Control – Orientation, Size, Scaling, Quality 236
Alignment Control – Margins, Centering Report 238
Headers and Footers, First Page Numbers 239
Controlling Sheet Properties During Printing... 241
Printing Charts.. 243
Four More Topics 244
    Massive Printing of Blank Pages 244
    Pages per Sheet Option 244
    Printing to PDF... 245
    Copying Page Setup Options Between Different Sheets............................ 246
For Further Study.. 247

Adding Interactivity and Publishing Reports on the Web 249
Saving as a Web Page.. 250
Publishing an Entire Workbook on a Web Page 253
Publishing One Worksheet / Range / Other Items....................................... 254
Publishing a Chart on a Web page 258
Publishing a PivotTable Report on a Web Page.. 259
Further Information… 261

An Introduction to VBA 263
What Is a Macro and What Is It Used for?... 264
Recording a Macro – the Toolkit... 265
Writing a Macro - the VBE Window 269
Running a Macro 270
Other Advanced Topics and Links 271

Case Studies 273
Peter F. Drucker's Advice to CEOs 274
    Duties of the CEO 274
    Key Decision Making Points 275
    OK, But Where Does Excel Come in? 276
Reviewing Projects and Their Profitability... 277
Checking Delivery Schedules Using Gantt Charts 282
Comparing Excel Worksheets/Workbooks 286
    Comparison Process 288
Financial Analysis Models – Creation and Automation 290
Having Your Own Menu Bar.. 294
Control Reports Using PivotTables 298
    Step-by-Step Construction of the Control PivotTable 301
Using Conditional Statements for Reporting 304
Controlling Entry of Dates – the Dating Problem!....................................... 309

Some Interesting Examples..**311**
    Using Word Count in Excel 311
    Showing Formulas in Different Color.................................... 311
    Deleting Empty Worksheets.. 312
    Sorting All Sheets by Name... 312
    Forcing Caps on Entry 312
    Deleting Every nth Row 313
    Merging Data of Multiple Columns into One Column 313
    Merging the Selection into One Cell 314
    Inserting a Blank Row Between Every Row of Data 314
    Coloring Alternate Rows with a Distinct Shade.................... 315
    Using VBA to Print Your File to PDF 315

Goal Seek and Scenario Builder **317**
Using Goal Seek...**317**
Using Scenario Builder **320**
Other New Techniques and Developments...........................**327**
    Dashboard Charting Techniques 327
    New Techniques with PivotTables 327
    New Techniques with Charting.. 327
    Resources and Examples for the Finance People................ 327
    Other Interesting Developments 328

One Journey Ends – Another Begins.....................................**329**
A Word of Conclusion **330**

Appendix A – Finding and Launching Excel **331**
Where to Find Excel **331**

Appendix B – Excel's Roots **333**
How Did It All Start – Weaving the Excel Magic......................**333**

Index **335**

Dedications

To my parents, who have raised me to be a knowledge-seeker, and my family and friends, who have always encouraged me to continue learning and sharing knowledge.

Acknowledgements

"We are what we repeatedly do. Excellence, then, is not an act, but a habit."

Aristotle

Though I am an accountant by profession, I am known more in my industry for my skills with the PC, and with Excel®, especially. This is so because I have spent a considerable portion of my life-time in refining and automating business processes. Having tried different spreadsheet programs, I settled on Excel as the best suited, since it has got a wide range of features and is almost fully customizable.

All the knowledge that I have acquired so far about Excel and automation possibilities is creditable to many individuals, to whom I owe a lot for sharing their terrific knowledge, support, and motivation. The list is long and nearly endless, but I shall include at least a few of them here for their specific and direct contributions to this project.

My thanks and appreciation goes to Mr. Sriram Vaidheeswaran (Scope Intl, India) for initiating me into a career in computers, to Mr. V. L. Parameshwaran (Senior Auditor) and Mr. K. R. Sundaram (Sr. Consultant-KG Group, India) for their continued support to me in developing automation tools, and also to Mr. L. Mallikharjuna Rao (Sr. Partner – Brahmayya & Co,

Auditors, India), Mr. R. Ramaraj (CEO, SIFY, India), Mr. K. Thiagarajan (CFO, Cognizant Technology Solutions, India), Mr. T. R. Santhana Krishnan (Co-Founder and Vice Chairman, Quscient Technologies, India), Mr. Sriram Subramanya and Ms. Anu Sriram (Directors – Integra Software Services Pvt Ltd, India), Mr. John P. Joseph (Director, Blue Rhine Group, Dubai) and to Mr. S. L. Jobanputra (Director, Henley Group, U.K.) for their continued support and wonderful opportunities provided to me during my professional career.

My interest in developing solutions with Excel took on a completely different dimension with the support and morale-lifting words of Anne Troy Pierson (aka Dreamboat), and also by interaction and support from experts in the field like Brad Yundt, Brett Dave, Bill Jelen, John Walkenbach, Jon Peltier, Debra Dalgleish, and many others.

Preparing and presenting the contents of this book required a lot of work, a tough task while trying to cope with pressures of work and home. But when you are assisted by someone who is able and understanding, it becomes a joyful journey – my wife Priya made it one such wonderful experience for me to complete this book well in time. She was my first-draft reader, the best critic, and helper of various sorts for me in this project, and she has sacrificed a lot of time from her personal life so that I can realize my dream.

Special thanks also goes to Linda DeLonais, editor of this book, who took a lot of care and interest in asking the most relevant editorial queries and sought better solutions from me so that the readers get the best input. I am short of words to express my gratitude to the publishers, who have given me such a wonderful opportunity to express and share my thoughts. Finally, my sincere thanks to each and everyone of you readers, for choosing to buy this title and in encouraging me further to develop more titles using my specialized "Do & Learn" approach.

To quote my favorite, Aristotle, again,

> "One must learn by doing the thing, for though you think you know it, you have no certainty until you try."

Do remember that you work hard to get good and then again work hard to get better. There is a simple 3P's recipe for success – it is Patience, Perseverance and Practice.

All the Very Best to Excel with Excel®,

P.K.Hari   Dubai

pkhariaiyer@gmail.com   June 2006

www.hari.ws

About the Author

P.K. Hari Hara Subramanian

P.K. Hari *FCA, ACS & CISA (US)* is an accountant by profession, and is working as the Group Financial Controller for a large group of companies. P.K. Hari is a certified Master of Microsoft Excel and is one of the features experts with www.experts-exchange.com. With a very rich and varied work experience acquired by his employment in three different continents of the world, P.K. Hari commands the best knowledge of the theory and use of various Computer Applications, especially Microsoft Excel. His experience as a mid-level and top-level manager and also as a business owner has provided the perfect angle of top management thoughts and an easy-learning solution model with which he has tailored the learning approach.

Starting off on the Right Foot

Welcome aboard! This book is your guide on a journey into the mysteries of Excel. This is a never-ending, ever-exploring adventure that tunnels you deep into Excel's secrets.

Let's start with the basics. You may already know some of this information; nevertheless, give it a quick read – you just might get to know some useful info that you haven't come across elsewhere. If you have never ventured into Excel before, take a look at Appendix A to find out how to locate and launch Excel. If you are really supremely confident of your basic Excel foundations, please feel free to skip this chapter and plunge into Chapter 2 – Excel-lent Tips starting on page 27 – for insights into the secrets of, and tips on using, Excel.

Topics in this chapter:

- Basic terminology

- Creating, saving, opening, and closing workbooks

- Navigating in Excel – within a worksheet and between workbooks

- Selecting cells, rows, and columns, and non-adjacent cells

- Editing data, updating and deleting data – ways available

- Formatting cells and data

- Worksheet background, name, hiding and unhiding

- Entering functions in Excel

- Entering formulas in Excel

- Creating charts – the basics

Basic Terminology

Before proceeding further, let's review some basic Excel terminology. It will make life simpler for you and speed your progress if you spare a couple of minutes to familiarize yourself with these terms.

The following figure shows the locations of the workbook components that we are going to discuss in this section:

Figure 1   Basic components in a typical Excel workbook

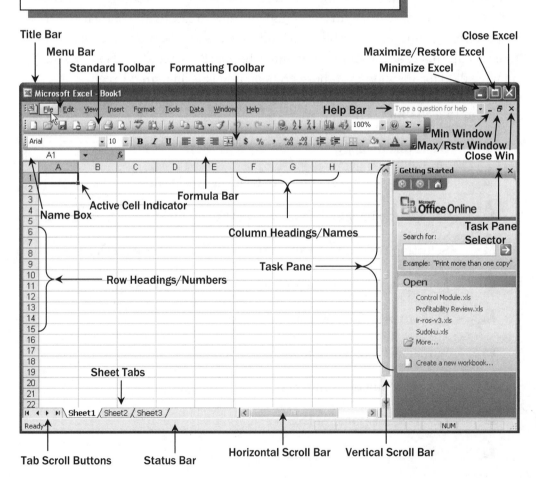

Title Bar

This bar reflects the names of both the Application and the Active File (the one that is currently open) – in this case, "Microsoft Excel – Book1". You can change the appearance to show your own name (amazing, but true!) like this – "Sam's Excel – Book1". Want to know how ? Hang in there – the answer is in the next chapter of tips and tricks!

Menu Bar

You probably know what a Menu bar is – it contains a collection of all the menu functions available in the application. But did you know that you can customize this, too – that you can have your own personalized menu of functions listed there like this – "John's Tools"? You will learn how in one of the case studies.

Active Cell

The current working cell is called the Active Cell in Excel as well as in VBA. The Active Cell is identified with a thick black border around the cell that makes it obvious.

 Note:

The row and column headings of the active cell are highlighted in different color shades than the others to make it easier to identify the current working row and column.

Toolbar Collections

You will see the Standard and Formatting toolbars in the snapshot in **Figure 1**, but these are but a small selection from a huge list of toolbars available in Excel. These two are the most widely used, and are normally placed within one row to maximize the working area. There are almost 20 different toolbars, and if you were to place each one of them in a separate row on the screen, you would be left with just one row in Excel's working area! We will get to know more about the relevant toolbars throughout the book. Certain tools are pretty cool and easy to work with. The more you explore and work with them, the more familiar and comfortable you will become with Excel.

Help Bar

This is available only with the latest editions of Excel, and it provides you with an instant search box, thus simplifying Help and making the Help bar preferable to the conventional F1 key (although that still works).

Minimize / Maximize and Close Buttons

There are two sets of these buttons – one at the Application level (Excel level) and another one at each worksheet or window level. You can choose to minimize, maximize or restore, and also to close Excel using one of these buttons.

 Tip:

Shortcut keys:

Ctrl+F9 keys – Minimize
Ctrl+F10 keys – Maximize / Restore
Alt+F4 keys   – Close application

Task Pane / Task Selector

The Task Pane is a standard component with all of Excel's latest editions; it helps you to "quick pick" a task. You can show or hide it by pressing the Ctrl+F1 keys or by clicking on Task Pane on the View menu. The Task selector (an arrow type of clickable indicator) lets you select one of several possible tasks such as Help, Workbook, Clip Art, Document Updates, and so forth.

 Note:

The Task pane always includes links to Microsoft Office online for various searches. You can easily turn off these links. Click on the tasks selector, select Help. Once you are in the Help screen, select the "See Also" section at the bottom and then click on the "Online Content Settings". Clear the checkbox on the item "Show content and links from Microsoft Office Online".

Rows and Columns

A worksheet is comprised of many cells, each of which is formed by the intersection of a row and a column. Until recently, the maximum number of rows available in Excel was 65,536 (numbered from 1 to 65536) and the maximum number of columns available was only 256 (named from A to IV). A cell is identified by its name, which is formed by a combination of the column name followed by the row number, such as C4.

Formula Bar

The formula bar displays the contents of the current selected cell (also called as the active cell), and is especially useful when you want to introduce or edit a formula. This is because Excel, by default, shows only the *results* of the formula in the cell. When you want to know what formula is

 Tip:

Press F2 to access a cell's formula.

being used or to edit that formula, you need to access it – either directly in the formula bar or by pressing F2 while in the active cell.

As with many other things in Excel, you can control whether or not you want to see the Formula bar. Go to Tools → Options → View tab and clear the checkbox under "Show: Formula Bar" – this will hide the Formula bar. The same option is also available under "View → Formula Bar". This will be especially useful when you want to protect your Excel file, which we will about learn in due course.

There are three more small buttons available to the left of the formula bar marked with arrows (see **Figure 2**). Of these three, the X and tick mark buttons (X, ✓) are available only when you are entering something in a cell. Use them either to cancel (X) or to go ahead with your entry in the cell (✓). The function wizard (f_x) helps you to select and insert the desired function into the active cell.

Figure 2

The formula bar and its accessories

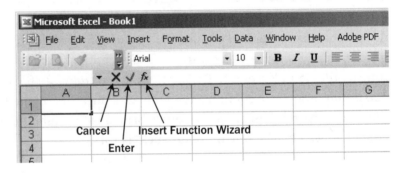

Name Box

The name box is one of the most ignored and least used features of Excel. However, it is very handy when you are navigating in a big worksheet and you have a fairly good idea of which row and column number you want to view. In that case, click on the name box, type your address (for example, AA375), and then press Enter. You go right there. The name box is also very useful when you have defined ranges; you can select one of the available ranges using the drop down box in the Name Box field.

Scroll Bars

No explanation required for this one – just a quick mention that Excel has both horizontal and vertical scroll bars that adjust with the size of the work area. The vertical area is almost full size when the worksheet is empty – indicating that there are only around 30 rows in the immediate working area. As you keep adding data to the file, the vertical scroll bar keeps adjusting to accommodate each addition.

Let us say you enter some info in A200 – you will see the vertical scroll bar become smaller in size; when you pull it down to the bottom, you will reach A200. This is a very helpful navigation feature. Pulling the vertical scroll bar to its last point has the same effect as pressing the Ctrl+End keys, which takes you to the last active cell in the current worksheet.

Tab Scrollers

You may have used tab scrollers in MS-Access® under the data sheets/ forms. In Excel, the tab scrollers are used in very much the same way. When there are too many sheets, you cannot see all of the names within the available work area. You can choose to see the left- or right-most sheet by selecting the left- or right-most scroll button. Or you can choose to browse through the left or right side, sheet by sheet, by using the second (browse left) or third (browse right) button.

Status Bar

The Status bar shows the current status of Excel – it says either "Ready" or "Enter" or indicates "Circular Reference" or "Calculate", and so forth, depending on the circumstances.

The right side portion of the status bar indicates whether the Num Lock and Caps Lock are on or off and also shows you the Sum Total of the values in the current selection. You can easily change it to show either the sum or average, count, min or max of the values currently selected. Just right-click on the right side of the Status bar, and you can select which of these operations to show. The default selection is Sum, and it is very handy to see the total of items in a selection without having to insert a SUM formula somewhere in the sheet.

The illustration in **Figure 3** will give you an idea of how this works.

Figure 3

Status bar – using it for quick, handy calculations

Tip:

The Status bar also can be turned on or off like the formula bar (either by Tools – Options or from View – Status Bar).

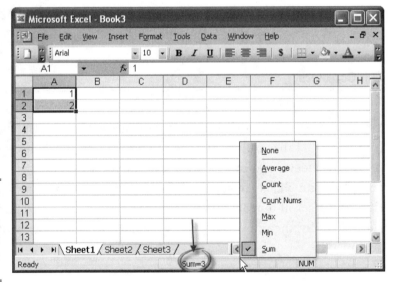

Creating, Saving, Opening, and Closing Workbooks and Worksheets

What we call a Workbook is actually a collection of Worksheets. Each Excel file is called a workbook, and each file can contain from one to as many as 1000+ worksheets (in Excel XP, the number of worksheets in a workbook is limited by available memory). In earlier versions, the default number of worksheets was 14, but in the latest versions, it is only three. You can customize Excel to open new workbooks with a specified number of worksheets by visiting Tools → Options and selecting your preferred number under "Sheets in new workbook:".

Creating Workbooks

Once you have opened up Excel, you will be welcomed with a new workbook, unless you have set up a different option (explained below).

To create a new workbook, just press Ctrl+N keys or select New from the File menu at the top.

Did you realize that you can select a set of files always to be opened up by default when you open Excel? You can set this option from the window in Tools → Options; specify a directory in the line marked "At Startup, open all files in:" (marked with an arrow in Figure 4).

 Tip:

You can use this feature to point to a standard directory containing just one or two files having your things to do or reminders.

 Caution!

Excel will open any and all files located in the specified directory. It will not make any distinction between Excel files or other files. If there are too many files in the directory, it will just try to open up all the files placed there, and you might end up getting stuck!

Figure 4   Setting up selected files to open by default at Excel startup

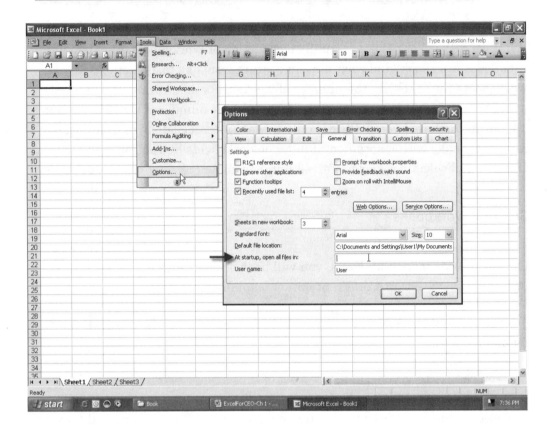

Saving Workbooks

It is simple to save workbooks – just press Ctrl+S or select Save from the File
Menu. You can also press F12 to bring up the **Save As** dialog box to save the
file as a new copy or to save a file with a new name.

 Note:

Even if you try to close a file by mistake without saving it, Excel prompts you with
this question: "Do you want to save changes to Book1?" and gives you options of
Yes, No, and Cancel.

Opening Workbooks

You can open workbooks in several different ways: by selecting File → Open from the menu, by clicking on the Open Folder icon in the standard toolbar, or by pressing Ctrl+O (O for Open). The Ctrl+F12 keys also do the same job, except that Excel will open up the My Documents page by default and ask you to select your file.

If you are really organized and you store your Excel documents in a properly identified location (let us say, D:\Assignments\Excel Docs), you will get tired of selecting this path every time you open Excel. There are two solutions – one is to create a shortcut to this location in the My Documents folder so that you can select it straightaway. The second option is to make this folder your default file location folder. This option is available from the menu item "Default file location", available under Tools → Options. (refer to **Figure 5** – the area marked with a double sided arrow).

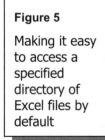

Figure 5

Making it easy to access a specified directory of Excel files by default

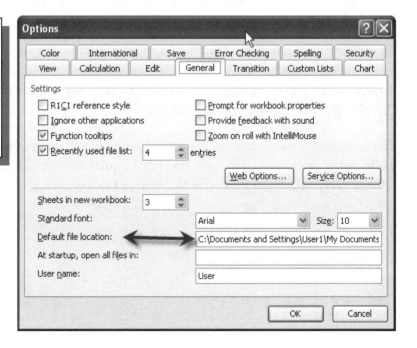

Closing Workbooks

You can close a file by any of these methods:

> ➢ Select File → Close from the menu.

> ➢ Click on the "X" button at the right corner of the window (Close Window).

> ➢ Press the Ctrl+W keys.

> ➢ Press the Ctrl+F4 keys.

If you have not saved your work so far, Excel will ask you to decide at the point of closing the file.

Navigating in Excel – Within a Worksheet and Between Workbooks

The tab scrollers are there to help you to see the different sheets. When you know the sheet that you want, just click on the Sheet name to go there. Alternatively, you can press the Ctrl+Pg Dn keys to go to the next sheet, and Ctrl+Pg Up keys for the previous sheet.

You can glide through the worksheet by using either the mouse or the keyboard. You can also use the name box to quickly jump to a location, or, alternatively, press the F5 key to bring up a **Go To** dialog box.

Tip:

You can scroll through the worksheet without changing the active cell by turning on Scroll Lock. This can be useful if you need to view another area of your worksheet and then quickly return to your original location.

Just press Scroll Lock and use the direction keys to scroll through the worksheet. When you want to return to the original position (the active cell), press Ctrl+Backspace. Then, press Scroll Lock again to turn it off.

When Scroll Lock is turned on, Excel displays SCRL in the status bar at the bottom of the window.

When you have two or more workbooks open, use the Ctrl+F6keys to cycle through the workbooks.

Selecting Cells, Rows and Columns, Non-adjacent Cells

Selecting a cell is as simple as pointing to it and clicking – or just moving there with the keyboard. When you are trying to select a range of cells, just keep pressing the Shift key until you finish your selection.

For example, when you want to select from B3 to F4, first go to B3, press the Shift key, and then click on F4. Or go to B3 first, press the Shift key, and then the right arrow and down arrow keys until you have selected through F4.

Selecting an entire row or column is very easy with the mouse – click on the row number or the column name – the entire row or column gets selected at one go.

When you are trying to select non-adjacent cells, you have to depend on the mouse with the Ctrl key combination. Select your first cell, press the Ctrl key, and then click on your second point; continue clicking on your

Tip:

Shortcut to select entire row – Shift+Spacebar

Shortcut to select entire column – Ctrl+Spacebar

selections while keeping the Ctrl key pressed. That's it – Cool!

Figure 6 shows you how to use the Ctrl key to select cells so that you can see the sum total of various cells in the status bar. This saves you a lot of time and effort.

Figure 6

Selecting and making a quick calculation with non-adjacent cells

 Tip:

A couple of very rarely known and seldom used shortcuts – Use the F8 key to select a continuous range of cells; use Shift+F8 keys to select non-adjacent cells – more details in Chapter 2.

Table 1

List of keys and resulting navigation

Key	Navigation
Up arrow	Moves the active cell up one row
Down arrow	Moves the active cell down one row
Left arrow	Moves the active cell one column to the left
Right arrow	Moves the active cell one column to the right
PgUp	Moves the active cell up one screen
PgDn	Moves the active cell down one screen

Table 1	Key	Navigation
List of keys and resulting navigation	Alt+PgDn	Moves the active cell right one screen
	Alt+PgUp	Moves the active cell left one screen
	Ctrl+Backspace	Scrolls to display the active cell

When Scroll Lock is on (Status bar displays "SCRL"), the following happens without any change of Active Cell position:

Table 2	Key	Navigation
List of keys and resulting navigation when Scroll Lock is on	Up arrow	Scrolls the screen up one row
	Down arrow	Scrolls the screen down one row
	Left arrow	Scrolls the screen left one column
	Right arrow	Scrolls the screen right one column

Other Keys in Used Navigation

It is vital to remember the shortcut keys for quick navigation in Excel. If you are using a wheel-mouse, the AutoScroll feature of the wheel makes things even simpler. Just click on the wheel and then select a direction to navigate – it will do the auto scrolling and the speed can be controlled by a subtle movement of the mouse.

Also, with a wheel-mouse you can quickly adjust the zoom level of the window by pressing the Ctrl key and then moving the wheel forward or backwards. This will zoom the window in or out, respectively.

 Tip:

Always experiment with the shortcut menus available with the right-click option of the mouse at various locations and under different conditions. You normally get options for cut, copy, paste, insert, delete, clear contents, format, hyperlink, plus a host of other things you can do, depending on where you are.

Editing, Updating, and Deleting Data – Ways Available

•

Editing data can take many forms such as copying, moving, updating, replacing, and deleting. Take a look at how to accomplish each of these actions.

Copying Data

This procedure copies information so that it remains in its original cell(s) and a duplicate appears elsewhere.

Step 1 – Select the cell(s) containing the information that you want to copy and then click on the Copy icon, located on the Standard toolbar.

Step 2 – Select the blank cell(s) into which you want to copy the information.

Step 3 – Click on the Paste icon (see Figure 7) located on the Standard toolbar, or press Ctrl+V, or just press the Enter key.

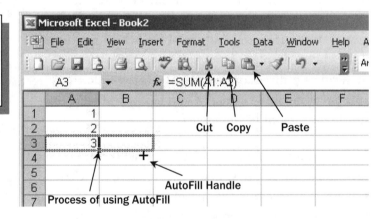

Figure 7

Cut, Copy, and Paste buttons, AutoFill in progress.

Keys	Navigation
Ctrl+C keys	Copy
Ctrl+V keys	Paste

Table 3

List of shortcut keys for copying data

Keys	Navigation
Ctrl+R keys	Copy right (copy formula from immediate left cell to active cell

Moving Data

This procedure moves information from one location to another.

Step 1 – Select the cell(s) containing the information that you want to move.

Step 2 – Click on the Cut icon (see Figure 7) or press the Ctrl+X keys.

Step 3 – Move to the cell where you want to place the item. Now Click on the Paste icon or press Ctrl+V, or just press the Enter key.

 Note:

When you use the Enter key in copy and move situations, Excel will paste the data into the active cell(s) and clear it from the clipboard. If you are using Ctrl+V or the Paste icon, it will retain the copied information in memory until you press the Esc key, which enables you to use the data in multiple non-adjacent cells before clearing it from the clipboard.

An alternative to using Copy and Paste to copy information or formulas to adjacent cells is to use the AutoFill feature. If you want to copy a cell to the cells below it or to its right, position your cursor over the small black box in the lower right corner of the cell. The big white plus sign cursor should change to a thin black one. Drag and drop to the left or right, up or down to copy the cell's data or formula to the empty cells (see **Figure 7**).

Updating and Deleting Data

When you want to replace some data in a field, just go to that field and start typing over it. It is as simple as that. If you want to alter or update the existing data, click on the formula bar to edit that data. Alternatively, once you are in the relevant cell, press the F2 key to start editing the data.

The Delete key on the keyboard is available at all times if you want to delete the entire contents of the cell or the selection. Equivalents of this are available in the Edit menu and also in the right-click shortcut menu as "Clear Contents". Under the Edit menu, the Clear selection offers more options – to clear only formats, contents, comments, or all.

To delete the cells and shift the other data closer, select the data and then select "Delete" from the right-click menu. You will be prompted to select from four options – to shift cells left or up after deleting current data and to delete the entire row or column. The options window is shown in **Figure 8**.

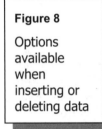

Figure 8

Options available when inserting or deleting data

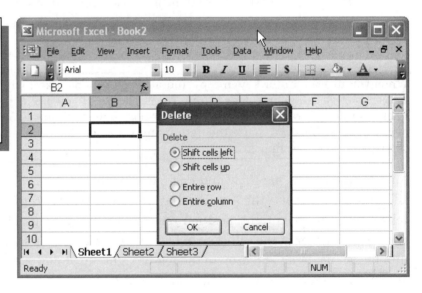

The same menu can be displayed from the Edit → Delete menu item or by pressing the Ctrl and – (Hyphen/Minus) keys together after selecting your data for deletion.

A similar set of four options is available when you are trying to insert some data in Excel. Select the area where you want to insert data and then go to

Edit → Insert. You will see choices very much like the Delete choices. You can also invoke this option can from the right-click menu or by pressing the Ctrl and + (Plus) keys together.

Formatting Cells

Formatting and Datacan take different forms – formatting of numbers, text, borders, colors and shades, patterns, visibility and protection, and alignment. We will see each one of these in brief below.

Formatting of numbers is easy with the Currency button (shown as $ in the toolbar) along with the "%" button, the "," button, and buttons for increasing and decreasing decimal points. Each of these is self-explanatory. Try your hand at it and you will see how easy it is.

Formatting text has many options with buttons on the toolbar for Font, Size, Color, and so on. Many more options are available under the Format → Cells menu, which can also be invoked from the right-click menu.

The Format menu also has a "Style" option available for more advanced users, where you can define your defaults for alignment, protection, font size, and so forth, and then store this configuration as one of your styles. You can then easily apply your custom style to your data.

There are many more functions available for formatting data such as the Borders, Color Shadings, Pattern Fills, Alignments – both horizontal and vertical, Shrink to Fit, Wrapping of Text, Text Orientation, and Strikethrough Effects. All of these are available under the Format → Cells menu item and are easy to use. Just play around with these effects in a dummy worksheet to understand more about them. The **Format Cells** dialog box (see Figure 9) provides a brief description of each option, making even easier to use.

Figure 9   Format Cells Dialog Box from menu choice, Format → Cells (or use Ctrl+1 to quickly bring up the Format Cells menu item)

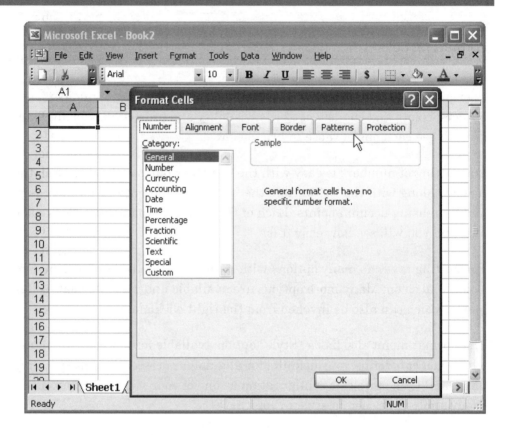

There is one last tab under the **Format** dialog box containing the "Locked" and "Hidden" properties. These are really useful only when you need to protect a workbook, which we will discuss in detail a little later on our journey.

Sheet Background, Name, Hiding, and Unhiding

The Format group on the Excel menu bar has "Sheet" as one of the sub items. Under this, we have options of Renaming the Sheet and Hiding and Unhiding Sheets. It is a logical requirement that at least one sheet should remain unhidden while all the other sheets can be hidden.

The latest versions of Excel also allow you to keep a different color for each worksheet under the same workbook. Once you select a color for a particular sheet, the sheet name will still remain black, but the background of the text will take the color that you have chosen. To see the color effect of the sheet you set, select some other sheet so that the set color is fully visible.

You can also customize Excel to show your Company's logo or corporate design in the background while you display or discuss certain vital MIS reports in the foreground. It is pretty easy to bring about this change through the menu item Format → Sheet → Background, where you can select any picture to use as the tiled background for the current Excel worksheet (remember, the worksheet only and not the workbook).

Entering Functions in Excel

Excel has more than 300 built-in functions for use in any worksheet, simplifying their use for the financiers, scientists, and statisticians alike. The functions are organized and categorized for the various types of users and are available under Insert → Function on the Main menu bar. SUM, MIN, MAX, COUNT, AVERAGE, ROUND, RAND, and IF are some of the most frequently used functions.

To enter a function into a particular cell, place your cursor in that cell and select Insert → Function from the menu. You can also invoke the Function Wizard from the button near the formula bar (also from AutoSum Wizard's dropdown menu in the Standard toolbar) (see **Figure 10**). The Function Wizard presents a window showing the list of available functions – select the one you want. The wizard will prompt you to enter the relevant criteria for the formula; once that is done, Excel will output the result into the same cell.

Figure 10   Invoking the Function Wizard (Shortcut key: Shift+F3)

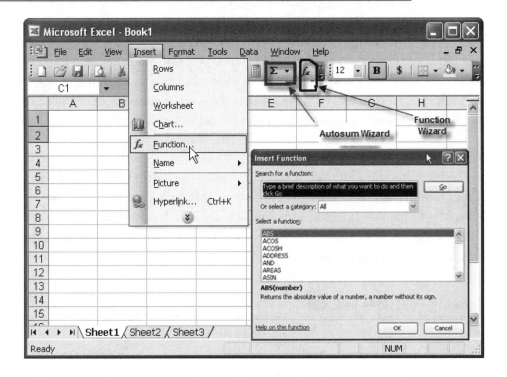

Excel also lets you write your own function using VBA and then to call (use) the function in your worksheet. We will discuss more about these advanced features in the chapters to come.

 Tip:

Call the Function Wizard by pressing Shift+F3 while in any cell.

Entering Formulas in Excel

With Excel, you can create your own small formulas to do the basic arithmetic and logical functions such as add, subtract, multiply, and divide by applying the standard operators available in Excel to any of the cells in a worksheet.

For example, Figure 11 shows how to add up the values of cell A1 and cell C3 and to display the result in cell F2.

Figure 11

Using a basic arithmetic formula in Excel

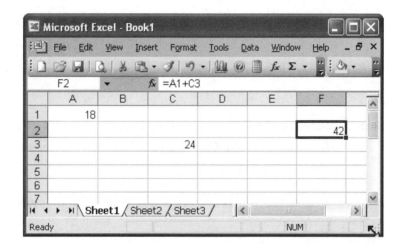

Formulas are different from functions only to the extent that we create them in the application interface using the standard operators available. In fact, you can write advanced formulas using VBA in the background and then call them for use as a custom function, which we will cover further down the road.

Creating Charts – the Basics

Charts allow you to graphically display the data. As it is said, a picture is worth a thousand words; information is more easily understood and assimilated if it is provided in a graphic form rather than as tens of hundreds of rows of numbers.

Excel lets you automatically generate more than 70 different varieties of charts, once you have the base data ready. There is a Chart Wizard on the Standard toolbar that you can also select by going to Insert → Chart on the Main menu bar.

With the Chart Wizard, creating a chart from your data is an easy four-step process:

Step 1 – Select the cells containing your data, including the headings as the first row (use the Ctrl key to select a non-adjacent set of data, as mentioned on page 13).

Step 2 – Invoke the Chart Wizard using one of the previously noted options.

Step 3 – Select the type of chart, feed in the legend, axis title, and other such options as required. Confirm the data source (it is already selected).

Step 4 – Select where to place the chart (the location) – whether as part of the current sheet or as a new sheet – and then click on Finish.

The process is so simple – you now have a wonderful chart in front of you that conveys much more than numbers alone.

 Tip:

If you are happy with the default settings for chart type – series names, and so forth – it is even simpler to create a chart. Just select the data and press the F11 key to create a chart and display it in a new worksheet. Cool, isn't it?

Figure 12 shows you an example of the Chart creation steps, as well as the source data and resultant Chart – all in one quick glance.

Figure 12   Using the Chart Wizard to create a basic 3D column chart

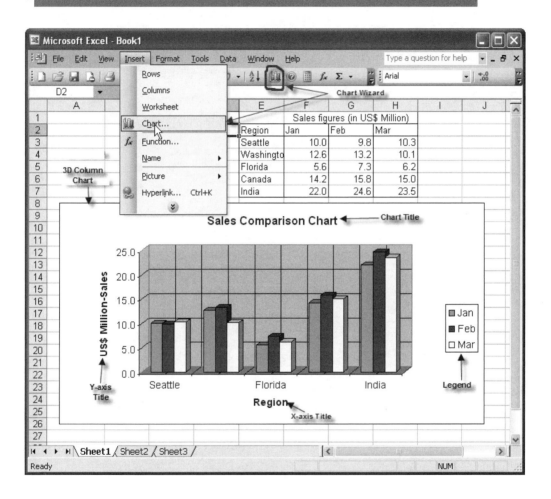

We will learn more about using the advanced features of charting as we go along.

Now that you have a handle on the basics, we can move ahead for a quick dip into the secrets behind Excel that can increase your operation speed and amaze your friends and colleagues alike.

Excel-lent Tips

Master the tips in this chapter, and you will be well on your way to being an Excel power user. You are about to enter a fascinating area that has mostly been the exclusive realm of professionals in this field. A great deal of effort has gone into preparing this chapter to make it as comprehensive as possible – and, false modesty aside, perhaps the best collection ever of tips on using Excel!

Topics in this chapter:

- Activating the menus
- Accessing the toolbars with the keyboard
- Basic and common shortcut keys
- Shortcuts using the Ctrl key
- Shortcuts using the Shift key
- Shortcuts using the Alt key
- Other shortcut keys
- Function keys
- Twenty terrific Excel tips
- Links for more tips

Activating the Menus

There are at least three different ways to activate the Menu bar from the keyboard.

➢ Press the F10 key.

➢ Press the Alt key.

➢ Press the Forward Slash (/) key.

Once the menu is activated, you can use the arrow keys to move sideward or to pull down the menu.

If you know your particular menu item's Hot Key (indicated by an underlined letter – for example, the letter D is underlined in the <u>D</u>ata menu item), then it is even easier to bring up that menu. To pull down the Data menu, simply press the Alt and D Keys together (Alt+D).

Similarly, each sub-menu item contains a hotkey to enable quick selection by keyboard. For instance, to select the Filter sub-menu item under the Data menu, press Alt+D first and then immediately press F.

The most important sub-menu items will have their own keyboard shortcuts (look for the underlined letters under the menus). The Print menu is an example. You can bring it up by first pressing Alt+F (to invoke the File menu) and then pressing P. You can also go directly to the Print menu by using its independent shortcut – pressing the Ctrl+P keys.

Accessing the Toolbars with the Keyboard

You may already know how to use the toolbars – to just click on a toolbar icon to do a particular action, such as Print Preview. But can you select the same toolbar icon without a mouse?

Here's how:

Step 1 – Activate the Menu bar by pressing Alt or Forward Slash (/) or F10.

Step 2 – Press Ctrl+Tab; you will go to the first toolbar set available.

Step 3 – Use your arrow keys to navigate; select an item by pressing Enter.

Step 4 – Press Ctrl+Tab to go to the next open toolbar set, say the Formatting toolbar.

Basic and Common Shortcut Keys

As a practiced user of Excel, I strongly recommend that you start using the keyboard shortcuts as often as possible. Don't worry if you cannot memorize or remember everything immediately. Pick some of the most important keyboard shortcuts and start using them. After using a shortcut three or four times, you will have it locked in your mind. Once you have a few of these under your belt, you will speed through tasks in Excel, and anybody seeing you working in Excel will be amazed at your speed with the menus and submenus.

Table 4 shows the most common shortcut keys.

Table 4 Chart of common Shortcut keys	Shortcut Keys	Effect
	SHIFT+F11 or ALT+SHIFT+F1	Insert a new worksheet.
	CTRL+SHIFT+PLUS SIGN	Insert blank cells.

		Shortcut Keys	Effect
Chapter 2	**Table 4** Chart of common Shortcut keys	F11 or ALT+F1	Create a chart that uses the current range.
		ALT+DOWN ARROW	Display the AutoComplete list.
		CTRL+9	Hide the active row.
		CTRL+SHIFT+9	Unhide the active row.
		CTRL+0	Hide the selected columns.
		CTRL+SHIFT+0	Unhide the active column.
		CTRL+D	Fill down (copy from cell immediately above).
		CTRL+R	Fill to right (copy from cell to immediate left).
		CTRL+; (semicolon)	Enter the date.
		CTRL+SHIFT+: (colon)	Enter the time.
		CTRL+ENTER	Fill the selected cell range with the current entry.
		SHIFT+F5	Display the **Find** dialog box.
		SHIFT+F4	Repeat the last **Find** action (same as **Find Next**).
		F5	Display the **Go To** dialog box.
		CTRL+1	Display the **Format Cells** dialog box.

Why bother with shortcuts? Often times it is more efficient to keep your hands on the keyboard rather than jumping from the keyboard to the mouse and back again, over and over. If time is money and wasted motion is wasted time … well, you get the point. Read on!

Shortcuts with the Ctrl Key Combination

Shortcuts with a Ctrl key combination can be grouped under four subheadings. Ctrl key plus:

> ➤ Numeric keys   1, 2, 3, ...

> ➤ Alphabet keys   a, b, c, ...

> ➤ Special / Other keys   !, @, #, ...

> ➤ Function keys   F1, F2, F3, ...

Ctrl Key with Number Keys

Table 5 shows common shortcuts with a Ctrl combined with a numeric key.

Table 5 Chart of common shortcuts with Ctrl/number keys	Shortcut Keys	Effect
	CTRL+1	Display the **Format Cells** dialog box.
	CTRL+2	Apply or remove bold formatting.
	CTRL+3	Apply or remove italic formatting.
	CTRL+4	Apply or remove underlining.
	CTRL+5	Apply or remove strikethrough.
	CTRL+6	Alternate between hiding objects, displaying objects, and displaying placeholders for objects.
	CTRL+7	Display or hide the **Standard** toolbar.
	CTRL+8	Display or hide the outline symbols.
	CTRL+9	Hide the selected rows.
	CTRL+0	Hide the selected columns.

Ctrl Key with Alphabet Keys

Table 6 shows common shortcuts with a Ctrl key combined with an alphabet key.

Table 6

Chart of common shortcuts with Ctrl/alphabet keys

Shortcut Keys	Effect
CTRL+A	Select the entire worksheet.
	If the worksheet contains data, CTRL+A selects the current region. Pressing CTRL+A a second time selects the entire worksheet. When the insertion point is to the right of a function name in a formula, displays the **Function Arguments** dialog box.
CTRL+ SHIFT+A	Insert the argument names and parentheses when the insertion point is to the right of a function name in a formula.
CTRL+B	Apply or removes bold formatting.
CTRL+C	Copy the selected cells.
	CTRL+C followed by another CTRL+C displays the Microsoft Office Clipboard.
CTRL+D	Perform the **Fill Down** command to copy the contents and format of the topmost cell of a selected range into the cells below.
CTRL+F	Display the **Find** dialog box.
SHIFT+F5 SHIFT+F4	Also displays this dialog box; Repeats the last **Find** action.
CTRL+G	Display the **Go To** dialog box.
F5	Also displays this dialog box.
CTRL+H	Display the **Find and Replace** dialog box.
CTRL+I	Apply or remove italic formatting.
CTRL+K	Display the **Insert Hyperlink** dialog box for new hyperlinks or the **Edit Hyperlink** dialog box for selected existing hyperlinks.
CTRL+L	Display the **Create List** dialog box.

Table 6

Chart of common shortcuts with Ctrl/alphabet keys

Shortcut Keys	Effect
CTRL+N	Create a new, blank file.
CTRL+O	Display the **Open** dialog box to open or find a file. CTRL+SHIFT+O selects all cells that contain comments.
CTRL+P	Display the **Print** dialog box.
CTRL+R	Perform the **Fill Right** command to copy the contents and format of the leftmost cell of a selected range into the cells to the right.
CTRL+S	Save the active file with its current file name, location, and file format.
CTRL+U	Apply or remove underlining.
CTRL+V	Insert the contents of the Clipboard at the insertion point and replace any selection. Available only after you cut or copy an object, text, or cell contents.
CTRL+W	Close the selected workbook window.
CTRL+X	Cut the selected cells.
CTRL+Y	Repeat the last command or action, if possible.
CTRL+Z	Perform the **Undo** command to reverse the last command or to delete the last entry you typed.
CTRL+ SHIFT+Z	Uses the **Undo** or **Redo** command to reverse or restore the last automatic correction when AutoCorrect Smart Tags are displayed.

Ctrl Key with Special Keys

Table 7 shows common shortcuts with a Ctrl key combined with a special key.

Table 7

Chart of common shortcuts with Ctrl/special keys

Shortcut Keys	Effect
CTRL+(	Unhide any hidden rows within the selection.
CTRL+)	Unhide any hidden columns within the selection.
CTRL+&	Apply the outline border to the selected cells.
CTRL+_	Remove the outline border from the selected cells.
CTRL+~	Apply the General number format.
CTRL+$	Apply the Currency format with two decimal places (negative numbers in parentheses).
CTRL+%	Apply the Percentage format with no decimal places.
CTRL+^	Apply the Exponential number format with two decimal places.
CTRL+#	Apply the Date format with the day, month, and year.
CTRL+@	Apply the Time format with the hour and minute, and AM or PM.
CTRL+!	Apply the Number format with two decimal places, thousands separator, and minus sign (-) for negative values.
CTRL+-	Display the **Delete** dialog box to delete the selected cells.
CTRL+*	Select the current region around the active cell (the data area enclosed by blank rows and blank columns).

	Shortcut Keys	**Effect**
Table 7		In a PivotTable, select the entire report.
Chart of common shortcuts with Ctrl/special keys	CTRL+:	Enter the current time.
	CTRL+;	Enter the current date.
	CTRL+`	Alternate between displaying cell values and displaying formulas in the worksheet.
	CTRL+'	Copy a formula from the cell above the active cell into the cell or the Formula Bar.
	CTRL+"	Copy the value from the cell above the active cell into the cell or the Formula Bar.
	CTRL++	Display the **Insert** dialog box to insert blank cells.

Ctrl Key with Function Keys

Table 8 shows common shortcuts with a Ctrl key combined with a function key.

	Function	**Effect**
Table 8	CTRL+F1	Close and reopen the current task pane.
Chart of common shortcuts with Ctrl/function keys	CTRL+F3	Displays the Insert Name → Define dialog box.
	CTRL+F4	Close the selected workbook window.
	CTRL+F5	Restore the window size of the selected workbook window.
	CTRL+F6	Switch to the next workbook window when more than one workbook window is open.
	CTRL+F7	Perform the **Move** command on the workbook window when it is not maximized. Use the arrow keys to move the window, and when finished press ESC.
	CTRL+F8	Perform the **Size** command (on the **Control** menu for the workbook window) when a

	Function	Effect
Chapter 2		
	Table 8	workbook is not maximized.
	Chart of common shortcuts with Ctrl/function keys	
	CTRL+F9	Minimize a workbook window to an icon.
	CTRL+F10	Maximize or restore the selected workbook window.
	CTRL+F11	Insert a new Excel 4.0 Macro Sheet into the workbook and make that the default screen.
	CTRL+F12	Bring up the File → Open command.

Shortcuts Using the Shift Key

Shortcuts with a Shift key combination can be grouped under three subheadings:

➢ Numeric Pad keys

➢ Function keys

➢ Other keys

Shift Key with Numeric Pad Keys

Table 9 shows common shortcuts with a Shift key combined with a numeric pad key.

	Function	Effect
Table 9	SHIFT+1	Effect of "End" key
Chart of common shortcuts with Shift/numeric pad keys	SHIFT+2	Effect of "Down arrow" key
	SHIFT+3	Effect of "Pg Dn" key
	SHIFT+4	Effect of "Left arrow" key
	SHIFT+6	Effect of "Right arrow" key

Table 9	Function	Effect
Chart of common shortcuts with Shift/numeric pad keys	SHIFT+7	Effect of "Home" key
	SHIFT+8	Effect of "Up arrow" key
	SHIFT+9	Effect of "Pg Up" key
	SHIFT+.	Effect of "Del" key
	SHIFT+Enter	Effect of "Up arrow" key
	SHIFT+/	Activates Menu Bar
	SHIFT+-	Effect of SHIFT + F8 (see table below)

Shift Key with Function Keys and Other Keys

Table 10 shows common shortcuts with a Shift key combined with function keys and other special keys.

Table 10	Function	Effect
Chart of common shortcuts with Shift/function and other special keys	SHIFT+SPACEBAR	Select the current row.
	SHIFT+TAB	Move one cell to the LEFT
	SHIFT+ENTER	Move one cell or row UP.
	SHIFT+ALT+F1	Insert a new blank worksheet.
	SHIFT+F2	Enter or edit a cell comment in the active cell.
	SHIFT+F3	Paste a function into a formula – Insert Function.
	SHIFT+F5	Pop-up the **Find** dialog box.
	SHIFT+F6	If task pane is open, alternate cursor between the task pane and work area. If there are split panes, switch to the previous pane in a worksheet that has been split.

	Function	Effect
Table 10 Chart of common shortcuts with Shift/function and other special keys	SHIFT+F8	Add a non-adjacent cell or range to a selection of cells by using the arrow keys. For instance, if you want to sum up the cell values in A1:A2 and also in E1:E2, simply block the cells A1:A2 first and press SHIFT+F8 (status bar will show "ADD"). Move to E1, press Shift, and select up to E2. Repeat the procedure for any additional cells; the status bar will show the sum of the selected cells.
	SHIFT+F9	Calculate the active worksheet.
	SHIFT+F10	Bring up the right-click menu (shortcut menu).
	SHIFT+F11	Insert a new blank worksheet in the current workbook.
	SHIFT+F12	Activate the "Save As" functionality of Excel.

Shortcuts Using the Alt Key

Shortcuts with Alt key combinations can be grouped under four subheadings:

➢ Numeric keys

➢ Alphabet keys

➢ Function keys

➢ Other keys

Alt Key with Numeric Keys

Table 11 shows common shortcuts with the Alt key combined with a numeric key.

Table 11

Chart of common shortcuts with Alt/numeric keys

Function	Effect
ALT+1	☺
ALT+2	☻
ALT+3	♥
ALT+4	♦
ALT+5	♣
ALT+6	♠
ALT+7	•
ALT+8	◘
ALT+9	○

Alt Key with Alphabet keys

Table 12 shows common shortcuts with the Alt key combined with an alphabet key.

Table 12

Chart of common shortcuts with Alt/alphabet keys

Function	Effect
ALT+D	Invoke Data menu.
ALT+E	Invoke Edit menu.
ALT+F	Invoke File menu.
ALT+H	Invoke Help menu.
ALT+I	Invoke Insert menu.
ALT+O	Invoke Format menu.
ALT+T	Invoke Tools menu.

	Function	Effect
Chapter 2 **Table 12** Chart of common shortcuts with Alt/alphabet keys	ALT+V	Invoke View menu.
	ALT+W	Invoke Window menu.

Alt Key with Function Keys

Table 13 shows common shortcuts with the Alt key combined with a function key.

Table 13 Chart of common shortcuts with Alt/function keys	Function	Effect
	ALT+F1	Insert a new chart based on selected data (same as F11 Key).
	ALT+F2	Invoke the **Save As** dialog box.
	ALT+F4	Quit Excel (Closing all open workbooks).
	ALT+F8	Invoke the **Macros** dialog box (to select and run or create a macro).
	ALT+F11	Open up the VBA interface – the VBA Editor.

Special Shortcut Keys

Table 14 shows common shortcuts with special keys in particular circumstances.

Table 14 Chart of shortcuts with special keys	Function	Effect
	ESC	Cancel an entry in the cell or Formula Bar; can also close an open menu or submenu, dialog box, or message window.
	TAB	Move one cell to the right in a worksheet. Move between unlocked cells in a protected worksheet.

Table 14

Chart of shortcuts with special keys

Function	Effect
	Move to the next option or option group in a dialog box.
SHIFT+TAB	Move to the previous cell in a worksheet or the previous option in a dialog box.
CTRL+TAB	Switch to the next tab in dialog box.
CTRL+SHIFT+TAB	Switch to the previous tab in a dialog box.
SPACEBAR	In a dialog box, perform the action for the selected button, or selects or clears a check box.
CTRL+SPACEBAR	Select an entire column in a worksheet.
SHIFT+SPACEBAR	Select an entire row in a worksheet.
CTRL+SHIFT+SPACEBAR	Select the entire worksheet.
	If the worksheet contains data, press CTRL+SHIFT+SPACEBAR to select the current region. Press CTRL+SHIFT+SPACEBAR a second time to select the entire worksheet. When an object is selected, press CTRL+SHIFT+SPACEBAR to select all objects on a worksheet.
ALT+SPACEBAR	Display the **Control** menu for the Excel window.
BACKSPACE	Delete one character to the left in the Formula Bar; can also clear the content of the active cell.
ENTER	Complete a cell entry from the cell or the Formula Bar, and select the cell below (by default).
	In a data form, move to the first field in the next record.
	Open a selected menu (press F10 to activate the menu bar) or perform the action for a selected command.

Table 14 Chart of shortcuts with special keys		

Function	Effect
	In a dialog box, perform the action for the default command button in the dialog box (the button with the bold outline, often the **OK** button).
ALT+ENTER	Start a new line in the same cell.
CTRL+ENTER	Fill the selected cell range with the current entry.
SHIFT+ENTER	Complete a cell entry and select the cell above.
ARROWS	Move one cell up, down, left, or right in a worksheet.
CTRL+ARROW	Move to the edge of the current data region (data region: a range of cells that contains data and that is bounded by empty cells or datasheet borders) in a worksheet.
SHIFT+ARROW	Extend the selection of cells by one cell.
CTRL+SHIFT+ ARROW	Extend the selection of cells to the last nonblank cell in the same column or row as the active cell.
LEFT ARROW or RIGHT ARROW	Select the menu to the left or right when a menu is visible. When a submenu is open, these arrow keys switch between the Main menu and the submenu.
DOWN ARROW or UP ARROW	Select the next or previous command when a menu or submenu is open.
	In a dialog box, use arrow keys to move between options in an open drop-down list or between options in a group of options.
ALT+DOWN ARROW	Open a selected drop-down list.
DELETE	Remove the cell contents (data and formulas) from selected cells without affecting cell formats or comments.

	Function	Effect
Table 14 Chart of shortcuts with special keys		In cell editing mode, delete the character to the right of the insertion point.
	HOME	Move to the beginning of a row in a worksheet.
		Move to the cell in the upper-left corner of the window when SCROLL LOCK is turned on.
		Select the first command on the menu when a menu or submenu is visible.
	CTRL+HOME	Move to the beginning of a worksheet.
	CTRL+SHIFT+ HOME	Extend the selection of cells to the beginning of the worksheet.
	END	Move to the cell in the lower-right corner of the window when SCROLL LOCK is turned on. Select the last command on the menu when a menu or submenu is visible.
	CTRL+END	Move to the last cell on a worksheet, in the lowest used row of the rightmost used column.
	CTRL+SHIFT+END	Extend the selection of cells to the last used cell on the worksheet (lower-right corner).
	PAGE DOWN	Move one screen down in a worksheet.
	ALT+ PAGE DOWN	Move one screen to the right in a worksheet.
	CTRL+ PAGE DOWN	Move to the next sheet in a workbook.
	CTRL+SHIFT+ PAGE DOWN	Select the current and next sheet in a workbook.
	PAGE UP	Move one screen up in a worksheet.
	ALT+PAGE UP	Move one screen to the left in a worksheet.

	Function	Effect
Table 14 Chart of shortcuts with special keys	CTRL+PAGE UP	Move to the previous sheet in a workbook.
	CTRL+SHIFT+ PAGE UP	Select the current and previous sheet in a workbook.

Chapter 2 (margin)

Shortcuts Using the Function Keys

Table 15 shows common shortcuts with function keys.

	Function	Effect
Table 15 Chart of shortcuts with function keys	F1	Activate Help function in Excel.
	F2	Edit the contents of the active cell.
	F3	Paste a defined name into a formula.
	F4	Repeat the last action done using the Menu bar (especially useful when inserting rows/columns, deleting rows/columns).
	F5	Display the **Go To** dialog box.
	F7	Activate the **Spelling & Grammar** dialog box (only in advanced versions).
	F8	Make your cursor sticky – in other words, start blocking the cells as you move along until you press F8 again. You can block a bunch of cells without holding the Shift key down at all. During this operation, you can see the letters "EXT" in the Status bar.
	F9	Calculate all sheets in all open workbooks.
	F10	Activate the Main menu bar.
	F11	Create a chart that uses the current range.
	F12	Activate the **Save As** dialog box.

Twenty Terrific Excel Tips

This is it – the hidden treasure trove that you always suspected must exist somewhere in Excel. Master these tips and accolades are sure to follow.

Table 16 Tips to make you a faster and better Excel user

Challenge	Solution
1. Close all workbooks quickly.	Click on the File menu while pressing the Shift key.
	Select the new command you see on the menu – Close All.
2. Copy a selection of your worksheet as a screenshot from within Excel.	Select your chosen area; click on the Edit menu while pressing the Shift key.
	Select the new command you see on the menu – Copy Picture.
	You now have the choice to copy it as a Picture or Bitmap and also to copy as it appears on screen or as it would appear on Print. Go ahead, use this little trick to amaze your colleagues!
3. Temporarily replicate a portion of your Excel screen in a different location so that you can see changes to the original area there. This is a really neat trick that is almost unknown. Suppose that B2 has a formula that pulls values from cells near V38, where you are currently working. You want to monitor cell B2.	Go to the target cell (in this case, B2) and select Copy from the menu.
	Select a clear area near cell V38 (the changing cell), and then click on the Edit menu while pressing the Shift key.
	Select the new command you see on the menu – Paste Picture Link.
	This pastes a picture of your target cell (B2) near your selected work area without affecting your current work. This floating image does not fit in to any cell at all, but accurately reflects each change happening in the target cell.

Challenge	Solution

p.s. Have you caught on that the Shift key unlocks hidden passages in the menus?

Challenge	Solution		
4. Did you know that some toolbar icons toggle between two purposes when they are used in combination with the Shift key? To the right you will find ten of these pairs – be sure to keep an eye out for others while you're working. They're great time savers.	1. File Open	< = >	File Save
	2. Print	< = >	Print Preview
	3. Sort Ascending	< = >	Sort Descending
	4. Increase Decimal	< = >	Decrease Decimal
	5. Center Align	< = >	Merge and Center
	6. Increase Indent	< = >	Decrease Indent
	7. Align Left	< = >	Align Right
	8. Underline	< = >	Double Underline
	9. Trace Precedents	< = >	Remove Precedent Arrows
	10. Trace Dependents	< = >	Remove Dependent Arrows

Challenge	Solution
5. Keep your file size to a minimum by avoiding unnecessary empty sheets.	Select Tools → Options and click General in the **Options** dialog box. Change the setting for "Sheets in new workbook". Now all new workbooks will have the number of sheets you specified. *Tip:* *Minimize the number of sheets in a new workbook to avoid bloating the file size with unused worksheets.*
6. Navigate quickly to one of several worksheets without repeatedly pressing the sheet navigator buttons.	Just right-click on any one of the sheet navigator buttons and you get a list of available sheets in the workbook, very much like a PowerPoint slides list. Select the sheet you want – you go there in ONE click.

Challenge	Solution
7. Pick and delete only selected cell without disturbing other cells containing formulas.	Press F5 and select Special. In the resulting dialog box, select Constants and ensure that only the Numbers check box is on; clear any others. Now press OK, and you will see that only the number values are selected, without affecting the formulas. Your specific cells are selected without affecting the other formulas in the sheet – use the delete key to remove them.

Tip:

This is an especially important tactic in a large worksheet full of constants and formulas interspersed in various cells.

Challenge	Solution
8. Show your financial results in thousands rather than in full figures and decimals.	Select all your numeric cells. Press Ctrl+1 to bring up the **Format Cells** dialog box. Now go to the last item in the list (Custom) – and type a zero followed by a comma (0,) under the Type on the right side. Press OK, and you will see that all figures still retain their original values, but appear only in thousands. If you want it to show only millions, type "0,," in the custom type box. Nice tip, huh?
9. Increase a full column of values by 10%. (This is just one of the benefits of the Paste Special Operation.)	Type in 10% in a blank cell and copy it. Now select the destination cells that you want to increase by 10%, go to Paste Special, and select Multiply in the Operations part of the dialog box. That's all there is to it – your job is done and time is saved.
10. Generate consecutive numbering in a column next to a column of data contained in non-consecutive rows.	In cell A1, enter this formula: =IF(B1<>"",COUNTA($B$1:B1),"") Copy this down in column A to the same extent that data is contained in column B. The consecutive numbering is automatically done for you.

Challenge	Solution
Chapter 2 For example, suppose that cell B1 contains data. The next cell containing data is B4, followed by B9, then B15 and so on. You want to have consecutive numbering in Column A for the data in Column B.	
11. Hide a worksheet in such a way that others do not even know that it exists – without protecting the workbook. You know how to hide a worksheet using the Format → Sheet → Hide menu item. However, anybody can unhide it using Format → Sheet → Unhide. To prevent this, you would have to protect the workbook itself to disable this menu, but you don't want to do this. What to do?	Press Alt+F11 in Excel to open up the VBA window. Ensure that your sheet (the one to be hidden) is selected there. In the **Properties** dialog box (Shortcut: F4), go to the last item in the alphabetized list, titled "Visible:", and set the drop down values to 2-XlsheetVeryHidden. Save and close the VBA Window. Even after using Format → Sheet → Unhide from the Main menu, your hidden sheet will not be listed at all. Note that, to revert to the old status, you will have to follow the same procedure and set the sheet visible property to -1-xlsheetVisible.
12. Include the current date and time of report printing in an Excel cell. It always helps to have this field in any report that you print, preferably included as part of Report Header.	Copy and paste the following formula into any cell, and see the result. This formula combines both text and functions, with text enclosed in quote marks. ="Report printed on "&TEXT(NOW(),"mmmm d, yyyy at h:mm AM/PM")
13. Apply the specific page setup settings for one worksheet to the eight other worksheets in the	What you need to do is very simple – first place your cursor in the sheet that has the page setup you want to use.

Challenge	Solution
same workbook. There is no built-in option to do this in Excel.	Now select the sheets where you want to apply the page setup using the mouse cursor while holding down the Ctrl key.
	Select File → Page Setup from the Main menu and just click on OK. That's all – your page settings are automatically transferred to the eight new sheets.
14. Format a report so that every other row is shaded. You have seen databases or reports with every alternate rows shaded with a background color to make the report easily readable. You always wanted to achieve the same effect in your Excel worksheet, but found it difficult and boring to manually color every other row.	Select the range that you want to format. Go to Format → Conditional Formatting. Select "Formula Is" and then enter this formula: =MOD(ROW(),2)=0 Now click on Format within the dialog box, select Patterns and then select any color that you want to use as the background filler. Click OK. You now have a worksheet or range that is filled with your chosen color on alternate rows.
15. Prevent an important workbook that is filled with formulas from having those formulas accidentally deleted or overwritten. You have three options:	➢ Lock these cells and protect the workbook. Go to Tools → Protection → Protect Sheet. ➢ Show them as formulas instead of the resulting values. Go to Tools → Options → View and select the checkbox against formulas. ➢ Mark the cells with formulas with a particular shade to make it obvious to anyone keying in data not to touch those cells. For this last option, press F5 and select Special. In the resulting box, click on Formulas and select OK. Your selection will now highlight all those cells that contain formulas. Select a color shade from the Formatting toolbar, and that's it – your formulas are marked.

Challenge	Solution
16. Display the total number of days in a month when a date is entered in a particular field. Although this is a common situation, there is no direct way to do it – but there is always a workaround.	Suppose that you have entered a date of 28-Nov-05 in cell A1 and you want to display the total number of days of Nov 05 in cell B1 (which, incidentally, will need to change automatically if A1 is changed to a different month). Just enter the following formula in cell B1, and it will do the trick: =DAY(DATE(YEAR(A1),MONTH(A1)+1,1)-1)
17. Open a protected file for which you have forgotten the password.	Take a quick look at the following link on the Web. This link contains a string of links to sites offering solutions: http://www.j-walk.com/ss/excel/links/pword.htm
18. Force the text into multiple lines within the same cell when you are entering text manually. You have two options:	➤ Press Ctrl+1 to go to Format Cells → Alignment tab and select the Wrap text checkbox. Now if you adjust the column width, the text will wrap automatically. ➤ Manually insert one or more line breaks within the same cell. Wherever you want to break the text into the next line, just press Alt+Enter. This is one of the very handy but obscure tricks in Excel.
19. Use shortcut keys for Data Grouping and UnGrouping functions.	The combination is Alt+Shift+Right Arrow for Group, and Alt+Shift+Left Arrow for Ungroup. We will get to know more about these functions in the chapters that follow.
20. Use a custom number format to display hour and minute totals correctly. You sum several cells containing Hours and Minutes, but the total never passes 24 hours. What is going on?	Activate the cell that contains your total time. Choose Format → Cells, and select the Number tab. Choose Custom from the Category list. Type [h]:mm into the box labeled Type.

Links for More Tips

For more information about keyboard shortcuts in Excel 2000, see the following:

Best Keyboard Shortcuts for Selecting Data

http://office.microsoft.com/assistance/2000/ExCommonKeys2.aspx

Best Keyboard Shortcuts for Moving in a Workbook

http://office.microsoft.com/assistance/2000/ExCommonKeys3.aspx

Best Keyboard Shortcuts to Use with Functions and Formulas

http://office.microsoft.com/assistance/2000/ExCommonKeys4.aspx

Chapter 2

Formulas, Functions, and More...

We started this journey off on the right foot by reviewing the basics of Excel and by learning some tips, tricks, and techniques to speed along. Now it is time to come to grips with the built-in formulas and functions available in Excel, so that you can use them to power your way through great thickets of data.

Topics in this chapter:

- What Is a Formula and How Does It Work?
- Introducing array formulas
- Common error messages
- How are functions different from formulas?
- What are the categories and components of functions?
- Financial functions
- Date and time functions
- Math, trig, and statistical functions
- Lookup and reference functions
- Database functions
- Text, logical, and information functions
- Nesting functions
- Troubleshooting and evaluating formulas and functions
- Conclusion

What Is a Formula and How Does It Work?

A formula performs calculations within Excel. Formulas helps you to calculate and analyze data on your worksheet. Basic formulas include addition, subtraction, multiplication, and division.

A formula is made up of operands and operators as illustrated below. In the example below, 23 and 5 are the "operands" and the plus sign (+) is the "operator".

$$= 23 + 5$$

The equals sign (=) is a starting tag; it starts every formula in Excel. It indicates to Excel that it is to evaluate the cell as a formula / function and not to treat it as text.

Operands can be any of the following:

> Absolute values   23, 12

> References to cells   B12, A35

> Ranges   A35:C38 or $A$2:$B$2

> Labels   myRange

> Functions   SUM(A1:C1)

 Note:

To ensure that Excel accepts labels as operands, turn on the option of "Accepting labels in formulas".

Access this from the Main menu by selecting Tools → Options → Calculation tab → "Workbook options" heading.

Operators in Excel generally fall into one of the following six categories:

➢ Addition	(+)	
➢ Subtraction	(-)	
➢ Multiplication	(*)	
➢ Division	(/)	
➢ Exponentiation	(^)	
➢ Percentile	(%)	

Chapter 3

Note:

When using a formula, you can change any of the values included in the formula and the formula result will automatically be updated.

A formula is always evaluated from left to right, and using the standard principles of operator precedence.

The Operator Precedence Rules

These are the rules for operator precedence:

Table 17

This table shows the Operators in the order in which Excel evaluates them in a formula.

Operator Precedence in Formulas		
Order of Priority	Type of Operator	Example
Start	Reference	: (colon) and , (comma)
	Negation	-1
	Percentage	%
	Exponentiation	^
	Multiplication and Division	* and /
	Addition and Subtraction	+ and $-$
	Concatenation	&
End	Comparison	$>, <, \geq, \leq, <>,$ and $=$

To understand the importance of the operator precedence rules, consider the following formula:

=2+5*2   Multiplying 5 by 5 and then adding 2 gives a result of 12.

=(2+5)*2   Adding 5 and 2 and then multiplying that result by 2 gives a result of 14.

The moral of the story: To be sure that you get the desired results, always place your preferred precedence of operators within parentheses, so that the marked blocks will be evaluated separately by Excel.

Relative vs. Absolute Referencing

At this stage of the journey, we need to note the key differences between relative and absolute referencing techniques. Depending on your level of expertise, these terms may or may not be familiar to you.

When a range of cells is referenced in a formula such as A1:C3, it is called a relative reference – meaning that when the formula is copied to the next cell down, it will automatically become A2:C4. In other words, the elements of a formula change based on their *relative* positions.

In some circumstances, you may require a formula to contain the same range of cells even if they are copied down elsewhere; for example, a cell containing a price factor that needs to be accessed only from one cell. Incorporating dollar signs ($) tells Excel to always reference that particular row and column. In other words, the elements of a formula will never change, but will *absolutely* always have the same values. This is called an absolute reference.

So, when you make a formula such as =A1*C3, in which A1 is the price field, you will edit the formula to make it =$A$1*C3, so that whenever the formula is copied to a different cell, the new cell will also take pricing information from cell A1. This is the advantage of having an absolute reference as opposed to a relative reference.

Note:

Want to *mix* things up a bit? Put a dollar sign in front of the letter in a cell reference ($A3) to stay in the same column while allowing the row reference to change. Switch the dollar sign to in front of the number (A$3) to always keep the same row reference. This is called a mixed reference.

Introducing Array Formulas

An Array, essentially, is a group of cells or values that will be treated as one single unit.

Array formulas can perform multiple calculations and then return either a single result or multiple results. Array formulas act on two or more sets of values known as array arguments.

You can create an array either by running a function that returns an array result or by entering an array formula, which is a single formula that either uses an array as an argument or enters its results in multiple cells.

 Tip:

Use Array formulas sparingly. Too many array formulas will bog down your computer when recalculating, saving, opening, or closing files. Only use Array formulas if they are really required.

Here's some points to keep in mind when working with Array formulas:

➢ Always complete an Array formula by pressing the Ctrl+Shift+Enter keys, not just the Enter key alone.

➢ Once this combination of keys is pressed, the formula will be surrounded by curly braces ({}), which indicate that it is accepted as an Array formula.

> ➤ Each argument within an array should have an equal number of rows and columns for it to work properly.

> ➤ An array formula cannot and should not be used on an entire column.

Chapter 3

With the introduction and simplification of Database functions in Excel, array formulas have taken a backseat. This works to your advantage because database functions are less costly in time and resources than Array formulas.

Figure 13 shows an example of an Array formula. Column C shows the results of the TREND function used in an Array formula.

 Note:

The TREND function is essentially a Statistical tool that takes in data points as inputs and returns numbers in a linear trend, matching the inputs by using the least squares method.

Step 1 – To get this result, enter the values as shown in row 1 and in columns A and B. Select the cells C2:C5 and then type the text as follows:

=TREND(B2:B5,A2:A5)

Step 2 – Next, press the Ctrl+Shift+Enter keys together.

As soon as it accepts the formula, Excel automatically puts curly braces ({}) around the formula and displays the results in each of the cells C2:C5.

| Figure 13 |
| Example using an Array formula |

C2		▼	f_x {=TREND(B2:B5,A2:A5)}	
	A	B	C	D	E
1	Month	Sales Value	Trend		
2	1	10000	10000		
3	2	12000	12250		
4	3	15000	14500		
5	4	16500	16750		

Common Error Messages in Formulas

When you enter an incorrect operand, value, or reference in a formula, Excel displays an error value in the cell.

Error values always begin with a pound sign (#). Here are the three most common errors:

	Error	Description
Table 18 Common errors	#VALUE	The references used in the formula or function contain numbers that will not return a logical value amount. Recheck all the values you used in the formula.
	#NAME!	Excel doesn't understand the function name that you entered in the cell. Make certain that you used the correct name and spelling. This happens very frequently when you are trying to call a function that is available under an Add-In that is not installed in your machine.
	#DIV/0	The formula is attempting to divide by zero. Check – have you referenced a blank cell or range by mistake? Have you deleted a value that is needed in the formula?

How are Functions Different from Formulas?

A formula is a simple mathematical operation performed on the contents of a cell. On the other hand, a function is a special type of formula that is programmed to return a specific result.

In other words, every function is a type of formula, but every formula is not necessarily a function.

Excel provides more than 300 functions with which you can perform complex calculations with amazing ease – calculations that would otherwise prove to be very difficult.

Every function is comprised of two significant elements:

> **Function name** – the name assigned to the function (for example, SUM)

> **Argument(s)** – the argument list includes one or more operands (arguments), enclosed in parentheses, that the function uses to produce its result

Also, like formulas, functions always start with an equal sign (=) starting tag to signify to Excel that it needs to evaluate the entry and not consider it as text.

Depending on the function in which it appears, an argument can be a numeric or text constant, a single cell reference, or a multiple cell reference (for example, a range).

What are the Categories and Components of Functions?

Microsoft Excel has nine different categories of functions in its stable of more than 300 different functions. These functions are all pre-programmed formulas that you can call into Excel either by typing (as you would formulas) or by using the Function Wizard (press Shift+F3) to fill in the arguments for you.

The nine different categories of functions are listed in the Function Wizard window – see **Figure 14**:

 Tip:

There are at least three more ways to invoke the function Wizard – for details, refer to Twenty Terrific Excel Tips on page 45.

Figure 14

Insert Function dialog box

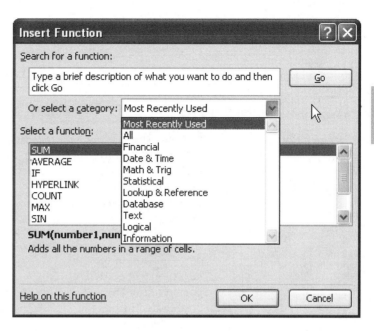

Now, we will briefly visit each of the nine categories, delving into detail only for the most important and valuable functions.

Financial Functions

The Financial suite of functions consists of about 16 main functions that cater to different needs such as computation of depreciation, calculation of interest payments, and working out the value of annuities.

We have reached another of the high points in this journey – a look at the basic models of financial functions along with the syntax and intended purpose for each, as classified by category.

 Note:

There are many more functions available in Excel if the Analysis ToolPak Add-in is installed; however, because it is not shipped by default, we will cover only the standard functions here.

Depreciation-related Functions

Table 19 shows the depreciation-related functions and their syntax.

Chapter 3

	Function	Purpose	Syntax
Table 19 Depreciation-related functions	DB	Returns the depreciation of an asset for a specified period using the fixed-declining balance method	=db(cost,salvage,life,period,[month])
	DDB	Returns the depreciation of an asset for a specified period using the double-declining balance method or other specified method	=ddb(cost,salvage,life,period,[factor])
	SLN	Returns the straight-line depreciation of an asset for one period	=sln(cost,salvage,life)
	SYD	Returns the sum-of-years' digits depreciation of an asset for a specified period	=syd(cost,salvage,life,per)
	VDB	Returns the depreciation of an asset for a specified or partial period using a declining balance method	=vdb(cost,salvage,life,start_period,end_period,[factor],[no_switch])

 Note:

Any arguments mentioned within square brackets ([]) are optional only, and may or may not be entered.

In the syntax shown above, the arguments have the following meanings:

Table 20

Depreciation-related function arguments

Argument	Meaning
cost	Cost of the asset to be depreciated, normally shown with a negative sign indicating the investment
factor	Rate at which the balance declines; default is 2, unless otherwise specified
life	Estimated useful life of the asset
month	Number of months in the first year
no_switch	Optional logical argument (TRUE / FALSE) that instructs Excel to switch to SLD model when the depreciation is greater than the declining balance calculation
per / period	Period for which depreciation is to be worked out (part of the useful life)
salvage	Estimated value at the end of useful life
start_period / end_period	Indicates the starting / ending periods respectively for which the depreciation needs to be calculated

Annuity-/Investment-related Functions

Table 21 shows the annuity- and investment-related functions and their

Table 21

Annuity- and investment - related functions

Function	Purpose	Syntax
FV	Returns the future value of an investment	=fv(rate,nper,pmt,[pv],[type])
IRR	Returns the internal rate of return for a series of cash flows	=irr(values,[guess])
MIRR	Returns the internal rate of return where positive and negative cash flows are financed at different rates	=mirr(values,finance_rate,reinvest_rate)
NPV	Returns the net present value of an investment based on a series of periodic cash flows and a discount rate	=npv(rate,value1,[value2],....[value29])
PMT	Returns the periodic payment for an annuity	=pmt(rate,nper,pv,[fv],[type])
PPMT	Returns the payment on the principal for an investment for a given period	=ppmt(rate,per,nper,pv,[fv],[type])
PV	Returns the present value of an investment	=pv(rate,nper,pmt,[fv],[type])

In the syntax shown above, the arguments have the following meanings:

Table 22	Argument	Meaning
Annuity- and investment - related function arguments	finance_rate	Rate of interest you pay on the money used in the cash flows (interest costs)
	fv	Future value that you want to attain after the last payment is made; if omitted, assumed to be 0
	guess	Can be any number that you guess is close to the result of the function used, such as IRR
	nper	Total number of payment periods in an annuity
	per	Period for which you want to find the interest; should be a value between 1 and nper
	pmt	Payment made each period – must remain even throughout the life of the annuity
		Ideally includes principal and interest only, but no other fees or taxes. If pmt is omitted, the pv argument is mandatory.
	pv	Present value of a series of future payments; if pv is omitted, pmt argument is mandatory
	rate	Interest rate per period
	reinvest_rate	Rate of interest rate you receive on the cash flows as you reinvest them (interest revenues)
	type	Default value is "0"; can be only "0" or "1", where 0 indicates payments are due at the end of the period, and 1 indicates that payments are due at the beginning of the period (arrears and advance, respectively)
	values	Array of cells that contain numbers (non-number cells will be ignored)
		These numbers represent a series of payments (negative values) and income

Table 22	Argument	Meaning
Annuity- and investment - related function arguments		(positive values) occurring at regular periods. At least one positive and one negative value is expected, failing which an error will be reported in MIRR function.

Functions for Interest Computation

Table 23 shows the interest computation functions and their syntax. See Table 22 for meanings of arguments.

Table 23	Function	Purpose	Syntax
Interest computation functions	IPMT	Returns the interest payment for an investment for a given period	=ipmt(rate,per,nper,pv,[fv],[type])
	ISPMT	Calculates the interest paid during a specific period of an investment	=ispmt(rate,per,nper,pv)
	NPER	Returns the number of periods for an investment	=nper(rate,pmt,pv,[fv],[type])
	RATE	Returns the interest rate per period of an annuity	=rate(nper,pmt,pv,[fv],[type],[guess])

Examples

Depreciation Functions

The following table summarizes the various types of depreciation functions available in Excel and shows how to use them.

Figure 15   Depreciation functions and their uses

	A	B	C	D	E	F
1	**Description**	**Data**				
2	Initial cost	1,000,000				
3	Salvage value	100,000				
4	Lifetime in years	3				
5						
6	**Description (Result)**	**DB Method**	**DDB Method**	**SLN Method**	**SYD Method**	**VDB Method**
7	First year's depreciation	$536,000.00	$666,666.67	$300,000.00	$450,000.00	$666,666.67
8	*Formula used above*	=DB(B2,B3,B4,1)	=DDB(B2,B3,B4,1,2)	=SLN(B2,B3,B4)	=SYD(B2,B3,B4,1)	=VDB(B2,B3,B4,0,1)
9	Second year's depreciation	$248,704.00	$222,222.22	$300,000.00	$300,000.00	$222,222.22
10	*Formula used above*	=DB(B2,B3,B4,2)	=DDB(B2,B3,B4,2,2)	=SLN(B2,B3,B4)	=SYD(B2,B3,B4,2)	=VDB(B2,B3,B4,1,2)
11	Third year's depreciation	$115,398.66	$11,111.11	$300,000.00	$150,000.00	$11,111.11
12	*Formula used above*	=DB(B2,B3,B4,3)	=DDB(B2,B3,B4,3,2)	=SLN(B2,B3,B4)	=SYD(B2,B3,B4,3)	=VDB(B2,B3,B4,2,3)
13	**Total Depreciation**	$900,102.66	$900,000.00	$900,000.00	$900,000.00	$900,000.00

Other Financial Functions

The following table summarizes the most important financial functions available in Excel and how to use them in typical situations.

Figure 16   Financial functions and their uses

	A	B	C	D	E	F	G	H	I	J	K
1	IRR Calculation			PMT Calculation			PPMT calculation (Principal pmt)			IPMT calculation (Interest pmt)	
2	Outflow	-2000		Interest rate p.a	12%		Interest rate p.a	10%		Interest rate p.a	10%
3	Inflow no 1	1500		Installments left	8		Installments left	2		Years of Loan	3
4	Inflow no 2	1500		Unpaid amt	-49680		Amount of Loan	2000		Present value of Loan	8000
5											
6	IRR =	31.87%		PMT=	$10,001		PPMT for Period 1=	($75.62)		IPMT for 3rd Year=	($292.45)
7		=IRR(B2:B4)			=PMT(E2,E3,E4)			=PPMT(H2/12,1,H3*12,H4)			=IPMT(K2,3,K3,K4)
8											
9	FV Calculation			PV Calculation			NPER Calculation			RATE calculation	
10	Interest rate p.a	12%		Interest rate p.a	12%		Interest rate p.a	12%		Monthly Installments left	48
11	Installments left	12		Installments left	240		Yearly Pmt	10000		Per Installment value	-1000
12	Per Installment value	-500		Per Installment value	-500		Unpaid amt	-49680		Amount of the Loan	40000
13											
14	FV=	$6,341.25		PV=	$45,409.71		NPER=	8.00		RATE per annum=	9.24%
15		=FV(B10/12,B11,B12)			=PV(E10/12,E11,E12)			=NPER(H10,H11,H12)			=RATE(K10,K11,K12)*12
16											
17	MIRR Calculation			NPV Calculation			ISPMT Calculation (Lotus support)				
18	Outflow	-2000		Discount Rate	10%						
19	Inflow no 1	1500		Initial Investment	-10000		Interest rate p.a	10%			
20	Inflow no 2	1500		Inflow-Year 1	3000		Years of Loan	3			
21	Loan Int rate	10%		Inflow-Year 2	4200		Amount of Loan	8000			
22	Deposit Int rate	12%		Inflow-Year 3	6800						
23	IRR =	26.10%		NPV =	$1,307.29		ISPMT for 1st year =	($533.33)			
24		=MIRR(B18:B20,B21,B22)			=NPV(E18,E20:E22)+E19			=ISPMT(H19,1,H20,H21)			
25											

Date and Time Functions

The Date and Time functions consist of about 19 main functions, out of which five functions relate just to Time, with the balance devoted to Date-related use.

Table 24 shows the basic Date and Time functions.

Table 24   Date and time functions

Function	Purpose	Syntax
DATE	Returns the serial number of a particular date	=date(year,month,day)
DATEVALUE	Converts a date in the form of text to a serial number	=datevalue(date_text)
DAY	Converts a serial number to a day of the month	=day(serial_number)
DAYS360	Calculates the number of days between two dates based on a 360-day year	=days360(start_date,end_date,[method])
HOUR	Converts a serial number to an hour	=hour(serial_number)
MINUTE	Converts a serial number to a minute	=minute(serial_number)
MONTH	Converts a serial number to a month	=month(serial_number)
NOW	Returns the serial number of the current date and time	=now()
SECOND	Converts a serial number to a second	=second(serial_number)
TIME	Returns the serial number of a particular time	=time(hour,minute,second)
TIMEVALUE	Converts a time in the form of text to a serial number	=timevalue(time_text)

Function	Purpose	Syntax
TODAY	Returns the serial number of today's date	=today()
WEEKDAY	Converts a serial number to a day of the week	=weekday(serial_number,[return_type])
YEAR	Converts a serial number to a year	=year(serial_number)

In the syntax shown above, the arguments have the following meanings:

	Argument	Meaning
Table 25 Date and time function arguments	date_text	Text that represents a date in an Excel date format; for example, "6/30/2006" or "30-Jun-2006"
	day	Number representing the day of the month
	end_date	One of the two dates between which you want to know the number of days (end date)
	hour	Hour is a number from 0 (zero) to 32767, representing the hour
	method	Method is a logical value that specifies whether to use the U.S. or European method in the calculation.
	minute	Minute is a number from 0 (zero) to 32767, representing the hour
	month	Number representing the month of the year
	return_type	Number that determines the type of return value.

Return type	Number returned
1 or omitted	Numbers 1 (Sunday) through 7 (Saturday)
2	Numbers 1 (Monday) through 7 (Sunday)
3	Numbers 0 (Monday) through 6 (Sunday)

	second	Second is a number from 0 (zero) to 32767, representing the hour
	serial_number	Any integer value that represents a date or time, to be worked on in a formula

Chapter 3

Table 25	Argument	Meaning
Date and time function arguments	start_date	One of the two dates between which you want to know the number of days (start date)
	time_text	Text string that represents a time in one of Excel's time formats; for example, "8:15 PM" and "20:15"
	year	Number representing the year – from one to four digits

Examples of Time-related Functions

The figure below summarizes the time-related functions available in Excel and how they are used.

 Note:

As mentioned earlier, we will cover only the standard functions here, not including those in the Analysis ToolPak add-in.

Figure 17

Time-related functions and their uses

	A	B	C
1	Examples of Time related Functions		
2		Case 1	Case 2
3	Date	Time (12 Hrs Format)	Time (24 Hrs Format)
4	13-Feb-06	6:12:24 AM	16:32:40
5			
6	Hour	6	16
7	Formula	=HOUR(B4)	=HOUR(C4)
8	Minute	12	32
9	Formula	=MINUTE(B4)	=MINUTE(C4)
10	Second	24	40
11	Formula	=SECOND(B4)	=SECOND(C4)
12	Time	6:12 AM	4:32 PM
13	Formula	=TIME(B6,B8,B10)	=TIME(C6,C8,C10)
14	Timevalue	0.258611111	0.689351852
15	Formula	=TIMEVALUE("06:12:24")	=TIMEVALUE("16:32:40")
16	Now	5/12/2006 23:59	
17	Formula	=NOW()	
18	Today	5/12/2006	
19	Formula	=TODAY()	
20			

Examples of Date-related Functions

These functions are used with dates in Excel.

In the following examples, there are three different samples for the WEEKDAY function, using the three different return_type flags (see Table 25 for a description of return types). Please note how the results differ.

	A	B	C
1	**Examples of Date related Functions**		
2		Case 1	Case 2
3		13-Dec-04	25-Jan-06
4			
5	YEAR	2004	2006
6	*Formula*	=YEAR(B3)	=YEAR(C3)
7	MONTH	12	1
8	*Formula*	=MONTH(B3)	=MONTH(C3)
9	DAY	13	25
10	*Formula*	=DAY(B3)	=DAY(C3)
11	DATE	12/13/2004	1/25/2006
12	*Formula*	=DATE(B5,B7,B9)	=DATE(C5,C7,C9)
13	DATEVALUE	38334	38742
14	*Formula*	=DATEVALUE("12/13/2004")	=DATEVALUE("25-Jan-2006")
15	DAYS360	-402	402
16	*Formula*	=DAYS360(C3,B3)	=DAYS360(B3,C3)
17	WEEKDAY	2	4
18	*Formula*	=WEEKDAY(B3,1)	=WEEKDAY(C3,1)
19	WEEKDAY	1	3
20	*Formula*	=WEEKDAY(B3,2)	=WEEKDAY(C3,2)
21	WEEKDAY	0	2
22	*Formula*	=WEEKDAY(B3,3)	=WEEKDAY(C3,3)
23			

Figure 18

Date-related function results

Math, Trig, and Statistical Functions

We are actually looking at two different categories of functions:

➤ Mathematical & Trigonometry functions

➤ Statistical functions

Chapter 3

There is a huge list of functions to be narrated and explained under both of these titles, but since many of these functions are not normally used in business (and because they are relevant to a separate field of study), we will only provide the function syntax for the ones you are most likely to use.

You may find that you already rely on some of these functions but are unfamiliar with others that also have good potential for day-to-day business applications.

Math and Trig functions

Table 26 shows the Math and Trig functions.

Table 26   Math and Trig functions

Function	Purpose	Syntax
ABS	Returns the absolute value of a number	=abs(number)
CEILING	Rounds a number to the nearest integer or to the nearest multiple of significance	=ceiling(number,significance)
EVEN	Rounds a number up to the nearest even integer	=even(number)
FLOOR	Rounds a number down, toward zero	=floor(number,significance)
INT	Rounds a number down to the nearest integer	=int(number)
MOD	Returns the remainder from division	=mod(number,divisor)
ODD	Rounds a number up to the nearest odd integer	=odd(number)

Function	Purpose	Syntax
PRODUCT	Multiplies its arguments	=product(number1,[number2]..)
RAND	Returns a random number between 0 and 1	=rand()
ROUNDDOWN	Rounds a number down, toward zero	=rounddown(number,num_digits)
ROUNDUP	Rounds a number up, away from zero	=roundup(number,num_digits)
SIGN	Returns the sign of a number	=sign(number)
SQRT	Returns a positive square root	=sqrt(number)
SUBTOTAL	Returns a subtotal in a list or database	=subtotal(function_num,ref1,[ref2]..)
SUM	Adds its arguments	=sum(number1,[number2]....)
SUMIF	Adds the cells specified by a given criteria	=sumif(range,criteria,[sum_range])
SUMPRODUCT	Returns the sum of the products of corresponding array components	=sumproduct(array1,[array2],...)
SUMSQ	Returns the sum of the squares of the arguments	=sumsq(number1,[number2]..)
TRUNC	Truncates a number to an integer	=trunc(number,[num_digits])

Chapter 3

In the syntax shown above, the arguments have the following meanings:

	Argument	Meaning
Table 27 Math and trig and statistical function arguments	array1, array2	Two to 30 arrays whose components you want to multiply and add using SUMPRODUCT
	criteria	Criteria in the form of a number, expression, or text that defines which cells will be added
	divisor	Number by which you want to divide a number
	function_num	Number from 1 to 11 that specifies which function to use in calculating subtotals within a list: 1-AVERAGE, 2-COUNT, 3-COUNTA, 4-MAX, 5- MIN, 6-PRODUCT, 7-STDEV, 8-STDEVP, 9-SUM, 10-VAR, 11-VARP
	num_digits	Number specifying the precision of the truncation (default is 0)
	number	Number on which you want to perform the calculations / apply the function
	number1, number2	One to 30 arguments on which to perform a function such as SUM or PRODUCT
	range	Range of cells you want evaluated while performing a SUMIF
	ref1, ref2	One to 29 ranges or references for which you want to apply the SUBTOTAL function
	significance	Multiple to which you want to round a number
	sum_range	Actual set of cells to sum (Refer to example for clarity.)

Here are some sample instances using Math and Trig functions.

Figure 19   Math and Trig function examples

	A	B	C	D	E	F
1	Readings during case studies					
2	Case No	Value				
3	1	-0.25				
4	2	0.63				
5	3	7.74				
6	4	1.98				
7						
8						
9	Function	=ABS(number)	=CEILING(ref,signif.)	=EVEN(number)	=FLOOR(ref,signif.)	=INT(number)
10	Result	0.25	0.70	8	0.60	1
11	Formula Used	=ABS(B3)	=CEILING(B4,0.1)	=EVEN(B5)	=FLOOR(B4,0.1)	=INT(B6)
12						
13	Function	=MOD(number,divisor)	=ODD(number)	=PRODUCT(val1,[val2])	=RAND()	=SIGN(number)
14	Result	1.74	9	-1.21905	0.349008239	-1
15	Formula Used	=MOD(B5,3)	=ODD(B5)	=PRODUCT(B3,B4,B5)	=RAND()	=SIGN(B3)
16						
17	Function	=ROUND(ref,no_digits)	=ROUNDDOWN(ref,no_digits)	=ROUNDUP(ref,no_digits)	=SQRT(number)	=SUM(n1,[n2]....)
18	Result	1.977	1.900	2.000	8	8.12
19	Formula Used	=ROUND(B6-0.003,3)	=ROUNDDOWN(B6-0.003,1)	=ROUNDUP(B6-0.003,1)	=SQRT(64)	=SUM(B3,B4,B5)
20						
21	Function	=SUMIF(range,criteria)	=SUBTOTAL(function_num,ref1,[ref2]..)		=SUMPRODUCT(array1,[array2],...)	
22	Result	-0.25		9.47	32.15	
23	Formula Used	=SUMIF(A2:A6,"1",B2:B6)	=SUBTOTAL(9,B3,B5,B6)		=SUMPRODUCT(A3:A6,B3:B6)	
24						
25	Function	=SUMSQ(n1,[n2]..)	=TRUNC(number,[num_digits])			
26	Result	0.4594	1.9			
27	Formula Used	=SUMSQ(B3,B4)	=TRUNC(B6,1)			

Statistical Functions

Table 28 shows the Statistical functions. See Table 27 for the meanings of the

arguments used here.

Table 28   Statistical functions

Function	Description	Function Syntax
AVERAGE	Returns the average (arithmetic mean) of the arguments.	=AVERAGE(number1,[number2]..)
AVERAGEA	Calculates the average (arithmetic mean) of the values in the list of arguments.	=AVERAGEA(value1,[value2]..)
COUNT	Counts the number of cells that contain numbers and also numbers within the list of arguments.	=COUNT(value1,[value2]..)
COUNTA	Counts the number of cells that are not empty and the values within the list of arguments.	=COUNTA(value1,[value2]..)
COUNTBLANK	Counts empty cells in a specified range of cells.	=COUNTBLANK(range)
COUNTIF	Counts the number of cells within a range that meet the given criteria.	=COUNTIF(range,criteria)
LARGE	Returns the k-th largest value in a data set.	=LARGE(array,k)
MAX	Returns the maximum value in a list of arguments.	=MAX(number1,[number2]..)

Function	Description	Function Syntax
MAXA	Returns the maximum value in a list of arguments, including numbers, text, and logical values.	=MAXA(value1,[value2]..)
MIN	Returns the minimum value in a list of arguments.	=MIN(number1,[number2]..)
MINA	Returns the minimum value in a list of arguments, including numbers, text, and logical values.	=MINA(value1,[value2]..)
PERCENTILE	Returns the k-th percentile of values in a range.	=PERCENTILE(array,k)
PERCENTRANK	Returns the percentage rank of a value in a data set.	=PERCENTRANK(array,x,[significance])
RANK	Returns the rank of a number in a list of numbers.	=RANK(number,ref,[order])
SMALL	Returns the k-th smallest value in a data set.	=SMALL(array,k)
STDEV	Estimates standard deviation based on a sample.	=STDEV(number1,[number2],..)
TREND	Returns values along a linear trend.	=TREND(known_y's,[known_x's], [new_x's],[const])
VAR	Estimates variance based on a sample.	=VAR(number1,[number2],…)

Figure 20 Sample applications of Statistical functions

	A	B	C	D	E	F	G
1	Salesman	Sales Achieved - Jan 06		For Trend			
2	Mark	50000		Month No	Sales		
3	Richard	70000		1	30000		
4	Krish	15000		2	45000		
5	Peter	25000		3	65000		
6	Sandy	45000		4	80000		
7	Mireille	Not Available					
8							
9	Function	=AVERAGE(range)	=AVERAGEA(range)	=COUNT(range)	=COUNTA(range)	=COUNTBLANK(range)	=COUNTIF(range,criteria)
10	Result	41000	34166.66667	5	6	1	1
11	Formula Used	=AVERAGE(B2:B7)	=AVERAGEA(B2:B7)	=COUNT(B2:B7)	=COUNTA(B2:B7)	=COUNTBLANK(B2:B8)	=COUNTIF(A2:B7,"Krish")
12							
13	Function	=LARGE(array,k)	=SMALL(array,k)	=MAX(range)	=MAXA(range)	=MIN(range)	=MINA(range)
14	Result	45000	25000	70000	70000	15000	15000
15	Formula Used	=LARGE(B2:B7,3)	=SMALL(B2:B7,2)	=MAX(B2:B7)	=MAXA(B2:B7)	=MIN(B2:B7)	=MINA(B2:B7)
16							
17	Function	=PERCENTILE(array,k)	=PERCENTRANK(array,x,[significance])	=RANK(k,range,[order])		=STDEV(range)	
18	Result	23000	0.5	5		21621.74831	
19	Formula Used	=PERCENTILE(B2:B7,0.2)	=PERCENTRANK(B2:B7,B2)	=RANK(B4,B2:B7,0)		=STDEV(B2:B7)	
20							
21	Function	=TREND(known_y's,[known_x's],[new_x's],[const])		=VAR(range)			
22	Result	29500		467500000			
23	Formula Used	=TREND(E3:E6,D3:D6)		=VAR(B2:B7)			

Lookup and Reference Functions

Table 29 shows Lookup and Reference functions.

Table 29 Lookup and Reference functions

Function	Purpose	Syntax
ADDRESS	Returns a reference as text to a single cell in a worksheet	=ADDRESS(row_num,column_num,abs_num, a1,sheet_text)
AREAS	Returns the number of areas in a reference	=AREAS(reference)

Function	Purpose	Syntax
CHOOSE	Chooses a value from a list of values	=CHOOSE(index_num,value1,value2,...)
COLUMN	Returns the column number of a reference	=COLUMN(reference)
COLUMNS	Returns the number of columns in a reference	=COLUMNS(array)
HLOOKUP	Looks in the top row of an array and returns the value of the indicated cell	=HLOOKUP(lookup_value,table_array,row_index_num,range_lookup)
HYPERLINK	Creates a shortcut or jump that opens a document stored on a network server, an intranet, or the Internet	=HYPERLINK(link_location,friendly_name)
INDEX	Uses an index to choose a value from a reference or array	=INDEX(array,row_num,column_num)
INDIRECT	Returns a reference indicated by a text value	=INDIRECT(ref_text,a1)
LOOKUP	Looks up values in a vector or array	=LOOKUP(lookup_value,lookup_vector,result_vector)
MATCH	Looks up values in a reference or array	=MATCH(lookup_value,lookup_array,match_type)
OFFSET	Returns a reference offset from a given reference	=OFFSET(reference,rows,cols,height,width)
ROW	Returns the row number of a reference	=ROW(reference)
ROWS	Returns the number of rows in a reference	=ROWS(array)
TRANSPOSE	Returns the transpose of an array	=TRANSPOSE(array)

Chapter 3

Function	Purpose	Syntax
VLOOKUP	Looks in the first column of an array and moves across the row to return the value of a cell	=VLOOKUP(lookup_value,table_array,col_index_num,range_lookup)

Chapter 3

In the syntax shown above, the arguments have the following meanings:

Table 30   Lookup and Reference function arguments

Argument	Meaning
abs_num	Type of reference to return 1-Absolute; 2-Absolute row, Relative column; 3-Relative row, Absolute column; 4-Relative
a1	Logical value that specifies the A1 or R1C1 reference style (TRUE returns A1-style, FALSE returns R1C1 style) Note: A1 and R1C1 are reference styles. In R1C1 style, R is followed by the row number and C is followed by the column number. Thus, you can refer to cell B1 as R1C2 or cell C4 as R4C3.
array	Array or array formula, or a reference to a range of cells for which you want the number of columns
col_index_num	Column number in table_array from which the matching value will be returned
cols	Number of columns, left or right, to which you want the upper-left cell to refer
column_num	Column number to use in the cell reference
friendly_name	Can be a value, a text string, a name, or a cell that contains the jump text or value
height	Number of rows that you want the returned reference to be; height must be a positive number

Argument	Meaning
index_num	Specifies which value argument is selected. Must be a number between 1 and 29
link_location	Path and file name to the document / URL / web address to be opened shown as text within quotes
lookup_array	Contiguous range of cells containing possible lookup values – must be an array or an array reference
lookup_value	Value to be found in the first row of the table. Lookup_value can be a value, a reference, or a text string
lookup_vector	Range that contains only one row or one column (should be sorted in ascending order)
match_type	–1, 0, or 1, where –1 = smallest value greater than or equal to lookup_value, 0 = first value exactly equal to lookup_value, 1 = greatest value lesser than or equal to lookup_value
range_lookup	Logical value that specifies whether an exact match is required (TRUE) or if an approximate match is acceptable (FALSE)
reference	Reference to a cell or range of cells and can refer to multiple areas, if included with extra sets of parentheses
ref_text	Reference to a cell that contains an A1-style reference, an R1C1-style reference, a name defined as a reference, or a reference to a cell as a text string
result_vector	Range that contains only one row or column – must be of the same size as the lookup_vector
row_index_num	Row number in table_array from which the matching value will be returned
row_num	Row number to use in the cell reference
rows	Number of rows, up or down, to which you want the upper-left cell to refer
sheet_text	Text specifying the name of the worksheet to be used as the external reference
table_array	Table of sorted information in which data is looked up. Use a reference to a range or a range name
value1, value2	One to 29 value arguments whose selection is based on the index_num; can be references, also

Chapter 3

Argument	Meaning
width	Number of columns that you want the returned reference to be; width must be a positive number

---

Figure 21 Examples of Lookup and Reference functions

	A	B	C	D	E	F
1	Salesman	Sales Achieved - Jan 06				
2	Krish	15000				
3	Mark	50000				
4	Mireille	Not Available				
5	Peter	25000				
6	Richard	70000				
7	Sandy	45000				
8						
9	Function	=ADDRESS(row,col)	=AREAS(range)	=CHOOSE(index,1,2)	=COLUMN(ref)	=COLUMNS(array)
10	Result	$C$2	3	50000	2	3
11	Formula Used	=ADDRESS(2,3)	=AREAS((B2:B7,A2,B1))	=CHOOSE(2,B2,B3,B4)	=COLUMN(B3)	=COLUMNS(B2:D7)
12						
13	Function	=INDEX(array,row,col)	=INDIRECT(ref_text)	=MATCH(lookup,array)	=ROW(ref)	=ROWS(array)
14	Result	Not Available	50000	1	3	6
15	Formula Used	=INDEX(A2:B7,3,2)	=INDIRECT("B3")	=MATCH(15000,B2:B7)	=ROW(B3)	=ROWS(B2:B7)
16						
17	Function	=LOOKUP(lookup_value,array)			=HLOOKUP(lookup_value,array,row_index_no)	
18	Result	15000			Peter	
19	Formula Used	=LOOKUP("Krish",A2:A7,B2:B7)			=HLOOKUP("Salesman",A1:B7,5)	
20						
21	Function	=VLOOKUP(lookup_value,array,col_index_no)			=HYPERLINK(cell,name)	=OFFSET(ref,rows,cols)
22	Result	25000			Mark	25000
23	Formula Used	=VLOOKUP("Peter",A2:B7,2)			=HYPERLINK(B3,"Mark")	=OFFSET(A2,3,1)
24						
25	Function	=TRANSPOSE(array)				
26	Formula Used	{=TRANSPOSE(A2:B7)}	(entered as Array formula in cells A29:F30)			
27	Result window	As seen in A29:F30				
28						
29	Krish	Mark	Mireille	Peter	Richard	Sandy
30	15000	50000	Not Available	25000	70000	45000

Database Functions

Table 31 shows the Database functions.

Table 31	Database functions

Function	Purpose	Syntax
DAVERAGE	Returns the average of selected database entries	=DAVERAGE(database,field,criteria)
DCOUNT	Counts the cells that contain numbers in a database	=DCOUNT(database,field,criteria)
DCOUNTA	Counts nonblank cells in a database	=DCOUNTA(database,field,criteria)
DGET	Extracts a single record that matches the specified criteria from a database	=DGET(database,field,criteria)
DMAX	Returns the maximum value from selected database entries	=DMAX(database,field,criteria)
DMIN	Returns the minimum value from selected database entries	=DMIN(database,field,criteria)
DPRODUCT	Multiplies the values in a particular field of records that match the criteria in a database	=DPRODUCT(database,field,criteria)
DSTDEV	Estimates the standard deviation based on a sample of selected database entries	=DSTDEV(database,field,criteria)
DSTDEVP	Calculates the standard deviation based on the entire population of	=DSTDEVP(database,field,criteria)

Function	Purpose	Syntax
	selected database entries	
DSUM	Adds the numbers in the field column of records in the database that match the criteria	=DSUM(database,field,criteria)
DVAR	Estimates variance based on a sample from selected database entries	=DVAR(database,field,criteria)
DVARP	Calculates variance based on the entire population of selected database entries	=DVARP(database,field,criteria)
GETPIVOTDATA	Returns data stored in a PivotTable	=GETPIVOTDATA(data_field,pivot_table, field1,item1,field2,item2,...)

In the syntax shown above, the arguments have the following meanings:

Table 32

Database function arguments

Argument	Meaning
criteria	Range of cells that contains the conditions you specify
	At least one column label and at least one cell below the column label is required for specifying a criteria.
data_field	Name, enclosed in quotation marks, for the data field that contains the data you want to retrieve
database	Range of cells that makes up the list or database, where rows are records, and columns are fields; first row of the list contains labels for each column
field	Indicates which column is used in the function
	The column label within double quotation marks can be given or the column number can be given.

	Argument	Meaning
Table 32 Database function arguments	field1, item1, field2, item2, ...	One to 14 pairs of field names and item names (enclosed in quotation marks) describing the data you want to retrieve For OLAP PivotTable reports, items can contain the source name of the dimension as well as the source name of the item.
	pivot_table	Reference to any cell, range of cells, or named range in a PivotTable report

The examples and practical usage tips related to Database functions are covered in the chapter on Advanced Data Management in Excel on page 137.

Text Functions

Table 33 shows Text functions.

Table 33 Text functions

Function	Purpose	Syntax
BAHTTEXT	Converts a number to text, using the ß (baht) currency format	=BAHTTEXT(number)
CHAR	Returns the character specified by the code number	=CHAR(number)
CLEAN	Removes all nonprintable characters from text	=CLEAN(text)
CODE	Returns a numeric code for the first character in a text string	=CODE(text)

Function	Purpose	Syntax
CONCATENATE	Joins several text items into one text item	=CONCATENATE(text1,[text2],..)
DOLLAR	Converts a number to text, using the $ (dollar) currency format	=DOLLAR(number,[decimals])
EXACT	Compares two text values to see if they are identical	=EXACT(text1,text2)
FIND	Finds one text value within another (case-sensitive)	=FIND(find_text,within_text,[start_num])
FIXED	Formats a number as text with a fixed number of decimals	=FIXED(number,[decimals],[no_commas])
LEFT	Returns the leftmost characters from a text value	=LEFT(text,[num_chars])
LEN	Returns the number of characters in a text string	=LEN(text)
LOWER	Converts text to lowercase	=LOWER(text)
MID	Returns a specific number of characters from a text string starting at the position you specify	=MID(text,start_num,num_chars)
PROPER	Capitalizes the first letter in each word of a text value	=PROPER(text)
REPLACE	Replaces characters within text	=REPLACE(old_text,start_num,num_chars,new_text)
REPT	Repeats text a given number of times	=REPT(text,number_times)
RIGHT	Returns the rightmost characters from a text value	=RIGHT(text,[num_chars])
SEARCH	Finds one text value within another (not case-	=SEARCH(find_text,within_text,[start_num])

Function	Purpose	Syntax
	sensitive)	
SUBSTITUTE	Substitutes new text for old text in a text string	=SUBSTITUTE(text,old_text,new_text, [instance_num])
T	Converts its arguments to text	=T(value)
TEXT	Formats a number and converts it to text	=TEXT(value,format_text)
TRIM	Removes spaces from text	=TRIM(text)
UPPER	Converts text to uppercase	=UPPER(text)
VALUE	Converts a text argument to a number	=VALUE(text)

Chapter 3

In the syntax shown above, the arguments have the following meanings:

Table 34

Text function arguments

Argument	Meaning
decimals	Number of digits to the right of the decimal point – if this is negative, number is rounded to the left of the decimal point
find_text	Text that you want to find
format_text	A number format in text form (from Format Cells → Number tab → Category box)
instance_num	Optional; specifies which occurrence of old_text you want to replace with new_text – if omitted, every occurrence is replaced
new_text	Text that will replace characters in old_text
no_commas	Logical value that, if TRUE, prevents FIXED from including commas in the returned text
num_chars	Specifies the number of characters you want the function to extract
number	Number you want to convert to text, or a reference to a cell containing a number, or a formula that evaluates to a number

Chapter 3

	Argument	Meaning
Table 34 Text function arguments	number_times	Positive number specifying the number of times to repeat text
	old_text	Text in which you want to replace some characters
	start_num	Specifies the character at which to start the search; if omitted, default is 1
	text	Any worksheet information (can contain printable as well as nonprintable characters.)
	text1, text2	Text items that can be text strings, numbers, or single-cell references (up to 30 items can be joined using CONCATENATE)
	value	Value that you want to test
	within_text	Text that contains the text you want to find

Examples of Text Functions

Figure 22	Examples of Text functions

	A	B	C	D	E	F
1	**Examples of Text Functions**					
2	Function Name	Function Used in Col C	Function Result	Additional Arguments		
3	Bahttext	=BAHTTEXT(D3)	สิบสองบาทถ้วน	12		
4	Char	=CHAR(49)	1			
5	Clean	=CLEAN(D5)	aabbcc	aa▯bb▯cc		
6	Code	=CODE(D6)	49	1		
7	Concatenate	=CONCATENATE(D7,E7)	abc123	abc	123	
8	Dollar	=DOLLAR(D8)	$1,235.00	1235		
9	Exact	=EXACT(D9,E9)	FALSE	Abc	ABc	
10	Find	=FIND(D10,E10)	3	b	tab	
11	Fixed	=FIXED(D11,,)	1,200.00	1200		
12	Left	=LEFT(D12,3)	Cha	Charles		
13	Len	=LEN(D13)	7	Charles		
14	Lower	=LOWER(D14)	charles	CHARLES		
15	Mid	=MID(D15,3,2)	ar	Charles		
16	Proper	=PROPER(D16)	Charles Keith	CHARLES keith		
17	Replace	=REPLACE(D17,2,2,E17)	Chatrles	Charles	hat	
18	Rept	=REPT(D18,5)	AmAmAmAmAm	Am		
19	Right	=RIGHT(D19,3)	les	Charles		
20	Search	=SEARCH(D20,E20)	2	Am	Pampers	
21	Substitute	=SUBSTITUTE(D21,E21,F21,2)	Pampad	Pampam	am	ad
22	T	=T(D22)	And	And		
23	TEXT	=TEXT(D23,"d-mmm-yy")	12-Jan-06	1/12/2006		
24	TRIM	=TRIM(D24)	materials	materials		
25	UPPER	=UPPER(D25)	CHARLES	charles		
26	VALUE	=VALUE("123.00")	123			

Logical Functions

Table 35 shows logical functions.

Table 35   Logical functions

Function	Purpose	Syntax
AND	Returns TRUE if all its arguments are TRUE	=AND(logical1,logical2, ...)
FALSE	Returns the logical value FALSE	=FALSE( )
IF	Specifies a logical test to perform	=IF(logical_test,value_if_true,value_if_false)
NOT	Reverses the logic of its argument	=NOT(logical)
OR	Returns TRUE if any argument is TRUE	=OR(logical1,logical2,...)
TRUE	Returns the logical value TRUE	=TRUE( )

In the syntax shown above, the arguments have the following meanings:

Table 36   Logical function arguments

Argument	Meaning
logical	Value or expression that can be evaluated to TRUE or FALSE
logical_test	Any value or expression using any comparison operator that can be evaluated to TRUE or FALSE
logical1	One to 30 conditions that you want to test that can be either TRUE or FALSE
value_if_false	Value to be returned if logical_test is FALSE
value_if_true	Value to be returned if logical_test is TRUE

Practical Application of Logical Functions

Figure 23   Examples of Logical functions

	A	B	C	D	E	F
1	Salesman	Sales Achieved - Jan 06				
2	Krish	15000				
3	Mark	50000				
4	Mireille	Not Available				
5	Peter	25000				
6	Richard	70000				
7	Sandy	45000				
8						
9	Function	=AND(logical1,[logical2]..)	=FALSE()	=NOT(logical)	=OR(logical1,[logical2]..)	=TRUE()
10	Result	TRUE	FALSE	FALSE	TRUE	TRUE
11	Formula Used	=AND(B2<20000,B4<>"")	=FALSE()	=NOT((B2<16000))	=OR(B3=50000,B5>25000)	=TRUE()
12						
13	Function	=IF(logical_test,true_value,false_value)				
14	Result			Less than 50k		
15	Formula Used	=IF(B5<50000,"Less than 50k","Equal to or greater than 50k")				

Information Functions

Table 37 shows information functions.

	Function	Purpose	Syntax
Table 37 Information functions	CELL	Returns information about the formatting, location, or contents of a cell	=CELL(info_type,reference)
	ERROR.TYPE	Returns a number corresponding to an error type	=ERROR.TYPE(error_val)
	INFO	Returns information about the current operating environment	=INFO(type_text)
	ISBLANK	Returns TRUE if the value is blank	=ISBLANK(value)

Chapter 3

	Function	Purpose	Syntax
Table 37 Information functions	ISERR	Returns TRUE if the value is any error value except #N/A	=ISERR(value)
	ISERROR	Returns TRUE if the value is any error value	=ISERROR(value)
	ISEVEN	Returns TRUE if the number is even	=ISEVEN(value)
	ISLOGICAL	Returns TRUE if the value is a logical value	=ISLOGICAL(value)
	ISNA	Returns TRUE if the value is the #N/A error value	=ISNA(value)
	ISNONTEXT	Returns TRUE if the value is not text	=ISNONTEXT(value)
	ISNUMBER	Returns TRUE if the value is a number	=ISNUMBER(value)
	ISODD	Returns TRUE if the number is odd	=ISODD(value)
	ISREF	Returns TRUE if the value is a reference	=ISREF(value)
	ISTEXT	Returns TRUE if the value is text	=ISTEXT(value)
	N	Returns a value converted to a number	=N(value)
	NA	Returns the error value #NA	=NA()
	TYPE	Returns a number that indicates a value's data type	=TYPE(value)

In the syntax shown above, the arguments have the following meanings:

	Argument	Meaning
Table 38 Information function arguments	error_val	Error value whose identifying number you want to find Commonly used in an IF function to test for an error value and return a text string, such as a message, instead of the error value.
	info_type	Text value specifying what type of cell information you want – can be any one of the following: "address", "col", "color", "contents", "filename", "format", "parentheses", "prefix", "protect", "row", "type", "width"
	reference	Cell about which you want information
	type_text	Text that specifies the type of information that you want returned – can be any one of the following: "directory", "memavail", "memused", "numfile", "origin", "osversion", "recalc", "release", "system", "Macintosh", "Windows", "totmem"
	value	Value that you want tested This can be a blank (empty cell), error, logical, text, number, or reference value, or a name referring to any of these, that you want to test.

Practical Application of Information Functions

Figure 24   Examples of Information functions

	A	B	C	D	E
1	Salesman	Sales Achieved - Jan 06		Error Flag Sample	#DIV/0!
2	Krish	15000		Error Flag Sample#2	#N/A
3	Mark	50000			
4	Mireille	Not Available			
5	Peter	25000			
6	Richard	70000			
7	Sandy	45000			
8					
9	Function	=CELL(info_type,ref)	=ERROR.TYPE(error_val)	=INFO(type_text)	=ISBLANK(value)
10	Result	$B$2	2	25	FALSE
11	Formula Used	=CELL("address",B2)	=ERROR.TYPE(E1)	=INFO("numfile")	=ISBLANK(B4)
12					
13	Function	=ISERR(value)	=ISERROR(value)	=ISLOGICAL(value)	=ISNA(value)
14	Result	FALSE	TRUE	FALSE	TRUE
15	Formula Used	=ISERR(E2)	=ISERROR(E1)	=ISLOGICAL(B3)	=ISNA(E2)
16					
17	Function	=ISNONTEXT(value)	=ISNUMBER(value)	=ISREF(value)	=ISTEXT(value)
18	Result	TRUE	FALSE	FALSE	FALSE
19	Formula Used	=ISNONTEXT(B3)	=ISNUMBER(B4)	=ISREF(2000)	=ISTEXT(B3)
20					
21	Function	=N(value)	=NA()	=TYPE(value)	
22	Result	50000	#N/A	1	
23	Formula Used	=N(B3)	=NA()	=TYPE(B3)	

Nesting Functions

Many functions can be nested together to create a more sophisticated or complex formula to address a specific need. In common practice, we find that IF is the most commonly used function in nesting at multiple levels.

Functions can become quite complex by nesting one within another. For example, we can nest an AND function within an IF function. Let us consider the following real-life example:

Suppose that the cell B2 contains a profitability figure and that the cell C2 contains the variance of cost – actual cost as a percentage of estimated cost. Furthermore, in cell D2 you want an indicator to flash the word "Review" if the profitability (B2) is negative *and* if variance (C2) is more than 100%. You would enter this formula in cell D2:

=IF(AND(B2<0,C2>1), "Review", "").

Alternatively, if you want the cell D2 to display "Review" if *either* of the two conditions prevail, you would replace AND with OR. Thus, the formula would become

=IF(OR(B2<0,C2>1), "Review", "")

Nesting the IF function has a small glitch, though. You can nest the IF function only up to a maximum of seven levels. Anything more than that, and the formula will produce nothing but an error.

So, how can we get around this issue to put IF to work in more than seven levels?

Let us take a look at a clever workaround suggested by Chip Pearson in his website – www.cpearson.com/excel.htm.

The logic suggested here is very simple and rather straightforward. What we are going to do is to create the nesting in two different stages, as distinct formulas or named ranges, and then call the nesting from *another* IF function, which has the capability to house up to seven levels within itself.

Theoretically, it is going to look like this:

=IF("Check out logic", "Matched", "Unmatched")

Matched and Unmatched are nested formulas within their own rights, each nesting up to seven levels. For clarity, here is an example of this multi-level nesting, as presented by Chip Pearson in his site:

 Tip:

Word to the wise:
Use the colors Excel assigns to match the closing and opening parentheses to make sure that they come out even.

Example of Multi-level Nesting

Assume that we wanted an nested IF formula to test the following:

IF A4 = 1   Then 11

Else If   A4 = 2 Then 22

Else If   A4 = 3 Then 33

.....

Else If   A4 = 13 Then 130   Else "Not Found"

Step 1 – Create a named formula called OneToSix, as shown below:

```
=IF(Sheet1!$A$4=1,11,IF(Sheet1!$A$4=2,22,IF(Sheet1!$A$4=3,33,
IF(Sheet1!$A$4=4,44,IF(Sheet1!$A$4=5,55,IF(Sheet1!$A$4=4,44,
IF(Sheet1!$A$4=5,55,IF(Sheet1!$A$4=6,66,FALSE))))))))
```

Step 2 – Create another named formula called SevenToThirteen, as shown below:

```
=IF(Sheet1!$A$4=7,77,IF(Sheet1!$A$4=8,88,IF(Sheet1!$A$4=9,99,
IF(Sheet1!$A$4=10,100,IF(Sheet1!$A$4=11,110,IF(Sheet1!$A$4=12,120,
IF(Sheet1!$A$4=13,130,"NotFound")))))))
```

Step 3 – Enter the "master" formula, which incorporates these two formulas, in the worksheet cell as follows:

```
=IF(OneToSix,OneToSix,SevenToThirteen)
```

This circumvents the nested function limitation because no single part of the formula exceeds the seven level limit, even though the "sum" of the components may do so.

Troubleshooting and Evaluating Formulas and Functions

There are two simple options to troubleshooting and evaluating the entry of formulas / functions.

The first option is available from near the Formula Bar on top of the Column Headings, with the button named f_x.

If you are not very sure of what entry is required in a particular function or want to understand why your formula is not producing the intended result, just click on the f_x button, which will pop-up a small dialog box with the relevant fields of arguments (syntax) going into the formula.

This dialog box will give you a step-by-step idea of what is happening to your formula or function once you enter your arguments into the respective fields. It is an impressive way to visualize the changes happening to your data as you go along feeding the inputs into the formula.

Refer to **Figure 25** for a screenshot of the dialog box.

Figure 25   Function Arguments dialog box

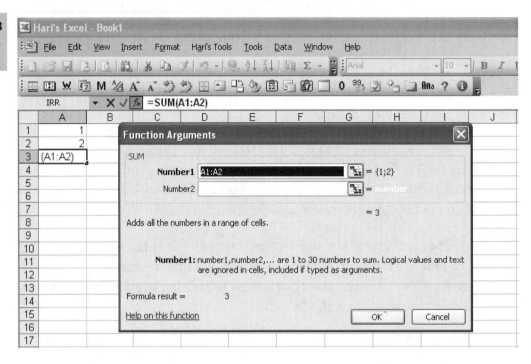

Still not sure about the function you're working on? Just click on "Help on this function" in the bottom-left portion of the dialog box to get more help and to correct your course.

An additional way to evaluate the formula's syntax is available under the Main menu bar. Select Tools → Formula Auditing → Evaluate Formula.

For example, using the formula shown above, assume that the cell A3 has been entered as =A1+A2 instead of Sum(A1:A2).

When we invoke the Formula Evaluator, we see the following dialog box:

Figure 26

Evaluate Formula dialog box

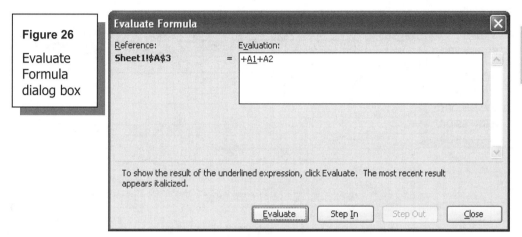

You can delve into the details of the current underlined expression by clicking on the Step In button. You will get the following screen, which shows the value of the first expression:

Figure 27

Using Step In to examine an element in a formula

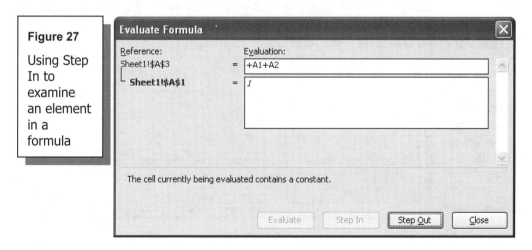

 Note:

The outline tree in the upper left helps you to keep track of where you are.

To continue the evaluation, use the Step Out button to come back out one level. Now you are ready to evaluate the second expression:

Figure 28

Ready to evaluate the second expression

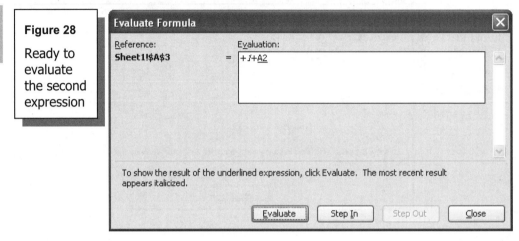

Use the Step In button to reveal the value of the second expression:

Figure 29

One of the last results of running Evaluate Formula tool shows the value of the second expression

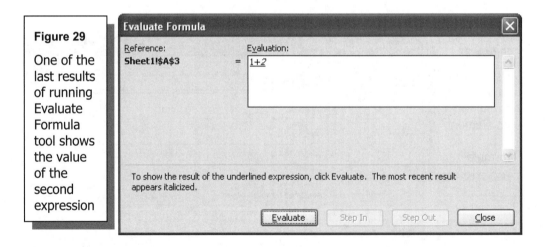

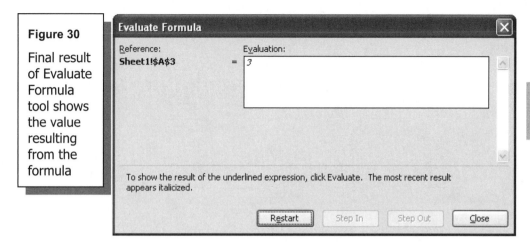

Figure 30

Final result of Evaluate Formula tool shows the value resulting from the formula

Conclusion

This brings us to the end of yet another leg of our journey through in Excel – through the thickets of Formulas and Functions. This is a wonderful treasure house that can simplify working with Excel to an unimaginable extent.

To get the most out of formulas and functions, keep learning about and exploring the available formulas. It always pays to keep in touch with the functions by practicing samples now and then, and also by visiting some websites that offer great advice on Excel formulas and customizations.

Some of the interesting websites worth a visit include the following:

http://www.mrexcel.com

http://www.experts-exchange.com/Applications/MS_Office/Excel/

http://www.tushar-mehta.com/excel/

http://www.mvps.org/dmcritchie/excel/

http://exceltips.vitalnews.com

Chapter 3

Data Management in Excel

Excel is widely known as a spreadsheet for bean counters, but there is another very important side to it:

The All-Powerful Data Management Toolset!

Excel can provide you with almost all of the data management and analysis functions available with any other powerful database management application.

In this chapter, we will review in detail the basic Data Management facilities and functions offered by Excel.

We will cover the more advanced topics concerning data tables, creating and managing lists, consolidation of data, importing external data, and handling xml data in the next chapter on Advanced Data Management in Excel, starting on page 137.

Similarly, PivotTable and PivotChart facilities will also be covered in a separate chapter (Introducing PivotTables starting on page 166) due to the importance and complexity of the subject.

Topics in this chapter:

- Database management – the basics

- Data management functions available in Excel

- Sorting data

- Filtering data – AutoFilter and Advanced Filter

- Subtotals, grouping and outlining

Data validation feature

Converting text to columns / importing text data

Sound interesting?

Chapter 4 **Database Management – the Basics**

A database is a collection of organized information. Normally, a database uses a table or list to hold data, which is made up of fields and records. An Excel worksheet list can be used as a database because the worksheet columns serve as fields while the rows serve as records.

A phonebook is an example of a database. Each company or listing within the phonebook is a "record". The names of the business, the city, and phone number are all separate "fields" within the "record". The entire list of records is referred to as the "database".

An organized database should be carefully planned from the beginning stage of design and should also contain elements of data validation and control.

For a successful data management application, there should be facilities to sort data, filter results, provision for grouping, outlining and subtotaling, and for importing data. All these elements are available with Excel and, in fact, the data management facilities keep getting better with each updated version of Excel.

Since Excel has all the features of a basic database management application, it is powerful enough to be considered as the first choice for any new database.

You should consider using a database program such as MS-Access only when one or all of the following issues begin to occur in Excel:

> ➤ When the size of the database simply becomes too large to manipulate data effectively.

> ➤ When you spend too much time analyzing data using filters and advanced filters.

> ➤ When Excel cannot create reports that look the way you need them to.

Data Management Functions Available in Excel

Figure 31   Excel's Data Management functions

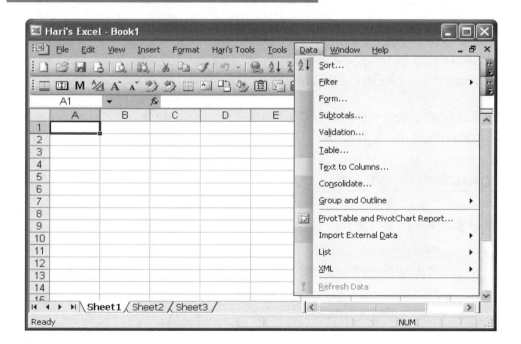

These are the data management functions available to you:

> ➢ Creating a database using manual data capture and using a data form

> ➢ Sorting a database (simple and advanced)

> ➢ Filtering data – AutoFilter and Advanced filter

> ➢ Creating subtotals

> ➢ Grouping / Ungrouping the Data and Outlining

> ➢ Implementing Data Validation routines

> ➢ Separating data and splitting data in a single cell across many columns

Let's analyze each one of these elements in detail.

Creating a Database

To recap the basics, a database is a collection of records that are comprised of fields. In Excel's language, it is a collection of rows (records), comprising column-wise information (fields).

In Excel, you can create a database either by manually keying in records, or by automating data capture using a form. Let's look at the first option in detail.

Manual Data Capture

Step 1 – Open a new Excel worksheet, name it Database, and enter the information as shown in **Figure 32** across the columns. You have just made a database design!

Figure 32 Blank database design for manual data capture

	A	B	C	D	E	F	G	H
1	Name	Address1	Address2	City	State	Country	Phone	Email
2								
3								
4								

In the preceding figure, all the data in range A1:H1 constitutes the column headings – in other words, the field names for the database.

Step 2 – Enter data about one new contact in row 2 – you will enter all the information in cells A2:H2. Row 2 now constitutes one record for your database, and all the information contained in A2:H2 are the fields for this record. Similarly, you can add more records by just entering the relevant information in row 3 and onwards.

The following figure shows the same database structure filled with some sample records, with the data capture done manually.

Figure 33 Database structure with sample records

	A	B	C	D	E	F	G	H
1	Name	Address1	Address2	City	State	Country	Phone	Email
2	Hari	No 40	Agm St	Chennai	TN	India	+91-44-000	pkhari@technologist.com
3	Priya	No 10	Ven St	Chennai	TN	India	+91-44-001	webmaster@hari.ws
4	Ananth	No 104	Ali Red St	Dubai	DXB	UAE	+971-4-001	webmaster@vedarahasya.net

Data Capture Using a Form

Step 1 – Start with the blank database example we used above. Time we will capture data using the Form feature of Excel.

Step 2 – Place the cursor in one of the field names, and click on Data → Form.

Step 3 – Click OK in the dialog box that follows, where Excel asks you to confirm if the first row contains the field labels.

Now you will be presented with a small, handy data capture form, as shown below.

Figure 34

Excel's Data Capture form

Note:

If you are planning to do data capture using a Form, there is a restriction of a maximum of 32 fields. However, when you are doing a manual data capture, you can have any number of fields in your database.

> Note that Excel uses the worksheet name (Database) as the Heading of the dialog box. You may see it as Sheet1 or Sheet3 or whatever, depending on your sheet name.

> The buttons in the form are straightforward.

  • New to create a new record

  • Criteria to specify some criteria

  • Find buttons to search for a particular record (based on the criteria)

  • Delete button to delete the current record

- Close button to close the data capture form

Step 4 – Enter new set of sample data into the form. Save it as a new record by press the Enter key. Excel will append it to your database as the last record.

Sorting a Database

Sorting is a function that gets used frequently when working with a database. Although a database is a collection of *organized* information, it can quickly become very large and unwieldy when you try to order your data in a specific way.

Sorting is the best way and the first step toward getting your records into a particular order. It can also facilitate a quick review of the total database.

Sorting allows you to check the extremes, or range, of your data. For instance, sorting employees' data by evaluation scores in descending order will put the top performer at the top of the list and take the lowest scorer to the bottom. You can also easily pick up the top 10 performers by just selecting the first 10 rows of the sorted data.

When you sort, Excel rearranges rows, columns, or individual cells using the sort order that you specify.

You can sort lists in ascending order (A to Z, 1 to 9) or descending order (Z to A, 9 to 1), and even sort based on the contents of one or more columns.

Steps in Data Sorting

Step 1 – When doing a data sort, you first need to select the data to be sorted. See example below, where the range A1:B9 has been selected.

	A	B
1	Employee	Eval Score
2	Sam	92
3	Rita	81
4	Bob	98
5	Mary	90
6	Cathy	76
7	Nicole	94
8	Gwyneth	81
9	Paris	91

Figure 35

Selecting the data to be sorted

Chapter 4

 Note:

Excel has an intuitive mechanism that allows it to select the data range automatically when you go to Data → Sort.

Keep the cursor in cell A3 and select Sort from the Data menu. Excel will automatically select the contiguous range of data nearby, which in the above case is range A1:B9.

 Caution!

If there is a blank row within the data range, the intuitive mechanism will stop at that blank row and may sort only a portion of your data, which can have disastrous results. If this happens, use the Undo button or press Ctrl + Z to reverse the sort.

Step 2 – Go to Data → Sort. The **Sort** dialog box displays:

Figure 36

Setting the data sort options

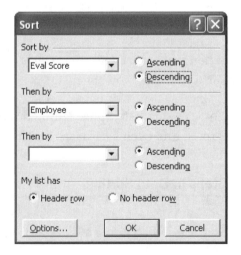

Here, you have a choice of selecting up to three different sorting keys. In the figure, you can see that Evaluation Score is selected as the primary sorting key and Employee is selected as the secondary sorting key.

We are able to see the field names in the drop down because the option "My list [data range] has Header Row" is selected. Alternatively, if "My list has No Header Row" is selected, you will see only Column A, Column B, and so on, in the Sort Key selection box.

 Caution!

Failure to specify a header row will result in the field names also being included in the sorting, which should be avoided. Be sure to select the has Header row option.

Step 3 – Click on the OK button to see the sorted data. The result for our current example is in the following figure.

Figure 37

Data sorted according to criteria specified in Step 2.

	A	B
1	Employee	Eval Score
2	Bob	98
3	Nicole	94
4	Sam	92
5	Paris	91
6	Mary	90
7	Gwyneth	81
8	Rita	81
9	Cathy	76

Note in rows 7 and 8 that both employees have the same evaluation score, but because the secondary sort key is "Employee-Ascending", Gwyneth comes first, followed by Rita.

Step 4 – In the **Sort Data** dialog box (see Figure 36), there is an Options button at the bottom left for more options. Click on this to open the **Sort Options** dialog box, where you can set whether case-sensitive sort is required or not.

You can also set the data sort orientation – from top to bottom or from left to right. This dialog box is meant for advanced users, and is shown in the figure below.

Figure 38

Advanced Sort Options available

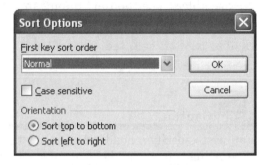

Filtering Data – AutoFilter and Advanced Filter

Filter is another important function on the Data menu. It has two variants – the AutoFilter and the Advanced Filter.

AutoFilter

AutoFilter also has an intuitive mechanism like the Sort function, and can select the nearest contiguous data and filter them based on the top most row as the Header row. But it is always advisable to select the range of data to auto filter, with the top row being the header row.

In the figure below, notice that we first select the range with the header row on top, and then we go to Data → Filter → AutoFilter.

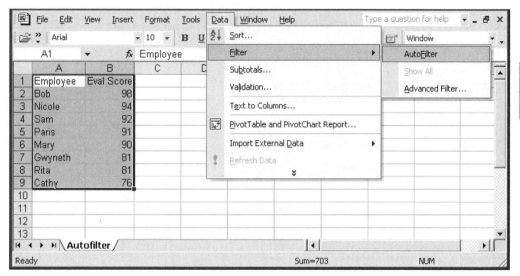

Figure 39 Selecting the AutoFilter option

The result is that you will be shown the header row with a drop down menu containing three different main options:

➤ All

➤ Top 10

➤ Custom

You will also see each record listed separately in the drop down. The options available in the drop down have increased with the latest versions of Excel, but these options are the only ones relevant to AutoFilter.

If you select All, you will see all records listed with no filtering. The option for listing the Top 10 only works in a column that contains numeric data. In our example, selecting Top 10 under the Employee column will not produce any result, whereas selecting Top 10 under the Eval Score column can list out the Top 10 performers and hide the rest.

You can modify the Top 10 option to list either the Top or Bottom items, and even set it to list between 1 to 500 items. Set this up in the Option box that opens when you select Top 10 from the drop down list.

Figure 40

Showing only the Top 5 items

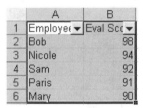

The figure above shows the AutoFilter option used to display the Top 5 items, based on the Eval Scores column.

But wait, there's more! Not only can you can choose to see the Top or Bottom items, you can also see the Top or Bottom Percentage of the data range. Thas is, you can see either the Top 5 items or the Top 5 Percentage of the data. As you can see, this is a very powerful feature in Excel and, unfortunately, a less familiar one as well.

Do you do a lot of juggling around to select the Top 10 customers each quarter? This option can straightaway pull out the data and immediately give you the result.

The Custom option under AutoFilter is for advanced users and enables you to filter the data for a particular condition.

For instance, you can set the filter to show where the employee name begins with B, or ends with H, or contains the letter a, or does not contain the letter z.

Similarly, numeric data can be checked with conditions set to list data which is greater than, equal to, less than, less than or equal to, or greater than or equal to a particular number.

To understand the condition better, let's set a custom filter condition on the Eval Scores column to show only those records where Eval Scores are less than 90. See the figure below for the custom filter settings.

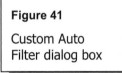

Figure 41

Custom Auto Filter dialog box

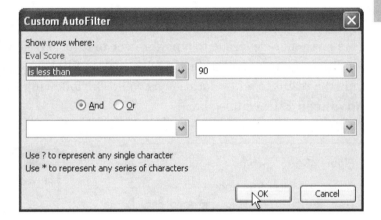

The result is reflected in the main window (see **Figure 42**). Note that some row numbers are missing. These rows are merely hidden to show you only the filtered results – they are not deleted or hidden forever.

Figure 42

Results of using the Custom AutoFilter

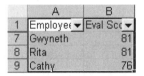

You can set a maximum of up to two conditions that can be mutually inclusive or exclusive. In other words, both the conditions can be enforced on an "either-or" basis or as "one-plus-other" basis.

Note:

There is only one indicator that shows which field has been filtered on. The field name drop down will be marked with a blue drop down arrow, as opposed to the others, which normally have black drop down arrows.

Chapter 4 | **Advanced Filter**

This is a function that is much more advanced than the custom filter function. This gives more leverage to a power user to filter based on more than two conditions (which is a limitation with custom filter) and either to display or to copy the result to a new location as well. The following figure shows the **Advanced Filter** dialog box.

Figure 43

Advanced Filter functions

The Advanced Filter dialog lets you choose to show the results in the original place or to copy the results to another location (which is a blessing).

You can select the list range, set the criteria, and select the destination to copy to; you can also set the option (see the check box at the bottom) to show only unique records or to include duplicates as well (checkbox unchecked).

Now let's look at four different scenarios using the Advanced Filter (with the result copied to a different location). This will give you an idea of how wonderful this feature is.

Scenario 1 – Filtering Data Based on One Condition

Figure 44 Advanced Filter – based on only one condition

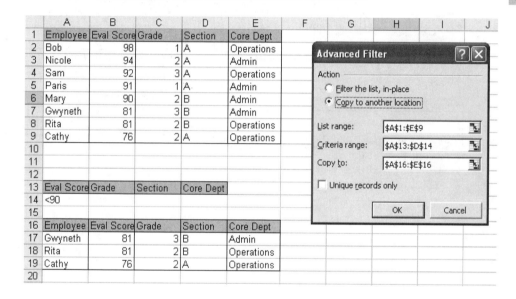

Scenario 2 – Filtering Data Based on Two Conditions

Figure 45 Advanced Filter – based on only two conditions

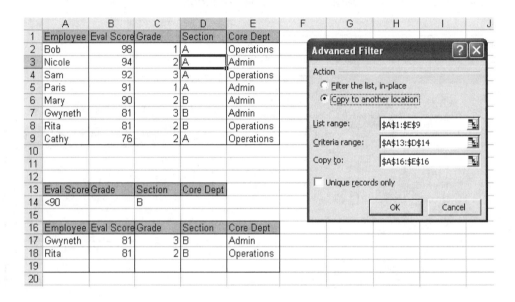

Scenario 3 – Filtering Data Based on Three Conditions

Figure 46 Advanced Filter – based on only three conditions

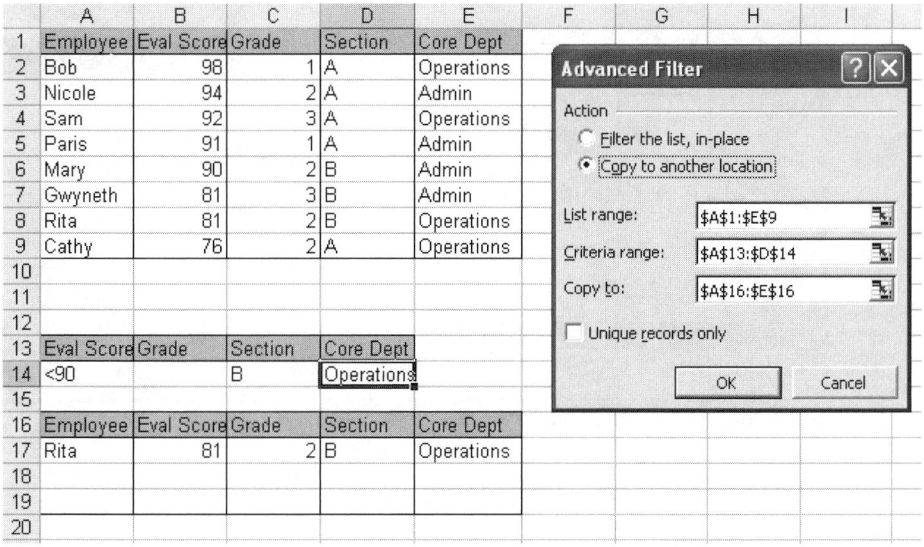

	A	B	C	D	E	F	G	H	I
1	Employee	Eval Score	Grade	Section	Core Dept				
2	Bob	98	1	A	Operations				
3	Nicole	94	2	A	Admin				
4	Sam	92	3	A	Operations				
5	Paris	91	1	A	Admin				
6	Mary	90	2	B	Admin				
7	Gwyneth	81	3	B	Admin				
8	Rita	81	2	B	Operations				
9	Cathy	76	2	A	Operations				
10									
11									
12									
13	Eval Score	Grade		Section	Core Dept				
14	<90			B	Operations				
15									
16	Employee	Eval Score	Grade	Section	Core Dept				
17	Rita	81	2	B	Operations				
18									
19									
20									

Advanced Filter

Action
- Filter the list, in-place
- Copy to another location

List range: $A$1:$E$9
Criteria range: $A$13:$D$14
Copy to: $A$16:$E$16

Unique records only

OK   Cancel

Scenario 4 – Filtering Data Based on Four Conditions

Chapter 4

> **Figure 47**   Advanced Filter – based on only four conditions

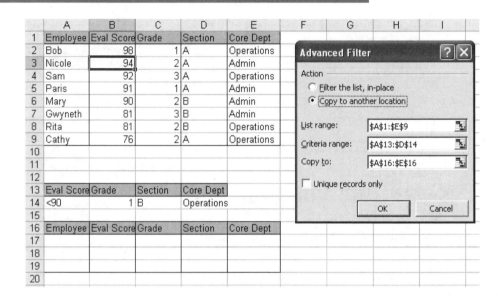

Subtotals, Grouping and Outlining

You can sort data and obtain subtotals on selected fields to get an abstract idea of the number of records that meet a specific condition.

Although called a Subtotal, this function can be used to get the Sum, Count, Min, Max, Average, Product, Variance, and Standard Deviation of the selected fields.

Before using Subtotal on a range of data, it is always advisable to sort the data with your chosen field as the primary sort key.

The field chosen as the primary sort key should be the one on which you are going to calculate the subtotals. Only this can give you a meaningful subtotal result.

Let's use our previous example to examine subtotals. We will see how to compute the count of records based on the field "Core Dept".

Step 1 – Select the range, then sort the data on Core Dept.

Figure 48 Sorting the data based on Core Dept field

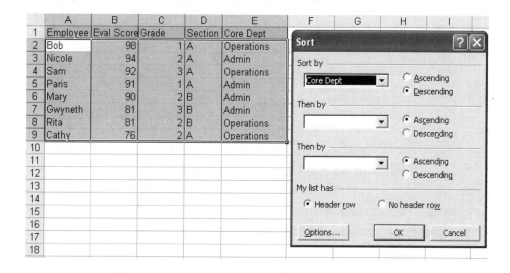

Step 2 – Select Data → Subtotal; set it as shown below:

Figure 49 Calculating a subtotal based on the Core Dept field

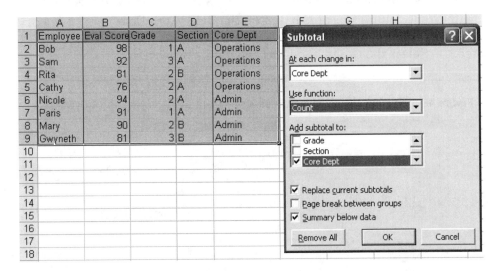

Now you will see the following result window:

 Note:

Figure 50 Results window after applying the subtotals

Expansion/
contraction bars
appear on the left.

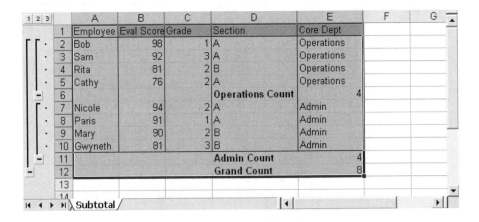

Step 3 – Click on the "2" on the left to see the abstract result.

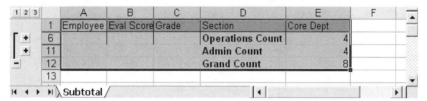

Figure 51   Results window viewing only the Outline result

Chapter 4

Grouping and Outlining

Do you like (if not love) the abstract result feature that you see in Step 3? Let's see how to create and apply this grouping feature, even if you are not planning to do a subtotal.

In the **Figure 52**, using our example case, we have done a manual grouping by first selecting the rows to group, then using Data → Group and Outline → Group, and finally clicking OK.

 Note:

You can choose to group and ungroup columns as well as rows.

Figure 52   Results window after performing manual grouping

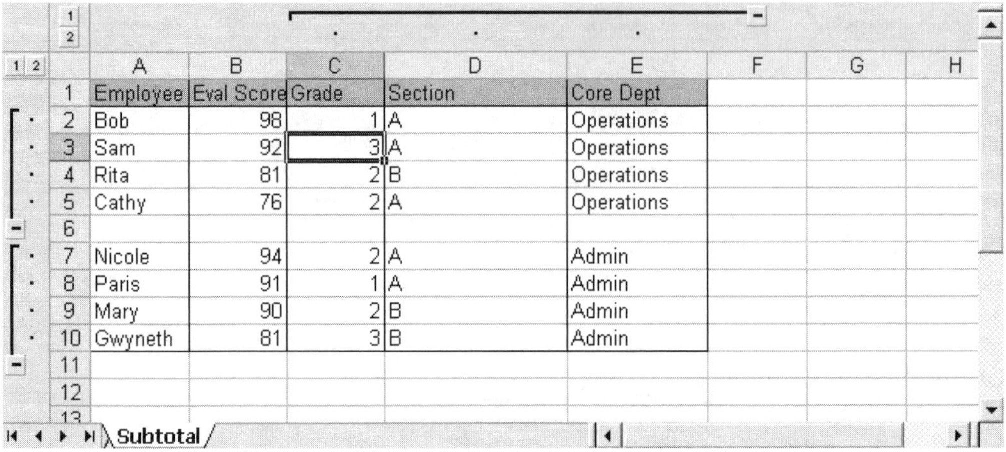

	A	B	C	D	E	F	G	H
1	Employee	Eval Score	Grade	Section	Core Dept			
2	Bob	98	1	A	Operations			
3	Sam	92	3	A	Operations			
4	Rita	81	2	B	Operations			
5	Cathy	76	2	A	Operations			
6								
7	Nicole	94	2	A	Admin			
8	Paris	91	1	A	Admin			
9	Mary	90	2	B	Admin			
10	Gwyneth	81	3	B	Admin			
11								
12								
13								

Subtotal

You can outline worksheets automatically if they have summary formulas that reference cells in the detail data. All columns containing summary formulas must be either to the right or to the left of the detail data; similarly, rows containing summary formulas must be either below or above the detail data.

To outline the data automatically:

Step 1 – Select the range of cells you want to outline.

Step 2 – To outline the entire worksheet, click any cell on the worksheet.

Step 3 – On the Data menu, point to Group and Outline, and then click Auto Outline.

To outline the data manually:

Step 1 – Select the rows or columns that contain detail data.
Detail rows or columns are usually adjacent to the row or column that contains the summary formula or a heading. For example, if row 6

---

contains totals for rows 3 through 5, select rows 3 through 5. If row 8 contains a heading that describes rows 9 through 12, select rows 9 through 12.

Step 2 – On the Data menu, point to Group and Outline, and then click Group. The outline symbols appear beside the group on the screen.

Step 3 – Continue selecting and grouping detail rows or columns until you have created all of the levels you want in the outline.

 Note:

You can ungroup the rows / columns, and you can also clear the Outline from the workbooks using the sub-menu items available under Data → Group and Outline.

Data Validation Feature

Excel provides you with a powerful data validation feature that you can use to designate valid cell entries. The validation settings can be different for each and every single cell, or can be applied for a range.

The following figure shows a snapshot of the **Data Validation** dialog box.

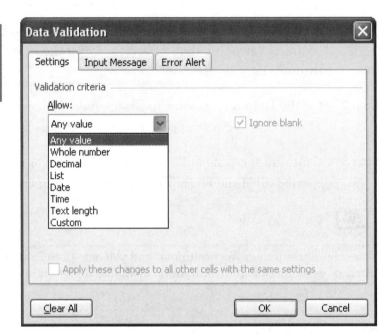

Figure 53

Data Validation dialog box

Chapter 4

The Data Validation dialog box has three tabs – one each for configuring:

> ➢ Settings

> ➢ Input Message

> ➢ Error Alerts

This example should make data validation features easier to understand. Using our employee database, let's assume that we want to restrict entries in column B (Eval Score) to ensure that only values less than 100 are entered.

In other words, no employee data should be entered with more than 100 as the evaluation score in any record. We will now see the step-by-step approach to implementing this control.

Step 1 – Select the Data in the entire column B by clicking on the column name, or by keeping the cursor anywhere in column B and pressing Ctrl+Spacebar.

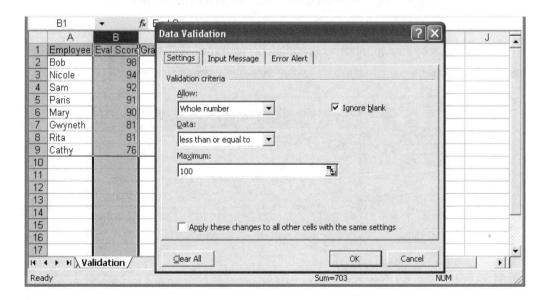

Figure 54

Selecting the entire column to apply Data Validation

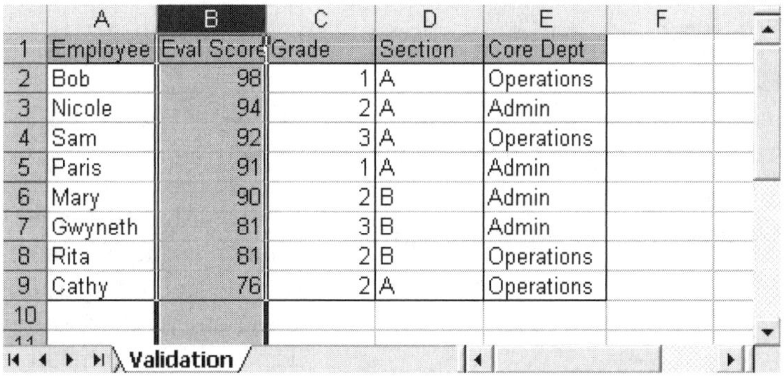

Step 2 – Apply Data Validation Rule.

Select Data → Validation, and make the settings as shown in the figure below. Click OK to apply the settings.

Figure 55 Applying a data validation rule to the entire column

These settings will only allow entry of whole numbers with a value less than or equal to 100.

All of these choices are available in the drop down menus, except for "less than or equal to 100", which we had to key in as the Maximum value. Also, as a general rule, tick the "Ignore blank" check box to allow blank cells. Of course, you can choose to prohibit blanks, as per your requirements and convenience.

 Note:

A data value filling a validated cell could have a blank value if it is being referenced from another cell or formula. To allow a blank value to appear in the validated cell, select the "Ignore blank" checkbox; otherwise, leave it open. In effect, if the checkbox is not ticked, Excel will not allow a blank value to be entered in a cell because it is against the validation rules. (The blank value is also considered as a value and not just as empty).

Step 3 – Specify an Input Message. If you want to add a comment on the cells to tell the data entry operator that "Only Whole numbers with value less than or equal to 100 are accepted", then go to the second tab of the Data Validation dialog box and set it as shown below.

Figure 56 Specifying an input message along with the validation

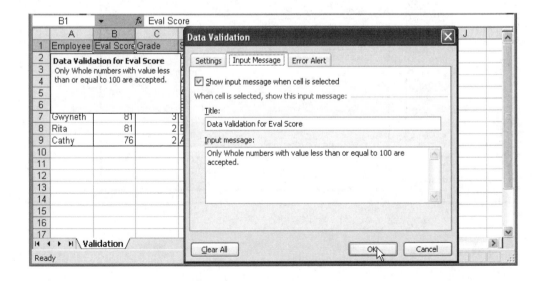

The input message in the pop-up box shows you how the comment will look when a user clicks on any cell in column B.

Step 4 – Specify Error Alert Dialog.

Now that you have defined the data validation rules, you need to enforce them. After all, rules that are not backed up by forceful implementation lack meaning. This enforceability is provided by the third tab of the Data Validation dialog box.

Open up the Error Alert tab and set it as shown below:

Figure 57

Specifying an Error Alert message along with the validation rule

Under Style, there are three types from which to choose:

> **Stop**   makes the rule mandatory

> **Warning**   asks for a reconfirmation if you violate the rule

> **Information**   allows you to continue but provides you with requirement and violation information

The Stop style is recommended here because it will not allow the user to proceed with a wrong entry at all and is the most certain choice to ensure a clear data validation.

This topic is normally not covered at great length by the standard text books on Excel because it is considered as a specialist's area and it requires greater understanding of the implementation side. However, using the above example as a guide, you should have a pretty good idea of how to design and implement data validation.

Converting Text to Columns / Importing Text Data

One of my personal favorites in the Data menu is the process of converting text to columns. It is an especially useful process when you are importing ASCII- or CSV-based data into Excel for further processing.

Let us assume that you have data in column A that contains first and last names, separated by a comma. This scenario is shown in the figure below.

Figure 58

Data to be converted using Text to Columns feature

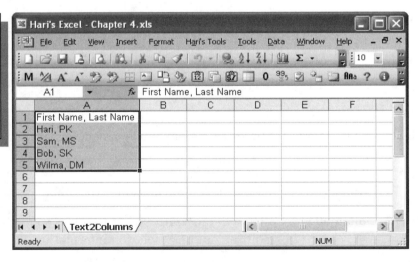

You want to have the first name and last name separated and available in two separate columns. What other option is there apart from typing each again separately?

Excel comes to your rescue with this wonderful "Text to Columns" option in the Data menu!

Start by selecting the data that you want to split into two columns (may be even more), then click on Data → Text to Columns. A Conversion Wizard pops-up that will take care of the splitting in just three steps. We will run through these steps using our sample data.

Step 1 of 3 – Decide the Data Type option for Splitting:

Figure 59

Selecting Delimited or Fixed Width and previewing data

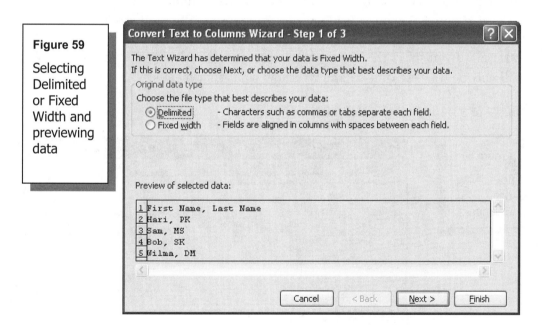

In this step, you tell Excel how you want to proceed with the splitting of the data. The two options available are:

➢ Delimited

➢ Fixed width

Use the first option (Delimited) if the data contains some identifier like a Comma, Space, or Tab on which the data can be split. Use the second option (Fixed width) if the data is standardized so that it can be easily broken by its position inside a cell (say every 5th element, or 8th number).

In our example, we have a comma as a delimiter, so we will go with Delimited. In some cases, Excel may detect a pattern in the data and suggest one particular option out of the two – but you are the ultimate judge in this matter. Be sure to select the appropriate option according to the nature of the data.

After all, if you select the Fixed width when you actually have identifiers, you will only be wasting time ... and we know what that means!

Step 2 of 3 – Identify the Delimiters.

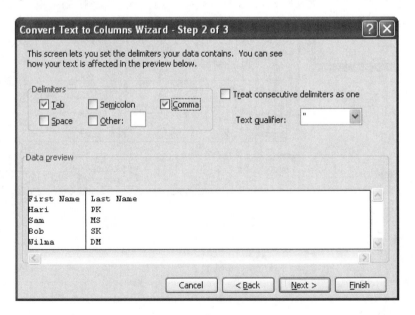

Figure 60

Identifying the delimiters

In this screen, Excel checks the Tab box by default, and gives us option to select one or more of the other delimiters.

Since Comma is the delimiter in our example, we check the Comma box, and immediately Excel shows the split up data in the "Data Preview" section in the bottom pane of the dialog box. Having done this, click on Next to proceed to Step 3 of 3.

Step 3 of 3 – Set the Formatting

In this third and final step, you have the choice of pre-setting the formatting for each and every column of split-up data.

Figure 61   Setting the formatting

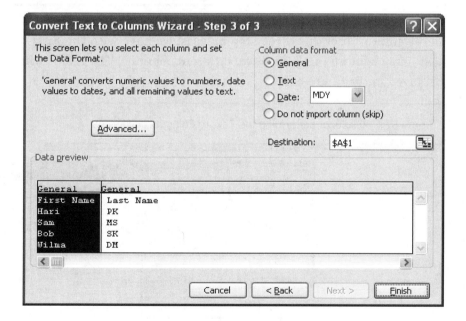

The figure above shows the last step of the conversion.

You may want to set some fields as Date type, some as Text type, and some fields you may not want to import at all.

Exercise the formatting options by clicking on the relevant column of data in the "Data Preview" section, then ticking the desired "Column data format" in the top right portion of the dialog box.

There is also an "Advanced" button that allows you to set the Decimal and Thousand separators. This also allows you to control "trailing minus sign for negative numbers" .

 Note:

Clicking on the "Trailing minus for negative numbers" checkbox tells Excel that numbers followed by a minus sign are negative numbers. It then moves the minus sign to the front of the number. Try this when you get an electronic bank statement where the all the debits are shown with a trailing minus sign. Just select those cells and use this feature to see Excel's magic at work.

As the end result of this three-step process, we have with the First name and Last name split up nicely into two different columns. The result window is displayed in the figure below.

Figure 62   Results of performing the Text to Column conversions

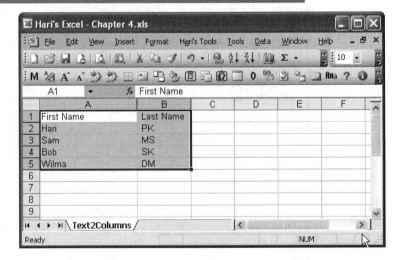

Sound Interesting?

Many of us really get involved and interested in the data management functions of Excel. If you are one such, watch out – there is a lot more to know about advanced data management and database functions, which will make them even more attractive. These topics are covered in the chapters on Formulas, Functions, and More... starting on page 53 and in Advanced Data Management in Excel starting on page 137.

Chapter 4

Chapter 4

Advanced Data Management in Excel

Thus far in our travels, we have checked out the basic data management tools available in Excel. We are now ready to proceed to the essentials of Excel's Advanced Data Management facilities.

In this chapter, we will review details concerning data tables, creating and managing lists, consolidating data, importing external data, and handling xml data.

However, before venturing into these topics, we first need to examine the database management functions available in Excel and how best to put them to use.

Topics covered in this chapter:

- Database functions – the concept

- Detailed listing of database functions

- Using database functions

- Working with data tables

- Creating and managing lists

- Consolidation of data

- Importing external data

- More terrific links

Database Functions – the Concept

We explored the basic database functions available in Excel in Formulas, Functions, and More..., which covered the description, syntax, and arguments for the database functions.

A database function is basically structured in the following form:

=Dfunction(database,field,criteria)

The function name begins with a D to indicate that it is a Database-related function. There are various functions, such as SUM, MAX, MIN, AVERAGE, and COUNT, that are available in the database segment as DSUM, DMAX, DMIN, DAVERAGE, and DCOUNT, respectively.

There are three elements in the arguments area:

> **Database** refers to a range of cells that makes up the list or database, in which rows are records and columns are fields. The first row of the range contains labels for each column.

> **Field** indicates which column is to be used in the function by giving either the column label within double quotation marks or the column number.

> **Criteria** is a range of cells that contains the conditions to be satisfied before executing the function on the specified range. At least one column label and one cell below the column label are required to specify a criteria.

In creating criteria, you have many options available, such as the following:

> Multiple conditions under one column

> One condition under multiple columns

> One condition in one column or another

The criteria are totally customizable, as per the requirements of the case under review.

Let's move on now to database functions and the situations in which we can use them.

Detailed Listing of Database Functions

Table 39 shows the database functions.

Table 39 List of database management functions

Function	Description	Function Syntax
DAVERAGE	Returns the average of selected database entries	=DAVERAGE(database,field,criteria)
DCOUNT	Counts the cells that contain numbers in a database	=DCOUNT(database,field,criteria)
DCOUNTA	Counts nonblank cells in a database	=DCOUNTA(database,field,criteria)
DGET	Extracts, from a database, a single record that matches the specified criteria	=DGET(database,field,criteria)
DMAX	Returns the maximum value from selected database entries	=DMAX(database,field,criteria)
DMIN	Returns the minimum value from selected database entries	=DMIN(database,field,criteria)
DPRODUCT	Multiplies the values in a particular field of records that match the criteria in a database	=DPRODUCT(database,field,criteria)
DSTDEV	Estimates the standard deviation based on a sample of selected database entries	=DSTDEV(database,field,criteria)

Function	Description	Function Syntax
DSTDEVP	Calculates the standard deviation based on the entire population of selected database entries	=DSTDEVP(database,field,criteria)
DSUM	Adds the numbers in the field column of records in the database that match the criteria	=DSUM(database,field,criteria)
DVAR	Estimates variance based on a sample from selected database entries	=DVAR(database,field,criteria)
DVARP	Calculates variance based on the entire population of selected database entries	=DVARP(database,field,criteria)
GETPIVOTDATA	Returns data stored in a PivotTable	=GETPIVOTDATA(data_field,pivot_table,field1,item1,field2,item2,...)

In the syntax shown above, the arguments or the variables in the brackets have the following meanings:

	Argument	Meaning
Table 40 Arguments and syntax used in database management functions	database	Range of cells that makes up the list or database, where rows are records, and columns are fields The first row of the list contains labels for each column.
	field	Indicates which column is used in the function The column label within double quotation marks or the column number can be given.
	criteria	Range of cells that contains the conditions you specify

	Argument	Meaning
Table 40 Arguments and syntax used in database management functions		At least one column label and at least one cell below the column label is required for specifying a criteria.
	data_field	Name, enclosed in quotation marks, for the data field that contains the data you want to retrieve
	pivot_table	Reference to any cell, range of cells, or named range in a PivotTable report
	field1, item1, field2, item2, etc.	One to 14 pairs of field names and item names (enclosed in quotation marks) that describe the data you want to retrieve
		For OLAP PivotTable reports, items can contain the source name of the dimension as well as the source name of the item.

Chapter 5

Using Database Functions

We will now continue our journey by examining the powerful functions of database management to see how they apply in real-life situations.

We'll use the database shown below for all our database function examples, in which the database is referred to by the range A1:E26 (it could also be referred to by a named range, created by blocking the range of cells, using Insert → Names → Define, and then naming the range).

Figure 63   Sample database used in this chapter

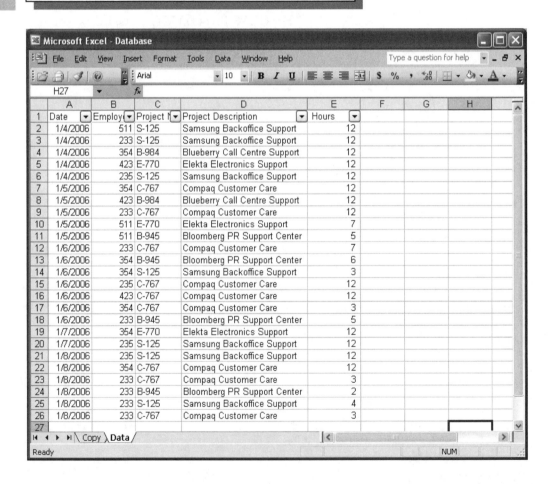

DSUM Function

The DSUM function is a good one to start with to ease your way toward understanding database functions. You can apply DSUM and obtain a result based on a single criterion or on one instance of multiple criteria.

DSUM Based on a Single Criterion

Figure 64

Setting the criteria range for the DSUM function

	G	H	I	J	K	L
1	Employee	Project No	Date	Employee	Project No	Hours
2	511	S-125	1/8/2006	233	C-767	>12
3	354	B-984		235		
4	423					

With the settings shown above in cells G1:L4, the formula =DSUM("A1:E26","Hours",I1:I2) gives a result of 36. The results are brought in as the sum total of all data under the field "Hours", where the date is equal to "1/8/2006".

DSUM Based on Multiple Conditions under the Same Field

Using the same information in the cells G1:L4, the formula =DSUM(A1:E26,"Hours",G1:G4) provides a result of 120. This is the sum total of all the hours for employees with numbers 511,354, and 423.

DSUM Based on Conditions under Different Fields

With the same criteria, the formula =DSUM(A1:E26,"Hours",G1:H2) yields a result of 12. This result is obtained by taking the sum of hours having the Project No S-125 and having the employee number 511 only.

DCOUNT Function

DCOUNT function is similar to the DSUM function but is used to obtain a count of the number of records matching a particular criteria rather than the sum total of a field.

The DCOUNT function can also be applied based on a single criterion or on one instance of multiple criteria.

DCOUNT Based on a Single Criterion

Using the same criteria settings as shown in **Figure 64**, the formula =DCOUNT("A1:E26","Hours",K1:K2) gives a result of 9, which matches the total number of records having the Project number C-767.

DCOUNT Based on Multiple Conditions under Same Field

The formula =DCOUNT(A1:E26,"Hours",J1:J3) provides a result of 12, which is the number of records having the employee number 233 or 235.

DCOUNT Based on Conditions under Different Fields

To get the count of the number of records with the employee number 233 and having the Project number C-767, we can use the formula =DCOUNT(A1:E26,"Hours",J1:K2).

Other Functions

The other database functions, such as DCOUNTA, DMAX, and DMIN, follow a similar syntax and structure and produce results based on the criteria selected.

Using the same sample database and criteria defined in cells G1:L4, let's take a look at the other functions and their results.

Figure 65

Various database functions and their results with criteria shown above

Formula Result	Function Usage
8.44	=DAVERAGE(A1:E26,"Hours",K1:K2)
8	=DCOUNTA(A1:E26,"Hours",J1:J2)
12	=DGET(A1:E26,"Hours",G1:H2)
4	=DMAX(A1:E26,"Hours",I1:J2)
2	=DMIN(A1:E26,"Hours",J1:J2)
756	=DPRODUCT(A1:E26,"Hours",J1:K2)
4	=DSTDEV(A1:E26,"Hours",J1:J2)
3.74	=DSTDEVP(A1:E26,"Hours",J1:J2)
16	=DVAR(A1:E26,"Hours",J1:J2)
14	=DVARP(A1:E26,"Hours",J1:J2)

Working with Data Tables

Working with data tables is one of those topics that is rarely elaborated upon because it is part of the "What-If Analysis" tools. As such, it is not detailed in the standard text books on Excel because it is specifically relevant for people who analyze information and options before making decisions. Sound like anyone you know?

Data tables can be structured either as a one-variable type or as a two-variable type. The single variable input cell can be row-oriented or column-oriented, depending on the table formation. Let us now create of a row-oriented data table, detailing the efforts involved in structuring it step-by-step, because this process is a little tricky.

 Note:

What-If analysis: A process of changing the values in cells to see how those changes affect the outcome of formulas on the worksheet. For example, varying the interest rate that is used in an amortization table to determine the amount of the payments

Step 1 – Key in the data and formula in one cell.

In the following example, we have entered the three different arguments required for the calculation of interest rate using the RATE function in cells A2:A4.

In the cell B5, enter the RATE function as follows:
=RATE(C2,B2,A2)*12

Figure 66

Setting up a data table based on a single variable

	A	B	C	D	E
	B5		f_x =RATE(C2,B2,A2)*12		
1	Loan Amount	Installment Amt	Term (months)		
2	$ 40,000.00	$ (1,000.00)	48		
3					
4					
5	Rate	9.24%			
6					

Now, we have one set of data and a function. We are ready to create a one-variable-based data table that is row-oriented.

Step 2 – Create the basis for the What-If scenario.

We have created additional terms to be used for What-If analysis across the cells C4:E4 (terms for 42, 52, and 60 months). In the next step, we will create a data table to perform the analysis.

Figure 67

Performing a What-If analysis – New Terms added

	A	B	C	D	E
1	Loan Amount	Installment Amt	Term (months)		
2	$ 40,000.00	$ (1,000.00)	48		
3					
4	New Terms		42	52	60
5	Rate	9.24%			
6					

Step 3 – Select the cells, and click Data → Table. Select the cells from B4:E5, and then go to Data → Table on the Main menu bar.

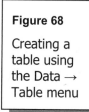

Figure 68

Creating a table using the Data → Table menu

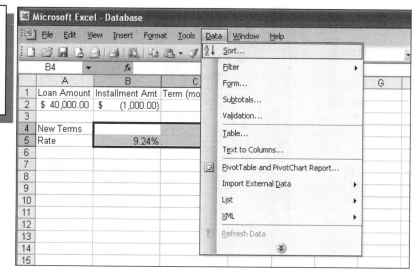

When you click on the Data → Table, a small dialog box pops up, as shown below:

Figure 69

The Table Input Cells dialog box

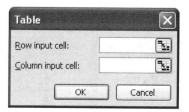

In this case, the data table is row-oriented, so enter the cell data in the field bearing the name "Row input cell:".

Step 4 – Mark the Input Cell by selecting C2 (it will appear as $C$2 – an absolute reference ensures that Excel will always look at the same cell) in the input cell field – and then click OK.

 Note:

In our row-oriented example, the input cell on which the entire what-if analysis revolves is cell C2, which contains the term that needs to be substituted with the new terms contained in C4:E4, and reviews the new results based on each new term.

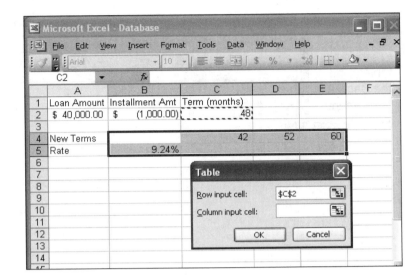

Figure 70

Marking the Input cells

Here comes the result!

The result window displays, with the new rates in the cells C5:E5, based on the substituted new terms available in cells C4:E4.

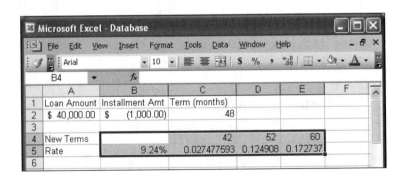

Figure 71

Data table results

Step 5 – Do the Formatting. Since the rates are now available in the cells C5:E5, we need to apply the Percentage formatting in the result area so that the results will display in the correct format.

Select cells C5:E5 and click on the Percentage button on the Formatting toolbar. Select the "Increase Decimal" button and set it for two decimal places.

Figure 72

Final formatted results

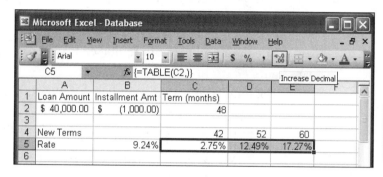

The final results present a clear What-If analysis, based on the input substitution data.

 Note:

A data table can be deleted only by deleting all the cells together. Excel creates the table by entering it as an array formula (see chapter on Introducing Array Formulas on page 56).

When you click through any of the cells in C5:E5, you will find that the formula bar just shows {=TABLE(C2,)}. The cells cannot be deleted individually, and the formula cannot be manually edited – any such attempt will produce an error, as shown in the following figure.

Figure 73

This error message pops up if you attempt to delete one of the cells within the data table

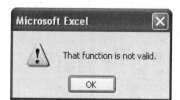

Data Table Based on Two Variables

Now let's take a look at the process of creating a data table based on two variables. The process is slightly more complex than that for one variable, but follows basically the same pattern.

Step 1 – Key in the data and formula in one cell. We have entered the different arguments / data in cells A2:A4.
In cell B5, enter the RATE function as follows: =RATE(C2,B2,A2)*12

Figure 74

Setting up a two-variable-based data table

	B5	▼	fx =RATE(C2,B2,A2)*12			
	A	B	C	D	E	
1	Loan Amount	Installment Amt	Term (months)			
2	$ 40,000.00	$ (1,000.00)	48			
3						
4						
5	Rate	9.24%				
6						

We are ready to create a two-variable-based data table that is both row-oriented and column-oriented.

Step 2 – Create the basis for What-If scenario.
We need to create the additional terms to be used for What-If analysis. Feed row-oriented variables into cells C5:E5, and column-oriented variables into B6:B7. See Figure 75.

Figure 75

Creation of new terms for performing the What-If analysis

	B5	▼	fx =RATE(C2,B2,A2)*12			
	A	B	C	D	E	F
1	Loan Amount	Installment Amt	Term (months)			
2	$ 40,000.00	$ (1,000.00)	48			
3						
4						
5	Rate	9.24%	42	52	60	
6		30000				
7		50000				
8						

Step 3 – Enter the variables for the data table. Select the cells from B5:E7, and then go to Data → Table on the Main menu bar. You will be presented with a small dialog box as follows:

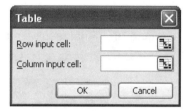

Figure 76

Table Input Cells dialog box

Our data table is based on two variables this time, so enter the following data in the input cells fields.

➢   Row input cell = C2

➢   Column input cell=A2

Figure 77

Marking the Input Cells

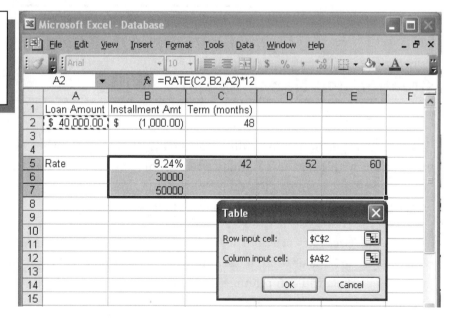

Step 4 – View the result window, which has the new rates in the cells C6:E7, based on the substituted new terms available in cells C5:E5 as well as in cells B6:B7. The Percentage formatting is applied, and is reflected in the results below.

Figure 78   Final result – a two-variable-based data table

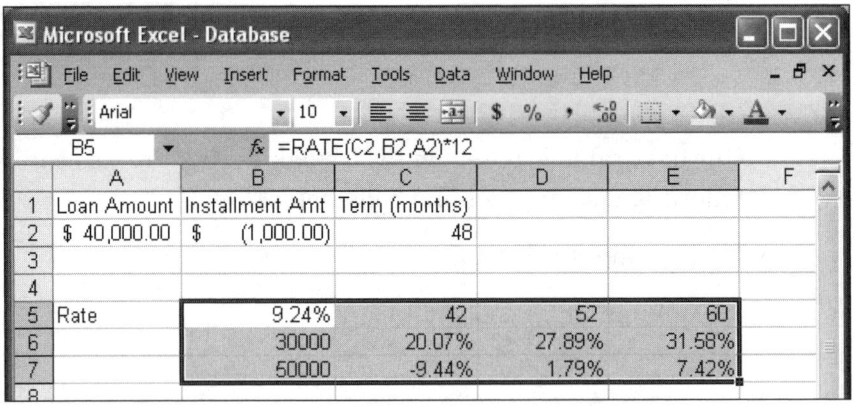

Creating and Managing Lists

Excel lists are designed to enable the sharing of data with other users through integration with Microsoft Windows SharePoint Services. If you have the Web address and authoring rights on a SharePoint site, you can share your list so other people can view, edit, and update the list.

A Microsoft Excel list provides features designed to make it easier to manage and analyze groups of related data in an Excel worksheet. When you designate a range as a list, you can manage and analyze the data in the list independently of data outside the list.

For example, you can create a PivotTable report and add a totals row and filter columns, using only the data contained within the list.

You can have multiple lists on your worksheet, which allows you a great deal of flexibility for separating your data into distinct, manageable sets according to your needs.

When you specify a range of cells as a list in Microsoft Excel, the List user interface brings up a lot of standard functionality that you can use on the data within that list.

 Note:

You cannot create a list in a shared workbook. You must first remove the workbook from shared use if you want to create a list.

Chapter 5

Advantages of Using a List

There are many advantages of using a list. Here are just a few of them:

> The data inside the list is auto-filtered, and can be sorted on a click.

> The list can easily be provided with a "total row". When you click on the cell within the total row, a drop down of aggregate functions is automatically available.

> The list is clearly marked by a blue border, which helps you to distinguish your list.

> The list size can be automatically increased or reduced by just dragging the border line.

> The penultimate row of the list is marked with a asterisk (*) by default. This is the "insert row", which will keep expanding automatically – when any new data is entered in that row, it will automatically insert another new row below that.

Step-by-Step Process of Creating a List

Let's go through the process of creating a list in a short sequence of steps.

Step 1 – Select the data, and click on Data → List → Create list on the Main menu bar.

 Tip:

You can also select the data and press the Ctrl+L keys to create the list.

Step 2 – Modify your selection of a data range if required, and then click on the OK button to proceed. The process, as used on our Database of Employee Hours, will produce the following result:

Figure 79

Creating a list from a database

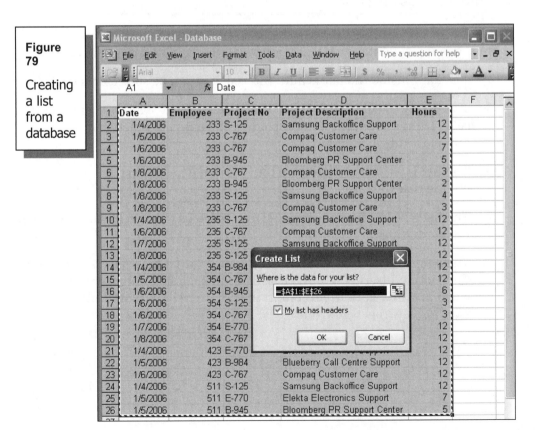

Step 3 – The list is now ready, with the borders marked in (see Figure 80). You have a floating tool bar for list management with options for inserting or deleting rows or columns, adding a total row and toggling it, sorting the list, creating a data form for the list, charting options, printing the list, etc. It also has features for publishing and resizing the list and for converting the list back into a normal working range. Once the list is published using a SharePoint service, more options for viewing and unlinking are enabled.

Figure 80   Floating tool bar for managing lists

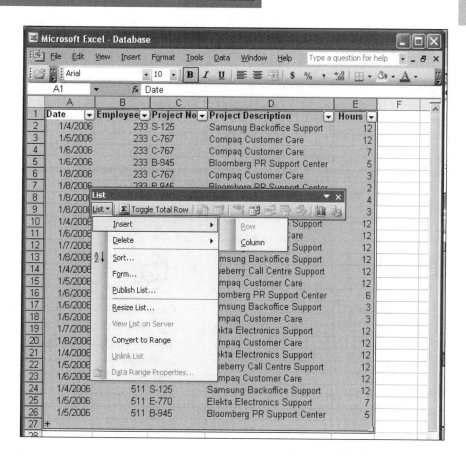

Step 4 – If you click any cell on the total row after toggling it on, you will see another drop-down of various aggregation functions that can be applied and displayed in that row, instead of just the Sum function. This list is shown below:

Figure 81   The last row of the List provides certain aggregation functions

---

27	*			
28	Total			216 ▼
29				None
30				Average
31				Count
32				Count Nums
33				Max
34				Min
35				Sum
				StdDev
				Var

Consolidation of Data

As the name itself indicates, this menu is just for combining values from different sheets or different ranges. The data can be pulled out and combined by:

> ➤ Using 3D formulas
>
> ➤ Position
>
> ➤ Category
>
> ➤ Creating a PivotTable report

Out of the different methods available to consolidate data, consolidation using 3D formulas is by far the simplest technique, so we'll take a look at that.

 Note:

Consolidate by Position when the worksheet data is identical in order and location; by Category when data is organized differently but has identical row and column labels; and by 3D formulas when worksheet data does not have a consistent layout or pattern. 3D formulas method is not as tricky as the others and is easier to implement and to maintain.

Consolidation Using 3D Formulas

Let's look at an example where three different worksheets have a similar format and type of data, pertaining to three different departments. We will create a sheet named "Sum" and use the consolidation technique there to pull out information from all three sheets and bring it in together.

Figure 82 Dataset of three sheets to be consolidated

Sheet named Dept A			Sheet named Dept B			Sheet named Dept C	
Dept - A			Dept - B			Dept - C	
Sales	20000		Sales	40000		Sales	50000
Direct Costs	10000		Direct Costs	18000		Direct Costs	20000
Gross Profit	10000		Gross Profit	22000		Gross Profit	30000
Indirect Costs	5000		Indirect Costs	7500		Indirect Costs	12500
Net Profit	5000		Net Profit	14500		Net Profit	17500

Each of the three sheets carries the data of Sales in cell B5, Direct Costs in cell B6, and so on to Net Profit in cell B9.

Step 1 – Create a sheet named "Sum" with the format shown in the following figure and enter formulas in the cells from B6 to B9 that will pull information from the three sheets.

The following figure shows the resulting cells, as well as the formulas used.

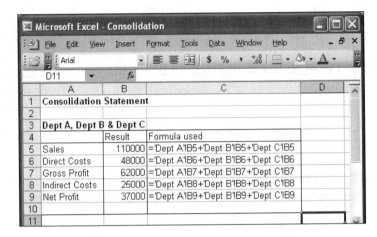

Figure 83

Consolidation using individually linked formulas

Because the format of all the three sheets is exactly the same, we have another consolidation style available. In this case, we can use the formula =SUM('Dept A:Dept C'!B5) and similar formulas in the other cells. Using this kind of formula has the distinct advantage that any new sheet inserted in between the three sheets already in the formula will automatically be included in the Consolidation function.

Step 2 – Enter the formulas as shown in the following screenshot.

Figure 84

Consolidation using Sum formulas

	A	B	C	D
1	Consolidation Statement			
2				
3	Dept A, Dept B & Dept C			
4		Result	Formula used	
5	Sales	110000	=SUM('Dept A:Dept C'!B5)	
6	Direct Costs	48000	=SUM('Dept A:Dept C'!B6)	
7	Gross Profit	62000	=SUM('Dept A:Dept C'!B7)	
8	Indirect Costs	25000	=SUM('Dept A:Dept C'!B8)	
9	Net Profit	37000	=SUM('Dept A:Dept C'!B9)	
10				

Step 3 – Insert another new sheet carrying the same format before Dept B, naming it Dept D. The value in cell B5 of Dept D will automatically be included in the consolidation statement without any modification in the formula =SUM('Dept A:Dept C'!B5).

Importing External Data

This is one of the advanced options available under Excel, and is primarily used by people reasonably familiar with database and web queries. We will not cover how to create a query, but instead will see how to use an existing query to import external data into Excel.

Note:

Query building is a separate topic of its own. Your best bet is to have them built for you by your IS department.

Step 1 – Select Data → Import External Data → Import Data from the Main menu bar.

Figure 85   Importing external data

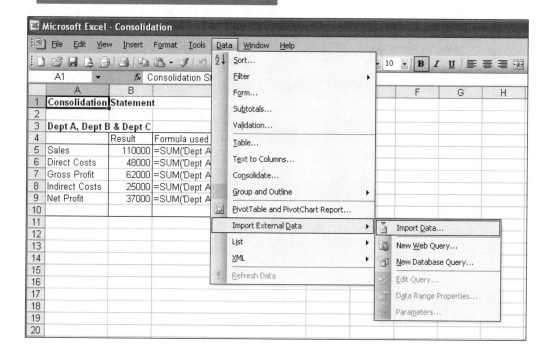

Step 2 – From the **Select Data Source** dialog box, select from one of the available queries and click on Open.

Figure 86 Selecting the Data Source to import external data

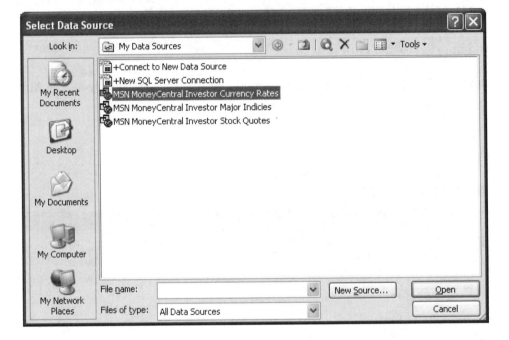

Step 3 – Specify where to place the results – this can either be in a cell within the existing worksheet or in a new worksheet.

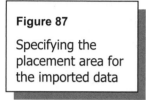

Figure 87

Specifying the placement area for the imported data

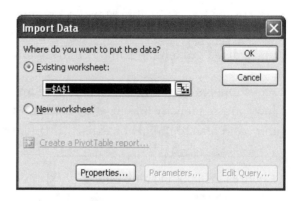

The results of your database/web query will be pumped into the given location. You can modify the query settings or change the Data Range properties by accessing the External Data toolbar, which is accessible from the list of toolbars. The toolbar has these buttons:

 ➢ Edit Query

 ➢ Data Range Properties

 ➢ Query Parameters

 ➢ Refresh Data

 ➢ Cancel Refresh

 ➢ Refresh All

 ➢ Refresh Status

Figure 88

Floating toolbar for managing external data

Handling XML data

XML stands for eXtensible Markup Language, which is a method for putting structured data in a text file following certain internationally accepted and standardized guidelines and by creating and utilizing customized tags.

Excel supports handling of XML data to an advanced level. The XML submenu allows you to identify and/or add an XML Map to the workbook, edit the XML query, and also to import or export XML data from Excel.

Figure 89 Importing XML Data

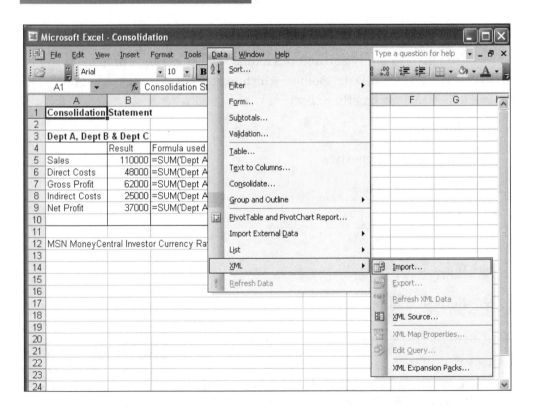

Working with XML is an interesting challenge, and is one of the ever popular topics in Excel. The flexible nature of XML allows different applications to export data in the XML format, so that it can be pulled into Excel and used according to the user's requirements.

More Terrific Links

There are quite a number of sites offering guidance and assistance in this topic of MS-Excel. A few of them are listed below for your reference. Click through them and expand your control over Excel.

Chapter 5

http://www.contextures.com/excelfiles.html

http://www.mvps.org/dmcritchie/excel/excel.htm

http://www.ozgrid.com/Excel/data-tables.htm

http://ask.support.microsoft.com/default.aspx?scid=kb;en-us;282851

Chapter 5

PivotTables, PivotCharts, and Reporting

Congratulations! You are a little over half way through this book – and you already well on your way to becoming an expert in Excel. The tips and techniques you have learned will help you to make the most of Excel's functions and its advanced database management facilities.

We will now take a giant leap into the world of PivotTables, starting with the basics, looking at the magic behind the scenes, and covering the smart working tips and practical applications of the different PivotTable components.

Chapter 6

Topics in this Chapter:

- Introducing PivotTables

- When should you use a PivotTable?

- Creating a PivotTable

- Filtering and modifying fields within a PivotTable

- Sorting data and listing only specific PivotTable items

- Drill-down facilities

- Adding calculated fields and modifying formulas

- PivotTable report formatting options

- PivotTable field settings

- Things you should know when using PivotTables

- Creating a PivotChart

- Links for more information

Introducing PivotTables

The PivotTable is an extremely powerful tool of Excel, and hence deserves an exclusive chapter in any book about Excel. In fact, there are books completely dedicated to just the matters of PivotTables and PivotCharts.

Excel's online help defines a PivotTable report as "an interactive table that quickly combines and compares large amounts of data". The rows and columns of the data can be juggled around in the report very easily by the drag-and-drop method, allowing you to see different summaries of the source data.

It can be said that PivotTables are a magical toolset enabling multiple different summary reports of the same source data within the shortest possible time. It also creates and shows the detailed data under each summary group, if you want to drill down into the details.

Chapter 6

PivotTables provide a way to easily summarize, analyze, consolidate, filter, prepare data for charting, and to report on large quantities of raw data in a fast, flexible, ad hoc manner. They are called PivotTables because you can change their layout by rearranging, or pivoting, the row and column headings quickly and easily.

However, pivoting is only possible if the data is properly prepared for the creation of a PivotTable. The data must be in a standardized format to make the most of the amazing PivotTable features.

When Should You Use a PivotTable?

PivotTables are interactive tables that make it possible to summarize, analyze, and manipulate data within any workbook. Many times an Excel worksheet contains so much data that it becomes difficult to interpret the data and make any useful meaning out of it.

We know that collection and accumulation of data is completely useless unless the data is reviewed, analyzed and made use of appropriately. A data collection that cannot be analyzed because of its sheer volume resembles a heap of junk – for which there is no use.

It is in this context that PivotTables come into play. PivotTables, in combination with PivotCharts, ensure that the data collection is organized, summarized, and presented appropriately to the user.

Visualizing alternative scenarios by analyzing reports from different angles is immediately possible with the power of PivotTables.

Effectively, we can conclude that wherever there is a need for data analysis, PivotTables should be the first choice, because they do not put a heavy payload on Excel, but provide maximum reporting features at an amazing speed.

Chapter 6

Creating a PivotTable

The PivotTable Wizard makes creating a PivotTable simple and ensures that even someone new to the concept will be able to get going on the first attempt.

In practical, real-life situations, you can get wonderful results using PivotTables. You need to think analytically to identify the situations that require PivotTables; once you have done that, half the problem is resolved.

Since the pre-requisite is a structured data set (normalized), let's take the following dataset as the example to be used throughout this chapter.

 Tip:

Though not mandatory, I always name the sheet containing the dataset "Data". When the PivotTable is created as a new worksheet, I rename it "Pivot". This ensures consistency and ease of use when accessing workbooks with multiple sheets.

Figure 90   Basic, structured dataset for creating a PivotTable

Chapter 6

	A	B	C	D	E	F
1	Date	Employee	Project No	Project Description	Hours	
2	1/4/2006	511	S-125	Samsung Backoffice Support	12	
3	1/4/2006	233	S-125	Samsung Backoffice Support	12	
4	1/4/2006	354	B-984	Blueberry Call Centre Support	12	
5	1/4/2006	423	E-770	Elekta Electronics Support	12	
6	1/4/2006	235	S-125	Samsung Backoffice Support	12	
7	1/5/2006	354	C-767	Compaq Customer Care	12	
8	1/5/2006	423	B-984	Blueberry Call Centre Support	12	
9	1/5/2006	233	C-767	Compaq Customer Care	12	
10	1/5/2006	511	E-770	Elekta Electronics Support	7	
11	1/5/2006	511	B-945	Bloomberg PR Support Center	5	
12	1/6/2006	233	C-767	Compaq Customer Care	7	
13	1/6/2006	354	B-945	Bloomberg PR Support Center	6	
14	1/6/2006	354	S-125	Samsung Backoffice Support	3	
15	1/6/2006	235	C-767	Compaq Customer Care	12	
16	1/6/2006	423	C-767	Compaq Customer Care	12	
17	1/6/2006	354	C-767	Compaq Customer Care	3	
18	1/6/2006	233	B-945	Bloomberg PR Support Center	5	
19	1/7/2006	354	E-770	Elekta Electronics Support	12	
20	1/7/2006	235	S-125	Samsung Backoffice Support	12	
21	1/8/2006	235	S-125	Samsung Backoffice Support	12	
22	1/8/2006	354	C-767	Compaq Customer Care	12	
23	1/8/2006	233	C-767	Compaq Customer Care	3	
24	1/8/2006	233	B-945	Bloomberg PR Support Center	2	
25	1/8/2006	233	S-125	Samsung Backoffice Support	4	
26	1/8/2006	233	C-767	Compaq Customer Care	3	
27						

Step 1 – Select the dataset and launch the wizard by clicking on Data → PivotTable and PivotChart Report.

 Note:

It is not essential to start by selecting the dataset, but it is preferable. If you do not select it now, you can do so in the next step.

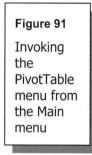

Figure 91

Invoking the PivotTable menu from the Main menu

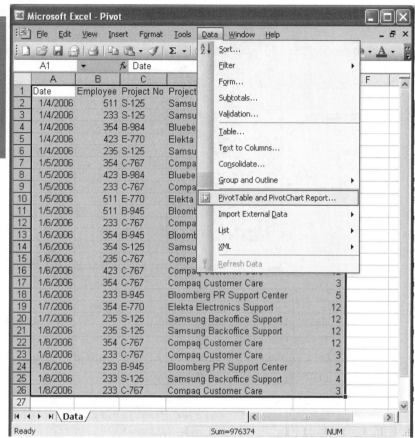

Step 2 – Work through the PivotTable Wizard.

    a. Once you have clicked on the "PivotTable and PivotChart Report", a dialog box containing the Wizard for creating the PivotTable pops up. The following screen shows the first step in the three-step process of the PivotTable wizard.

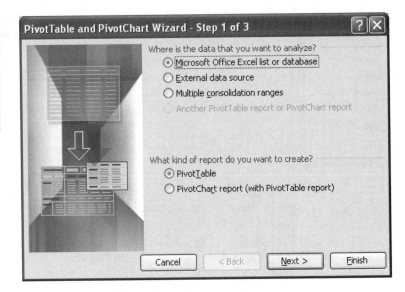

Figure 92

PivotTable Creation Wizard – Step 1 of 3

b. Select whether the source of data is a contiguous range of data from within the current Excel workbook or comes from an external data source using queries or from multiple ranges of data from within the current workbook.

c. Select between creating a PivotTable or a PivotChart (with a PivotTable as the backend).

d. If you selected the first choice of "Microsoft Office Excel list or database" within the current workbook, you will be presented with a range selector dialog box, that is pre-filled with your selection (if done earlier). Otherwise, select the desired data range.

Figure 93

PivotTable Creation Wizard – Step 2 of 3

e. In Step 3 of 3, specify whether the PivotTable should be created and placed in the current worksheet or if it should be created in a new blank worksheet.

Figure 94

PivotTable Creation Wizard – Step 3 of 3

f. Click on Finish. You will see a new worksheet with blank PivotTable settings and a list of fields from which to pull data.

 Note:

Use the "Layout" button and report "Option" button from Step 3 of 3 of the dialog box to configure the layout of the PivotTable.

Step 3 – Populate the PivotTable fields.

The framework of PivotTable we have now created looks like this:

Figure 95

Populating the PivotTable

There are four distinct areas in which you can place data

> **Page area**   Used to filter the row and column data for a particular Page field value
> A Page dropdown will contain all the unique values for the field(s) contained in Page.

> **Row area**   Field(s) to be used as row titles

> **Column area**   Field(s) to be used as column titles

> **Data area**   Summary data that is reported inside the rows and columns of the PivotTable
> At least one field must be placed in the Data area. You can either place one of the data fields here or insert a calculated field, but at least one item must be present in the Data area for the PivotTable to display any results.

Drag and drop certain fields onto the respective areas, as shown below:

- ➤ **Page area**   Employee
- ➤ **Row area**   Date
- ➤ **Column area**   Project No
- ➤ **Data area**   Hours

With these settings in place, you have a populated PivotTable report that should look similar to this:

Figure 96   PivotTable with information pulled up from the dataset

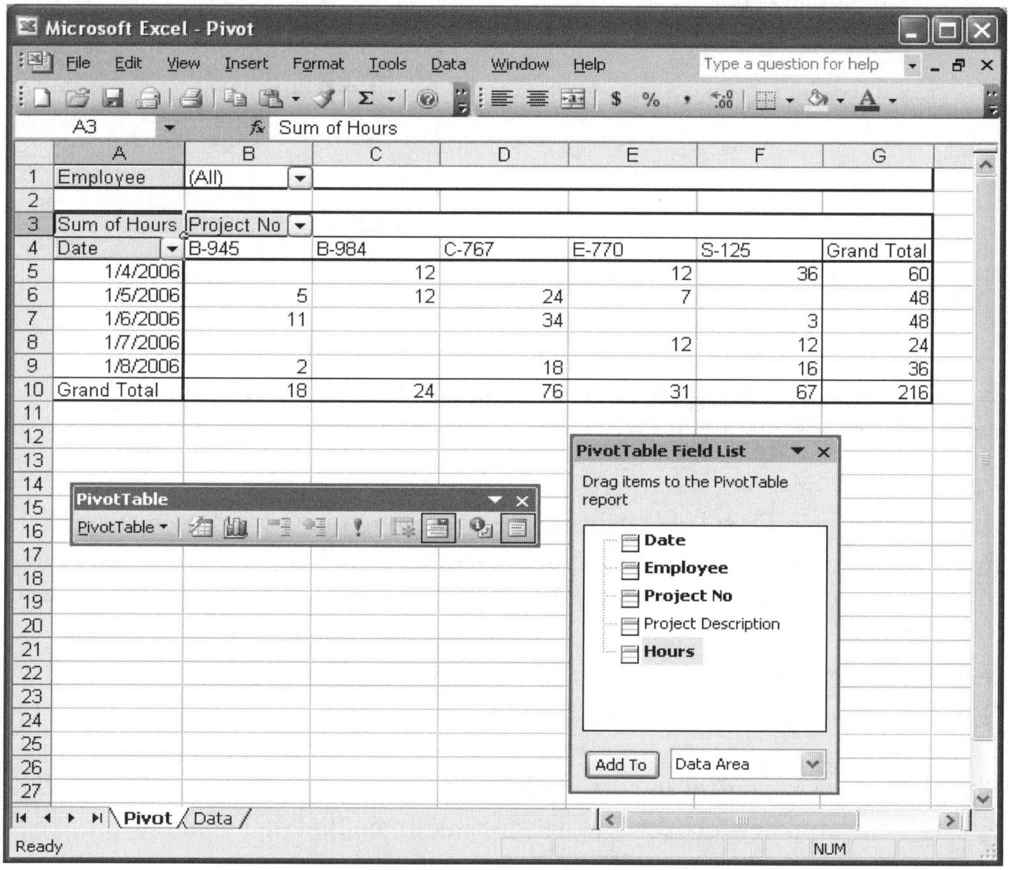

Date	B-945	B-984	C-767	E-770	S-125	Grand Total
1/4/2006		12		12	36	60
1/5/2006	5	12	24	7		48
1/6/2006	11		34		3	48
1/7/2006				12	12	24
1/8/2006	2		18		16	36
Grand Total	18	24	76	31	67	216

Depending on the internal settings of the field, when you drag and drop a field onto the Data area, it may be presented as one of the different types of aggregated data. The aggregation can be done using Sum, Count, Average, Max, Min, Product, Count Nums, StdDev, StdDevp, Var, or Varp function.

For instance, if the data is shown as "Count of Hours" instead of "Sum of Hours", (see A3 above), you can either double-click on the field name or select "Field Settings" from the right-click menu and then select Sum under the "Summarize" options.

Figure 97

Field Settings dialog box

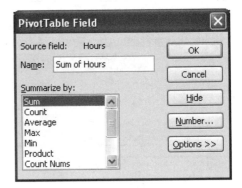

Filtering and Modifying Fields within a PivotTable

Once you set up a PivotTable, you can program it to display only specific data from the overall data table. For example, in our sample database, we can have the PivotTable display all the records pertaining to Employee number 354 only.

To accomplish this, just click on the drop down arrow in the Page field called "Employee" and from the list, select 354.

Similarly, you can control the display of Row fields and Column fields as well by using the drop down boxes and deselecting items that you do not want to display (remove the tick mark from the checkbox).

It is worth noting that you can add multiple Page fields to the PivotTable to filter the table even further; you can select and apply different filters from those different Page fields.

Tip:

For multiple Page fields, just click and drag the additional fields up into the Page area.

Data within the PivotTable can easily be manipulated to display an entirely different set of data. You can rearrange existing fields within the table, add new fields, even remove unwanted fields quite easily.

To add a field to the PivotTable, click on the field you wish to add from the Field List and drag it into one of the four field positions – Row field, Column field, Page field or Data item.

You can add the same field more than once onto the Data items area, but for the other three zones, a particular field can be added only once. Within the Data zone, each instance of a field can have the same or different sets of aggregation functions – such as Sum, Count, or Average.

To remove a field from the PivotTable, click on the field header and drag the field out of the PivotTable range. The mouse cursor will show an "x" mark to indicate that the field is being deleted.

This deletion does not mean that the field is being removed from the database itself, it just means that the field is being deleted from the table view. The original data is not affected at all.

Chapter 6

Sorting Data and Listing Specific PivotTable Items

The data within a PivotTable is set to be sorted manually, which is the default setting. This means that the sort order can be changed just by dragging the data within the table. As you drag the different fields between one another, the data will be sorted automatically and the sorted result will appear instantly. If you want to modify the sort settings, you can do so by following these steps:

Step 1 – Select the row or column field header by which you wish to sort.

Figure 98   Invoking the "Sort and Top 10" menu

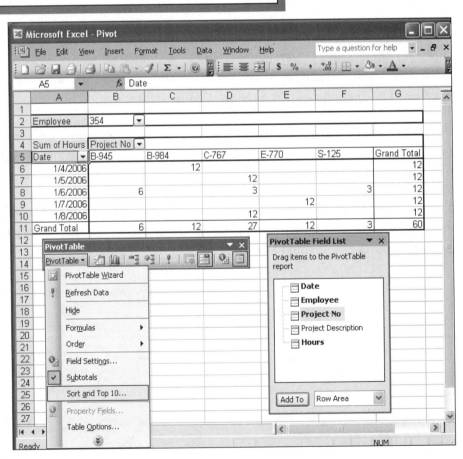

Excel for the CEO

Step 2 – Select the "Sort and Top 10" menu item from the PivotTable toolbar, which shows the following dialog.

Figure 99   Setting up the Sorting options

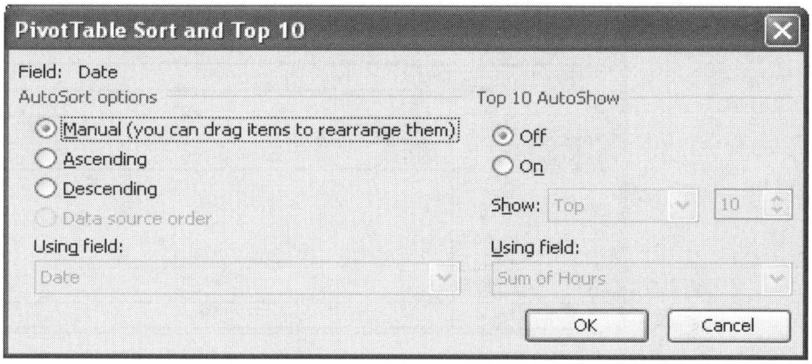

Step 3 - Within the AutoSort options on the left side of the dialog box, specify whether you want to have the data sorted in Ascending or Descending Order. Once you click on one of those options, the "Using field:" option will be enabled, allowing you to specify the field by which you wish to sort.

Before the sorting option modification, the PivotTable window looks like this:

Figure 100   PivotTable before applying the Sorting Options

	A	B	C	D	E	F	G
1							
2	Employee	354					
3							
4	Sum of Hours	Project No					
5	Date	B-945	B-984	C-767	E-770	S-125	Grand Total
6	1/4/2006		12				12
7	1/5/2006			12			12
8	1/6/2006	6		3		3	12
9	1/7/2006				12		12
10	1/8/2006			12			12
11	Grand Total	6	12	27	12	3	60

After setting the sort options in Descending order based on the Date field, the PivotTable window looks like this:

Figure 101   PivotTable after applying the Sorting Options

	A	B	C	D	E	F	G
1							
2	Employee	354	▼				
3							
4	Sum of Hours	Project No ▼					
5	Date ▼	B-945	B-984	C-767	E-770	S-125	Grand Total
6	1/8/2006				12		12
7	1/7/2006					12	12
8	1/6/2006	6			3		3	12
9	1/5/2006				12		12
10	1/4/2006			12			12
11	Grand Total	6	12	27	12	3	60

Listing the Top / Bottom Items

The data within a PivotTable can be short listed to display only the top or bottom few items (from 1 to 255) of the dataset, based on a particular field selection. To achieve this, we will use our sample dataset and click on the "Sort and Top 10" menu item.

Step 1 – Once the dialog box pops-up, keep the default AutoSort options (manual); just change the of the Top 10 AutoShow settings on the right side, as shown below:

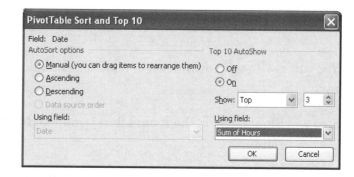

Figure 102

Listing the top /
bottom lists from
the PivotTable

We set the sort options to show only top three items, but you can make it top or
bottom and from 1 to 255 items, using the drop down and spin button controls
in the fields.

Chapter 6

Step 2 – Click OK; the PivotTable result window changes to the following:

Figure 103   The filtered top three items from the entire dataset

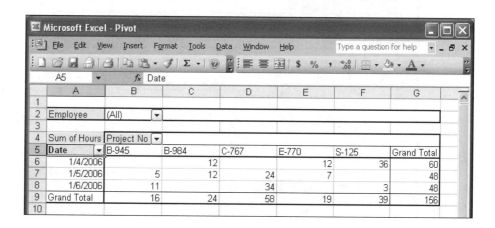

Notice that the text in the field on which the filtering is done can be identified
by its blue color (as you can see on your computer screen, cell A5 (Date) is
highlighted in blue).

Drill Down Facilities

You can get an easy drill-down of details from any single data item in the Data zone.

Step 1 – Right-click on the item; select Group and Show Detail.

Step 2 – Click on the Show Detail from the sub-menu. You have the details of the item in a separate worksheet.

Tip:

You can achieve the same effect by just double-clicking on any single item within the Data area.

Chapter 6 | **Figure 104** Drilling down to the details of a particular cell

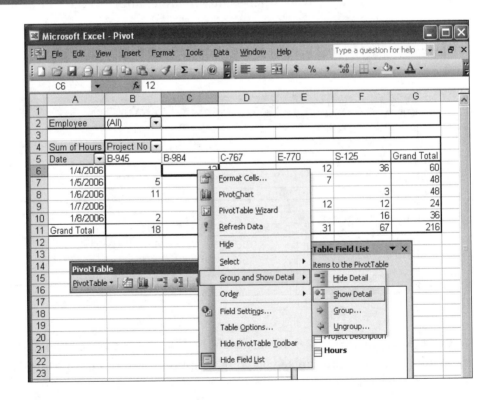

Grouping and Ungrouping

Besides the drill-down facility, there is also a facility to Group and Ungroup the Data items.

Step 1 – Right click on the "Date" field; from the "Group and Show Detail" menu, select the "Group" option. The **Grouping** dialog box displays, as shown below:

Figure 105

Fine tuning the Grouping of fields

Step 2 – In the Grouping dialog box, the "Starting at" and "Ending at" selections are automatically filled in by the system, based on the available data. From the bottom pane of the window, you can set the Grouping by any one of the many options such as Days, Months, or Quarters.

Clicking on the grouping by month option reduces the PivotTable window to produce the following result:

Figure 106 Results after grouping the results by month

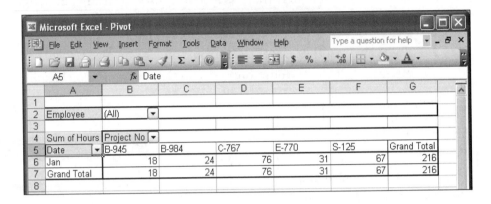

Step 3 – You can bring the setting back to the original by selecting Ungroup from the "Group and Show detail" menu in the PivotTable menu bar.

 Note:

The core data is not at all affected by any of these changes; it remains intact. Furthermore, when you drill down on a data item, the detail that opens up in a new sheet is only a copy and can be deleted without affecting the original data.

Using Calculated Fields

Besides providing organized summaries of the base data, a PivotTable allows you to introduce your own calculated fields into the report. Now we will discover how to create and add a calculated field and then how to modify and/or delete that field.

Adding and Modifying Calculated Fields

Step 1 – To make the illustration more relevant, keep "Project No" as the Page field, "Employee number" as the Row field, and "Date" as the Column field.

With these changes made to the structure, the PivotTable report will look like this:

Figure 107

Dataset modified for setting up a Calculated field

	A	B	C	D	E	F	G
1							
2	Project No	(All) ▾					
3							
4	Sum of Hours	Date ▾					
5	Employee ▾	1/4/2006	1/5/2006	1/6/2006	1/7/2006	1/8/2006	Grand Total
6	233	12	12	12		12	48
7	235	12		12	12	12	48
8	354	12	12	12	12	12	60
9	423	12	12	12			36
10	511	12	12				24
11	Grand Total	60	48	48	24	36	216

Step 2 – Click anywhere on the PivotTable area; from the PivotTable menu bar, select Formulas → Calculated Field. (see the following figure).

Figure 108   Introducing a Calculated Field from the PivotTable menu

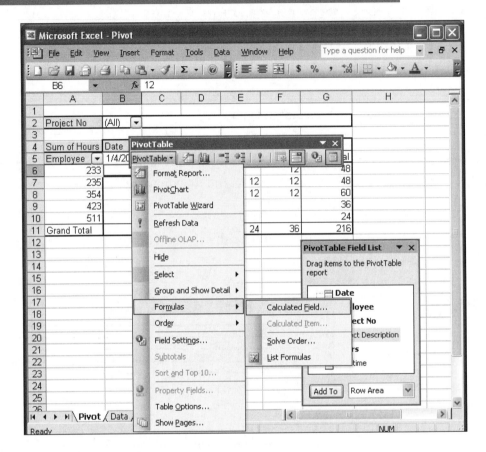

Chapter 6

Step 3 – The **Insert Calculated Field** dialog box pops-up as shown below. Note the provision to enter a name for the calculated field, and also to create a formula by combining different available fields. Note also the standard functions as well as arithmetic and logical operators and expressions.

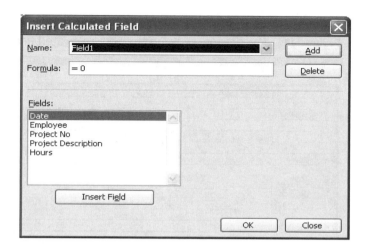

Figure 109

Insert Calculated Field dialog box

Step 4 – Create a calculated field named "Overtime", for which the formula calculates the total hours in excess of 10. Build the calculated field formula using the Hours field from the list in combination with the subtraction operator as shown below.

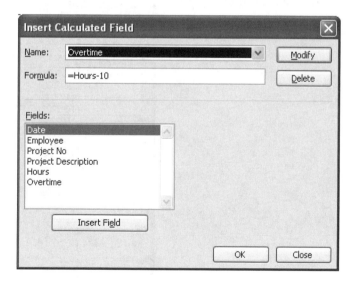

Figure 110

Creating a new field named Overtime

Step 5 – Click on OK to insert the field into the PivotTable report. This brings the PivotTable report to the following condition.

Figure 111 Pivot report showing the new calculated field

	A	B	C	D	E	F	G	H	
1									
2	Project No	(All)							
3									
4		Date	Data						
5		1/4/2006		1/5/2006		1/6/2006		1/7/2006	
6	Employee	Sum of Hours	Sum of Overtime	Sum of Hours	Sum of Overtime	Sum of Hours	Sum of Overtime	Sum of Hours	Sum of
7	233	12	2	12	2	12	2		
8	235	12	2		(10)	12	2	12	
9	354	12	2	12	2	12	2	12	
10	423	12	2	12	2	12	2		
11	511	12	2	12	2		(10)		
12	Grand Total	60	50	48	38	48	38	24	

Chapter 6

Step 6 - Click and drag the Date field to the Row area. This makes the report more easily readable and gets all the data into a comparable form.

Figure 112

Modified form of final report, including the calculated field

Microsoft Excel - Pivot

File Edit View Insert Format Tools Data Window Help

B25

	A	B	C	D	E
2	Project No	(All)			
3					
4			Data		
5	Employee	Date	Sum of Hours	Sum of Overtime	
6	233	1/4/2006	12	2	
7		1/5/2006	12	2	
8		1/6/2006	12	2	
9		1/8/2006	12	2	
10	235	1/4/2006	12	2	
11		1/6/2006	12	2	
12		1/7/2006	12	2	
13		1/8/2006	12	2	
14	354	1/4/2006	12	2	
15		1/5/2006	12	2	
16		1/6/2006	12	2	
17		1/7/2006	12	2	
18		1/8/2006	12	2	
19	423	1/4/2006	12	2	
20		1/5/2006	12	2	
21		1/6/2006	12	2	
22	511	1/4/2006	12	2	
23		1/5/2006	12	2	
24					

Pivot / Data

PivotTable

Ready NUM

Modifying and Deleting Calculated Fields

You can use the same dialog box that you accessed to insert a Calculated Field to modify and/or delete that field.

Step 1 – From the dialog box, in the Name field, select "Overtime" using the drop-down menu, and then click on the Formula field to change it.

Step 2 – Assume that the new formula should be **=Hours – 8**. Make the change, then click on the "Modify" button on the right hand side and click OK to apply it.

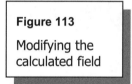

Figure 113

Modifying the calculated field

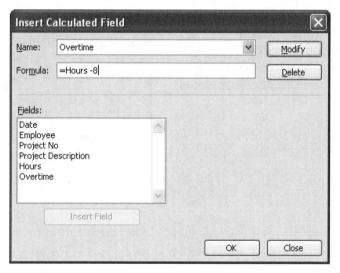

As soon as you modify the formula and apply it, the results in the PivotTable immediately refresh and change to reflect the modified formula.

Step 3 – To delete the calculated field, follow the same procedure to select the Overtime formula from the drop down box and then click on "Delete" to remove it.

PivotTable Report Formatting Options

The PivotTable not only lets you summarize and view organized information, but also lets you present the summaries in professional formats. Excel has more than 20 different styles of pre-defined report and table formats that you can apply to a PivotTable report.

The pre-defined report formats for the PivotTable are available under the menu "Format Report", which is one of the menu items under the Pivot Table menu bar, as shown below:

Chapter 6

Figure 114

Format Report option in the PivotTable menu

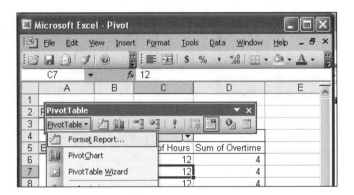

Step 1 – Select the Format Report menu item to bring up the **AutoFormat** dialog box, which shows a report preview and allows you to browse through, select, and apply one of them to the current report.

Figure 115

Various types of Report formats

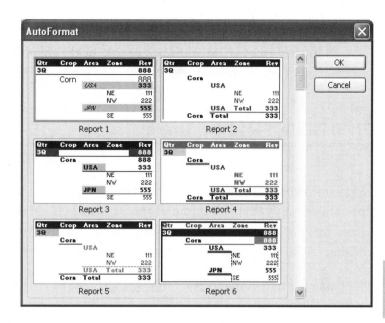

Chapter 6

Step 2 – Apply the "Report6" format. Your report is formatted as shown below.

Figure 116

Example report in one of the predefined formats

Employee	Date	Hours	Overtime
233			
	1/4/2006	12	4
	1/5/2006	12	4
	1/6/2006	12	4
	1/8/2006	12	4
235			
	1/4/2006	12	4
	1/6/2006	12	4
	1/7/2006	12	4
	1/8/2006	12	4
354			
	1/4/2006	12	4
	1/5/2006	12	4
	1/6/2006	12	4
	1/7/2006	12	4
	1/8/2006	12	4
423			
	1/4/2006	12	4
	1/5/2006	12	4
	1/6/2006	12	4
511			
	1/4/2006	12	4
	1/5/2006	12	4

Step 3 – There are many different options and styles available under AutoFormats that you can use to quickly give your reports the look you want. Experiment with them to see which ones work best for you.

PivotTable Field Settings

Every individual field within the PivotTable report can be customized with different settings that can be fine-tuned using the field settings option. You can access this option either by double-clicking on the field name itself or by right-clicking in the field name and selecting Field Settings from the sub-menu.

The following figure shows the field settings for the first Row field, "Employee".

Figure 117

Fine-tuning the Employee field settings

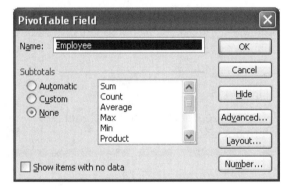

You have many different options that you can set for each field. One of the most important is to control the display of subtotals for the field – which can be Automatic, None, or a Custom function selected from the list.

You can also instruct Excel to "Show items with no data" by clicking on the check box at the bottom left of the dialog box.

The Hide option button enables you to hide the field completely.

Chapter 6

The Advanced option button opens up a dialog box, similar to the "Sort and Top 10" dialog box, that has a couple of additional options for handling external data. See the screenshot below:

Figure 118

Setting up Advanced Options for the Employee field

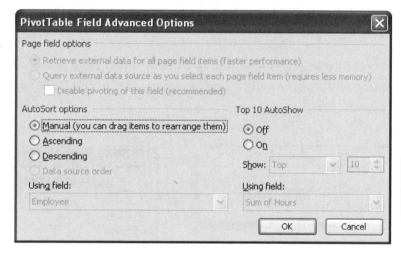

The Layout option button lets you control the field layout, as shown below:

Figure 119

Controlling the Field Layout

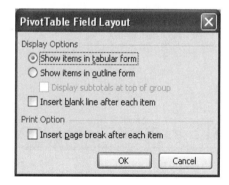

You can chose to display the items either in tabular form or in outline form; you can also opt to have a line break between each item in the field.

Additionally, you can insert a page break after each item for printing purposes.

Depending on the nature of the field, you may or may not see some of the options in the **Field Settings** dialog box. For example, the Number option button only displays for fields that contain numeric data. The **Number Format** dialog box lets you specify the number of decimals, formatting of negative numbers and a host of features that you will get from the "Format → Cells" item of the Excel Main menu.

The field settings of any field in the Page field zone provides the additional option of hiding specific items that form part of the Page area. See the example below.

Figure 120

Fine tuning the settings of Page fields

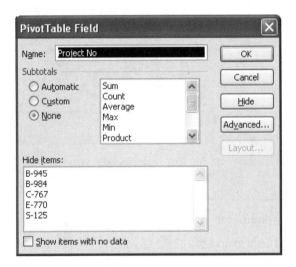

Things You Should Know When Using PivotTables

Refreshing Data

When any changes are made to the original data source, it is advisable to refresh the PivotTable before making any printouts.

Normally, if any change is made to the PivotTable, the table will refresh automatically, but it always pays to refresh manually to ensure that the report is accurate and up-to-date.

The icon on the PivotTable toolbar bearing an exclamation mark (!) is the option to be used for this. It is also accessible in the right-click menu from anywhere within the PivotTable.

Changing the Range of Source Data

Whenever there is a change in the range or address of source data itself, you should make the modification in the PivotTable report as well to keep the report up-to-date. To do this, select the "PivotTable Wizard" option from either the right-click menu or from the PivotTable toolbar. In the resulting dialog box, click on the Back button.

Figure 121

Modifying the source data range

This will take you again to Step 2 of 3 of the PivotTable creation process (see figure above), where you can alter the range of data to be used and then click on Finish to get the revised PivotTable report.

Table Options

There are many more options available when setting up of the PivotTable. Right-click anywhere on the PivotTable and select the "Table options" from the right-click menu.

The resulting dialog box provides you with options for controlling the display of some of the following items.

➢ Format Options:

- Grand totals for rows / columns
- Subtotal hidden page items
- Merging of labels
- Preserve formatting

➢ Data options:

- Enable drill-to-details
- Refresh on open

Figure 122

PivotTable Options

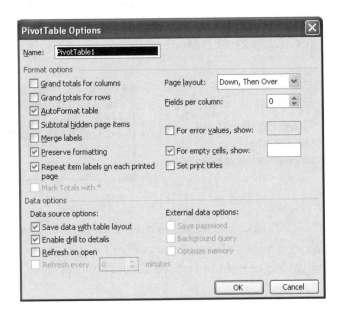

The figure above is a screenshot of the **PivotTable Options** dialog box.

Show Pages

Another option available from the PivotTable toolbar is the "Show Pages" menu item, which allows you to select and show individual pages of each Page field.

This option gives rise to the following dialog box, where you can select the Page field for which you want to show the pages separately.

Figure 123

Selecting a page to view complete details separately

Once this option is selected, you will see multiple sheets created automatically for each one of the items appearing in the Page field – and these will be individually populated with a copy of the data, without affecting the original database. You can play around with this copy of the data set without worrying about the reliability and accuracy of the original dataset.

Excellent! You have made it all the way through PivotTable reports.

On to PivotTable Charts!

Creating a PivotChart

PivotCharts can be created either from the Data → PivotTable and PivotChart Report on the menu bar or directly a from PivotTable using the PivotChart menu item available on the right-click menu.

Let us run through the process of creating a PivotChart from the scratch, rather than from within the PivotTable, because that process is so simple.

Step 1 – Select the data, and then go to Data → PivotTable and PivotChart Report. From the Step 1 of 3 dialog box, select the PivotChart Report in the bottom pane of the dialog, and click Next to proceed.

Chapter 6

Figure 124

PivotChart Creation Wizard – Step 1 of 3

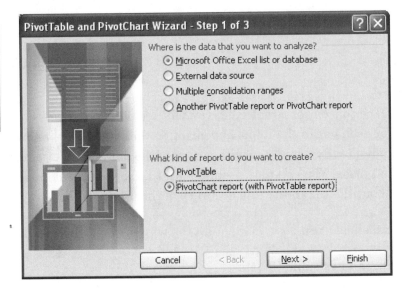

Step 2 – Confirm the data range, using the Browse button if necessary. Click Next to proceed.

Figure 125

PivotChart Creation
Wizard – Step 2 of 3

Step 3 – Confirm whether the PivotChart should be pasted within the existing
worksheet or in a completely new worksheet.

Figure 126   PivotChart Creation Wizard – Step 3 of 3

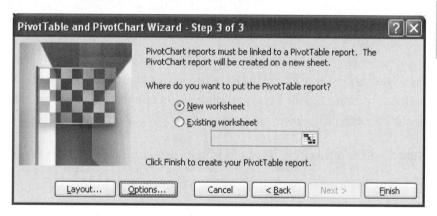

Step 4 – Click on Finish. You will be presented with a new worksheet that
looks similar to the following:

Figure 127

Populating a
PivotChart

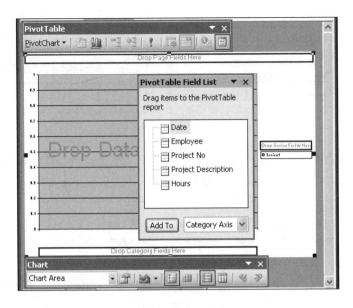

Now, let us create a PivotChart to present a visual representation of the total number of hours spent by all employees on the different dates, categorizing them by different project numbers.

Step 1 – From the PivotTable field list, drag and drop the fields as given below:

➤ Employee field	Drag to Page axis
➤ Date field	Drag to Category axis
➤ Project No field	Drag to Series axis
➤ Hours field	Drag to Data Items area in the center of the chart area.

Once these settings are in place, the Chart takes shape on the lines expected. You can move the fields around the different axes, without any worry about the integrity of the original dataset.

Figure 128   Final PivotChart result

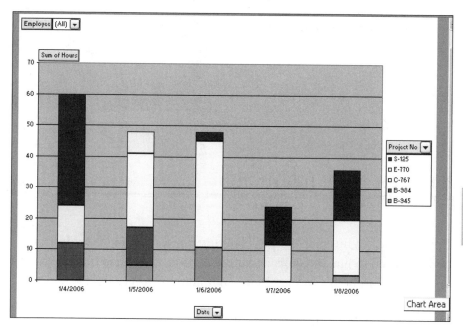

Chapter 6

Step 2 – Drag and drop the fields to modify the Chart to suit your requirements. All the other regularly available chart formatting options are available and effective with PivotCharts as well.

Step 3 – Hide the field names and series names that show up as drop-down items in the PivotChart by toggling them with the Hide PivotChart Field Buttons option from the PivotTable menu bar.

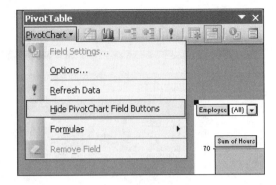

Figure 129

Hiding the PivotChart field buttons from view

Links for More Information

PivotTables, an interesting and complex topic, will require additional reading and research to master. For your information, some useful links are provided below that can help you to achieve complete mastery.

http://www.contextures.com/tiptech.html

http://peltiertech.com/Excel/Pivots/pivotstart.htm

http://peltiertech.com/Excel/Pivots/PivotCharts.htm

http://peltiertech.com/Excel/Pivots/pivotlinks.htm

Auditing Tools

Excel possesses in its armory a wonderful but less known toolset –the "Auditing Tools". We decided to dedicate one small but exclusive chapter for this topic, because it is not dealt with in depth by many other standard textbooks on Excel.

Topics in this chapter.

- Introducing auditing tools
- Formula auditing toolbar
- Error checking feature
- Tracing precedents
- Tracing dependents
- Removing tracing arrows
- Trace error option
- New comment / edit comment option
- Circling invalid data
- Clearing validation circles
- Showing Watch Window
- Evaluate Formula option
- Tracking changes made to a workbook
- Viewing and printing formulas in any sheet

Viewing and printing comments and errors

 Related links

Introducing Auditing Tools

Excel provides us with a comprehensive set of tools to perform basic auditing functions – all put together and presented in a toolbar called "Formula Auditing toolbar".

In its initial editions, Excel used to have just an Auditing toolbar, but over time, the toolbar has been expanded to accommodate the growing needs of business analysis.

Chapter 7

It is worth noting that in the process of editing any formula by pressing the F2 key, all the cells used in the formula are identified by different color coding, which can be used to trace them.

Although difficult to differentiate in this black and white book, in the following screenshot, B2 is blue, B3 is green, B4 is pink, and B5 is red.

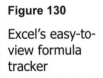

Figure 130

Excel's easy-to-view formula tracker

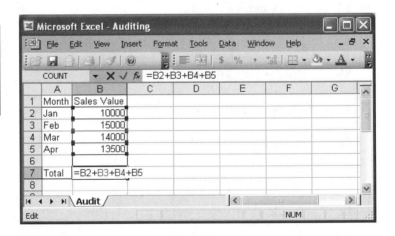

Formula Auditing Toolbar

The current version of Excel 2003 provides the following toolbar:

Figure 131 Formula Auditing" Toolbar	

The toolbar has a total of 12 buttons, each one catering to a specific need. This toolset helps you to identify and trace the formulas and links between different cells and worksheets.

You can use the Formula Auditing toolbar to graphically display, or trace, the relationships between cells and formulas with blue arrows. Among other things, you can trace the precedents (the cells that provide data to a specific cell) or you can trace the dependents (the cells that depend on the value in a specific cell).

Chapter 7

The buttons available in the formula auditing toolbar are examined in more detail in the following section.

Error Checking Feature

The very first button in the formula auditing toolbar provides the error checking feature. This feature checks all the cells in the worksheet (as selected in the **Options** dialog box) for any sort of error and provides a report of errors, allowing you to either ignore the error or to edit the formula to bring it out of the error condition.

Figure 132   Error-checking toolbar button

The toolbar button for the Error Checking feature is shown above. We will use the following example to review the Error Checking result window. We have entered a formula in cell B9 of =B7/0, which tries to divide a value of 52500 by 0, resulting in an error.

With this setting, let us analyze the error checking status.

Figure 133   Results of the Error Checking operation

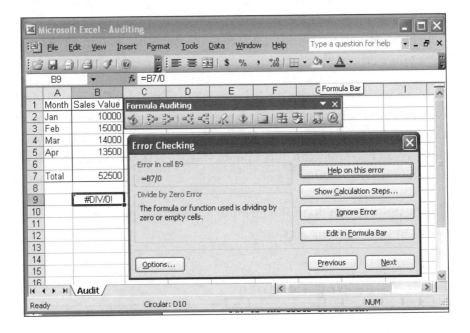

If you click on the Options button in the **Error Checking** dialog box, the Options dialog box pops up, in which you can decide which error types should be tracked and reported. The dialog box looks like this:

Figure 134

Setting the error checking options and rules

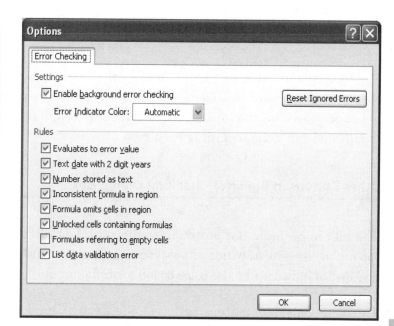

Note:

You can also access this dialog box from Tools → Options → Error Checking.

As you can see in the Options box, Excel uses certain rules to check for problems in formulas. The best part about these rules is that you can turn them on or off individually.

Depending on the settings made in this dialog box, Excel can point out the errors in real time as you key in data or review them all one-by-one, like the spell-checker. The real-time error checking will be familiar to many Office 2003 users, which indicates when a potential problem is found by a small triangle in the top-left corner of the cell.

You can resolve a problem using the options that appear, or ignore it. If you ignore a problem, it will not appear in further error checks. However, you can reset all previously ignored errors so that they appear again using the Reset Ignored Errors button.

The Rules and What They Check for

The text used for each rule should make the rule and its purpose fairly clear. However, if you want more details about each rule, just access Excel's online help and search for the topic "About Correcting formulas", where you can find detailed descriptions regarding each rule.

Other Buttons in the Error Checking Dialog Box

The Edit in Formula Bar button immediately takes you to the formula bar on top of the worksheet, which allows you to edit the formula from there to correct any errors indicated by the color coded formula links

The Show Calculation Steps button on the **Error Checking** dialog box leads you to the Evaluate Formula option, which is detailed later in the chapter.

If there are no errors in the worksheet or if all the errors have been analyzed and addressed, this will be indicated by the following information box.

Figure 135

Final message indicating cleansing all errors

Chapter 7

Tracing Precedents

The second button in the auditing toolbar (see figure below) allows you to track the precedent cells relevant to the current selection.

Figure 136	Trace Precedents toolbar button

Applying this tool in our current example – in the Cell B7 – we get the following result.

Figure 137 Results of using the "Trace Precedents" tool	

B7	▼		*fx* =B2+B3+B4+B5				
	A	B	C	D	E	F	G
1	Month	Sales Value					
2	Jan	• 10000					
3	Feb	• 15000					
4	Mar	• 14000					
5	Apr	• 13500					
6							
7	Total	52500					
8							

Chapter 7

To identify the next level of cells that provide data to the active cell (if any), click Trace Precedents button again.

Double clicking on the blue (or red) arrow, transports you to the other end of the arrow.

To display all the dependencies and relationships in one worksheet by the quick and dirty method, just enter the Equals sign (=) in any empty cell and then click on the "Select All" indicator, which is the intersection area between row 1 and column A.

Note:

The precedent cells are normally indicated by blue arrows and dots. Any red arrows call for attention, as they indicate errors. Again, if the precedent cell is on another worksheet or workbook, a black arrow points from the selected cell to a worksheet icon, which must be opened to trace further dependencies.

	A
1	Month
2	Jan
3	Feb
4	Mar

Figure 138

Select All indicator/button

Now your empty cell will have the formula =1:65536, and is likely to throw up a Circular Reference error. Do be too concerned; just select this cell and click twice on the "Trace Precedents" button.

You will see that all relationships within the worksheet are now highlighted.

Tracing Dependents

The fourth button in the auditing toolbar (depicted below) provides you with the ability to track the cells that are dependent on the cell(s) currently selected.

Figure 139   Trace Dependents" toolbar button

The steps involved in tracing dependents are similar to those used to trace precedents. Just select the region under question and click on the Trace Dependents button. Click once more to identify the next level of cells dependent on the active cell.

In our example, clicking on the cell B3 and then clicking on the Trace Dependents button will produce the following result:

Figure 140

Results of using the
Trace Dependents Tool

	A	B	C	D	E	F	G
1	Month	Sales Value					
2	Jan	10000					
3	Feb	15000					
4	Mar	14000					
5	Apr	13500					
6							
7	Total	52500					
8							

Removing Tracing Arrows

The third and fifth buttons in the auditing toolbar (depicted below) are
designed to remove the tracing arrows for Precedents and Dependents
respectively.

However, there is also a sixth button that is designed to remove all arrows
from the worksheet without any specific regard to precedents or dependents.

These buttons are shown below.

Figure 141   Remove Precedent tracer arrows

Figure 142   Remove Dependent tracer arrows

Figure 143   Remove all tracer arrows from the worksheet

Trace Error Option

The seventh button on the auditing toolbar (as shown below) is designed to trace the error path of the active cell. It is similar to the Trace Precedents option, but is specifically designed to trace the field causing the error.

Figure 144   Trace error path of the active cell

You can delete the tracer arrows created by this option by using the "Remove all arrows" feature discussed above.

If the active cell does not contain an error and you try to activate the trace error option, you will get the following warning dialog:

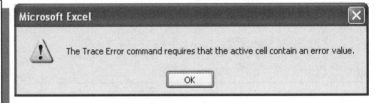

Figure 145

Dialog box showing that active cell contains no error values

New Comment / Edit Comment Option

It is widely known among auditors and senior managers that Excel allows comments to be entered in each and every single cell. This is especially useful to reviewers and management people to record their points of view and pass it on for further updates.

You can insert a comment by using the Insert → Comment from the Main menu bar, or from the right-click menu available in any cell. However, this option is also included as part of the Auditing toolbar because it is widely used in review and audit situations.

The notable advantage of this button is that it senses the availability of a comment in the active cell, and automatically toggles to an "Edit comment" button from the original "Insert new comment" button.

The image this button takes depends on the availability of a comment in the active cell.

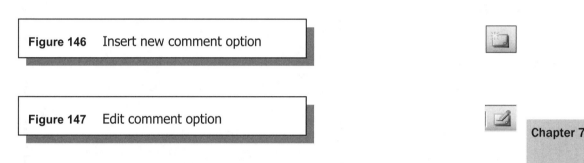

Figure 146   Insert new comment option

Figure 147   Edit comment option

Circling Invalid Data

This is one of the last set of buttons available under the Formula Auditing toolbar. When you enter any validation rule for a cell, you can set the rule to allow any invalid entry also, with a pop-up warning box, or even without a warning. If you decide to review any data not meeting the validation rules, you can use this option of circling invalid data.

Figure 148   Circle Invalid Data tool

This option compares each cell's value/contents against the data validation rules set for the cell; wherever the cell contents do not match the validation rules, it circles the cell to notify you of the mismatch.

This procedure illustrates the data validation application of this tool.

Step 1 – Set a data validation rule for the cell B3 to only allow data with a value less than 10000, as per the following screen.

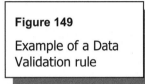

Figure 149

Example of a Data Validation rule

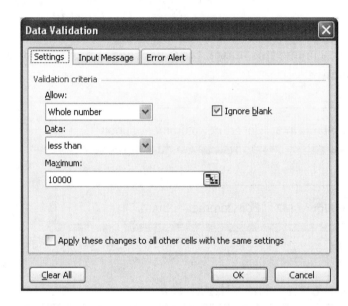

Step 2 – Remember to go to the Error Alert tab of the **Data Validation** dialog box, and set it to the "Information" Style, as shown below.

Figure 150

Setting the Error Alert tab in the Data Validation rule

Step 3 – After making this setting, re-enter a value of 10000 in the cell B3; it will pop-up an information box, but it will accept the data. This data content has been accepted, even though it is against the validation rule.

Step 4 – Now click on the "Circle Invalid Data" button on the toolbar, and you will see the result of using this handy tool to validate data.

Chapter 7

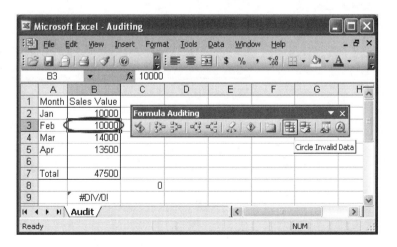

Figure 151

Result of using the Circle Invalid Data tool

Clearing Validation Circles

This option will undo and clear all the validation circles created on screen by the previous option, Circle Invalid Data.

Figure 152 Clear Validation Circles tool	

After reviewing the invalid data in the above example, if you click on the Clear Validation Circles button, the result window will change to reflect the following screen.

Figure 153

Results of applying the Clear Validation Circle button

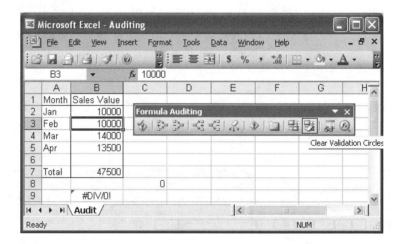

Showing Watch Window

The Watch Window option allows the user to watch cells and their formulas on the Watch Window toolbar, even when the cells are out of view.

Figure 154	Option to set a watch on any cell

To use this option, follow these steps:

Step 1 – Select the cells that you want to watch.

Step 2 – Click on the Show Watch Window button to bring up the **Watch Window** dialog box. Click on the Add Watch button; the active cell B7 will be added to the Watch Window after your confirmation.

Figure 155

Watch Window dialog box

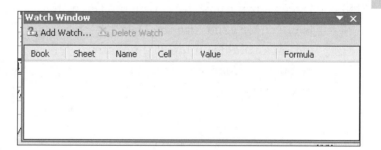

With the watch added in, the Watch Window now appears like this:

Figure 156

Adding a cell to be watched

Watch Window					▼ ×
🔲 Add Watch... 🔲 Delete Watch					
Book	Sheet	Name	Cell	Value	Formula
Auditin...	Audit		B7	47500	=B2+B3+B4+B5

Step 3 – Once the Watch Window is set up, you can dock it anywhere in the window – top, bottom, left or right. Also, you can move around freely anywhere in the worksheet, modifying the cells affecting the cell you are watching, and instantly seeing the effect of your modification in the watch window itself.

Step 4 – Once your purpose for setting up the watch is no longer valid, use the Delete Watch option available on top of the Watch Window to clear out the watches you have already set.

 Tip:

You can double click on the Watch window (on the particular cell entry) to go the relevant cell being watched.

 Note:

A cell that has links to another workbook(s) only display in the Watch Window toolbar when the other workbook(s) is open.

Chapter 7

Evaluate Formula Option

This is the last button available on the Formula Auditing toolbar, and is an item we already touched upon in our chapter on Formulas, Functions, and More... starting on page 53.

Figure 157   Option to start the Evaluate Formula tool

By using this function, you can see the different parts of a nested formula evaluated in the order in which the formula is calculated. By way of example, let us look at how our cell B7, with the formula =B2+B3+B4+B5, is evaluated.

Step 1 –   Select the cell B7 and click on the Evaluate Formula toolbar button. You will be presented with the **Evaluate Formula** dialog box, which shows the first step.

Figure 158

Initial dialog box of Evaluate Formula tool

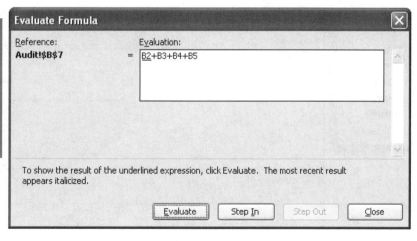

Step 2–   Click on the "Evaluate" to go to the next step, where the initial underlined expression is evaluated first (B2). The process continues

sequentially through each expression until the last expression (B5) is evaluated and final result is provided.

The following are intermediate result windows (not shown in sequence):

Figure 159

Inter-
mediate
dialog box
of
Evaluate
Formula
tool

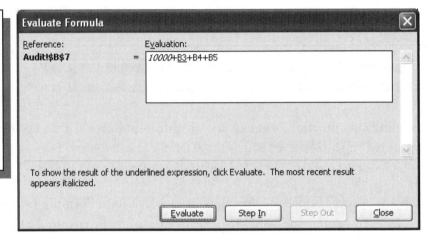

Figure 160

Pen-
ultimate
result
window of
formula
evaluation

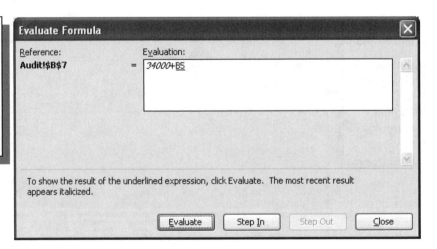

Final Result window:

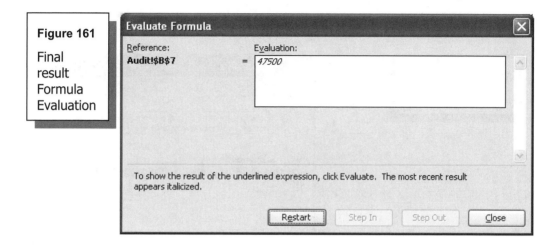

Figure 161

Final
result
Formula
Evaluation

Tips for Using Formula Evaluator

> If the underlined part of the formula is a reference to another formula, click Step In to display that formula in the Evaluation box.
> Click Step Out to go back to the previous cell and formula.

> Continue until each part of the formula has been evaluated.

> Click on the Restart button to see the evaluation again.

> Click on the Close button to end the evaluation.

Tracking Changes Made to a Workbook

You can track changes made to a workbook, much as you would use the Track Changes facility in MS-Word. This option is available and useful only for Shared Workbooks, which can be used by multiple users at the same time over a network.

Step 1 – For this option to take effect, you first need to enable Sharing by going to Tools → Share workbook → Editing tab and selecting the Allow changes by more than one user at the same time check box.

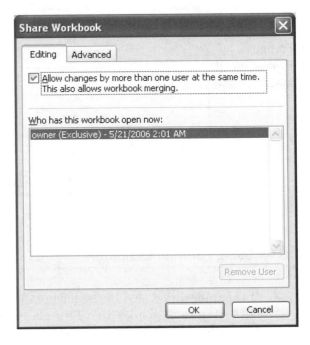

Figure 162

Sharing a workbook

Step 2 – Click on the Advanced tab; under the Track Changes option, key in or use the arrows to select your preferred number of days for which the change history needs to be maintained.

Step 3 – Set the priority for saving changes – when the file should be saved and, in times of conflicting changes by different users, which change should be saved, whether to save your personal view of filtered data and print settings – all these factors can be controlled from this Advanced tab, as indicated in the figure below.

Figure 163

Setting up the Change History Features in shared workbooks

 Note:

It is a good idea to keep the "Include in personal view" check boxes checked. That way, all the users of a shared workbook can have their print area and filtered data setups saved for their own use.

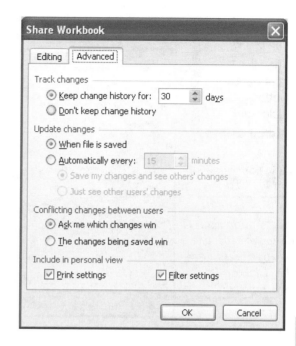

Chapter 7

Step 4 – Click OK to apply your settings; if prompted, save the file.

Viewing and Printing Formulas in Any Sheet

This option does not appear as part of the Formula Auditing floating toolbar, but it is still very useful as part of the auditing tools.

Step 1 – You can be enable or disable this option by accessing the it from the menu Tools → Options → View.

Step 2 – Under the Window options section at the bottom of the "View" tab, tick the Formulas checkbox. All the formulas in the workbook will then be displayed as formulas, instead of the results.

Here is a screenshot of the **Options** dialog box.

Figure 164

The all-important Options dialog box

Tip:

This formula view option can be toggled on or off by pressing the Ctrl and ~ keys together.

Example Using the Formulas Checkbox

If the Formulas checkbox is un-ticked (the default), the example worksheet will show the result in B7.

Figure 165

Viewing formula as final result value

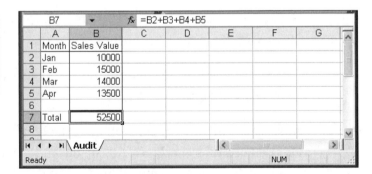

However, if the Formulas checkbox is ticked in the Tools → Options → View, then the example file will change to show the Total formula in B7.

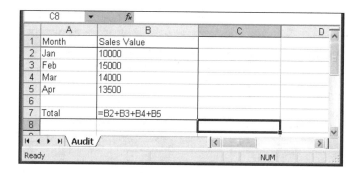

Figure 166

Viewing formula as formula itself instead of final result

Viewing and Printing Comments and Errors

Viewing comments and errors on screen and having the ability to print them in an Excel file is tremendously helpful when you need to sit down and analyze the files in hard copy.

Step 1 – It is quite simple to display all the comments onscreen. This facility is available through the Tools → Options → View tab. Select the "Comment & indicator" option from the section on Comments, as shown below.

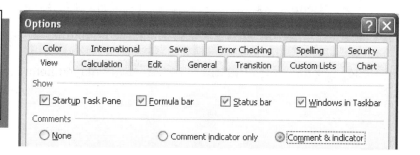

Figure 167

Viewing comments as well as the indicators

Step 2 – On the Error Checking tab of the Options window, set up the error-checking rules and enable background error checking to ensure that errors will be noted by indicators on screen. See below.

Figure 168

Viewing comments as well as the indicators

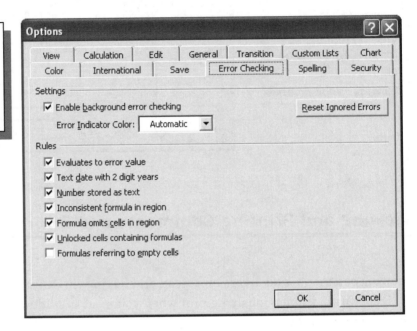

Step 3 – Control the printing of comments and errors. Go to File → Page Setup and select the Sheet tab. In this tab, you can see a section titled Print in the middle of the dialog box, wherein there is an option to display Comments and Errors as follows:

➢ Comments – None / At end of sheet / As displayed on sheet

➢ Cell errors as – #N/A / Displayed / <blank> / —-

The dialog box for controlling these options is displayed below for clarity.

Controlling the Printing of Comments

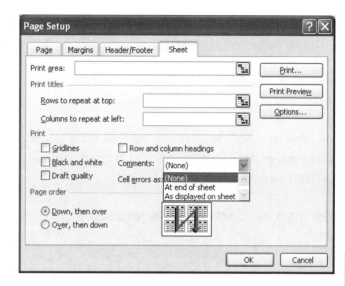

Figure 169

Controlling the print style of Comments

Controlling the Printing of Cell Errors

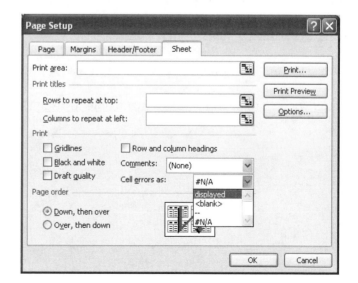

Figure 170

Controlling the printing of Cell Errors

Related Links

Some of the international audit firms use Excel to the fullest to automate their analyses, documentation requirements, financial modeling, and valuations.

As you can see, Excel is quite capable of delivering high level, extremely accurate services, provided that you know how to tap the power lying within.

You may want to visit some of the following websites to gain further insight into how the auditing toolsets and related capabilities of Excel are used in practical situations.

http://www.auditnet.org/spreadsheets.htm

http://panko.cba.hawaii.edu/ssr/auditexp.htm

Chapter 7

http://www.erlandsendata.no/english/

http://www.aicpa.org/pubs/jofa/oct1999/hormann.html

http://www.auditexcel.co.za/issue.html

http://www.lacher.com/

(This site has lots of downloadable examples for auditors)

http://www.mang.canterbury.ac.nz/people/jfraffen/sscom/links.htm

Formatting and Printing Reports

Thus far we have learned to perform some of the most complex tasks in Excel by identifying and using the right function and toolsets. However, most senior managers depend, to a large extent, on their subordinates to properly format and print their reports.

Though it is not usually necessary for a senior manager to be able to format and print reports, it is always useful to know the extent of customization and set-up options available in Excel.

Being aware of these features can not only save you from some embarrassing situations, but also put you in the driver's seat when you are able to produce an impeccably formatted, professional-looking report – say, if you and your laptop are at an off-site meeting with no support staff.

Keeping this point of view in mind, it is essential to know more in detail about the various printing options and formatting techniques.

Chapter 8

Topics in this chapter:

- Print preview options and zooming

- Controlling print selection, page, cells, and copies

- Setting, removing page breaks; page break preview

- Print area – setting, clearing

- Page control – orientation, size, scaling, quality

- Alignment control – margins, centering report

- Headers and footers, first page numbers

🛍   Controlling sheet properties during printing

🛍   Printing charts

🛍   Four more topics

🛍   For further study

Print Preview Options and Zooming

The first tool you'll want to know in Excel's range of Print controls is the Print Preview button. This button is part of the Standard toolbar, and is identified by an icon containing a magnifying glass over a sheet of paper (see figure below). You can also access this button from the File → Print Preview menu on the Main menu bar.

Figure 171   Print Preview button on the Standard toolbar

Clicking on the Print Preview option brings up a snapshot preview of the selection or of the entire worksheet if no print area is defined.

Tip:

Some programmers and experienced Excel operators prefer to use Alt+F keys followed by the "V" key, to invoke the Print Preview. (Alt+F → V).

Within the print preview window, you have a Zoom button that lets you zoom into and out of the selection.

There are also a few other buttons in the Preview window whose uses are detailed in the table below.

Figure 172   Other buttons inside the Print Preview screen

| Next | Previous | Zoom | Print... | Setup... | Margins | Page Break Preview | Close | Help |

Table 41

Functions of Print Preview screen buttons

Button	Description
Zoom	Zooms in/out of Print Preview
Print	Invokes the **Print Options** dialog box; same as pressing Ctrl+P
Next	Enabled if there is a next page beyond the current one; used for navigation
Previous	Enabled if there is a page previous to the current one; used for navigation
Setup	Pops-up the **Page Setup** dialog box (accessible from File → Page Setup)
Margins	Displays or hides the margins currently in use in the worksheet
Page Break Preview	Invokes Page Break Preview mode (discussed later in this chapter)
Close	Closes the Print Preview and returns to the worksheet

Chapter 8

Controlling Print Selection, Page, Cells, and Copies

You can open the **Print** dialog box in Excel by pressing Ctrl+P keys from the File → Print Menu or the Standard toolbar. The Print window looks like this:

Figure 173

Print dialog box

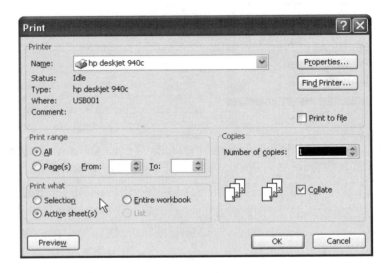

The "Print what" section in the bottom left area allows you to define what to print. You can choose to print only one particular range or one entire worksheet or the entire range of active worksheets by just clicking on the relevant radio button.

Before selecting the Print dialog box, you should first mark/select your range of data by using a combination of Shift and arrow keys or by dragging through the range with your mouse. If you click on the Print Selection button with no range highlighted, you will only print out a blank page.

To select multiple non-contiguous worksheets, hold the Control key down while clicking on each individual sheet name to print multiple sheets. See below.

Figure 174	
Selecting non-contiguous sheets to print	

To select multiple contiguous worksheets, click on the first sheet, hold the Shift key down, and click on the last sheet to be selected to print multiple sheets. See below.

Figure 175	
Selecting contiguous sheets to print	

Selecting Pages to Print

If you have already previewed the printout and only want to print selected pages from the whole set, use the "Print range" section in the middle left area of the Print dialog box.

You can either print all of the pages or specify the range of pages that you want to print.

Controlling Print Copies

The other section on the lower right side of the dialog box (Copies) allows you to print multiple copies and to organize the numbered pages.

Click on the Collate check box to print one full set of copies before printing the next set. That enables you to pull out the copies as complete sets.

Printing to a File

The Print to File checkbox allows you to print the information to a file. The output file will basically be a print spool file, so the page breaks, font spacing, and such may change if you print the file to a different printer (other than the one for which you originally created it).

 Note:

Do not mistake this process for printing to a soft copy file such as Word or other such formats. It is designed only to generate a print file.

Setting, Removing Page Breaks; Page Break Preview

There are two ways in which you can view a worksheet in "Page Break Preview" mode. The first is to invoke it from the Print Preview screen, and the other is to invoke it from the View → Page Break Preview from the Main menu bar.

Chapter 8

Figure 176

Switching to the Page Break Preview mode

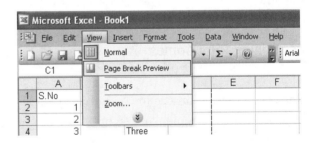

You can insert page breaks into any region by clicking Insert → Page Break from the Main menu. Similarly, you can remove page breaks by selecting the Insert → Remove Page Break from the Main menu.

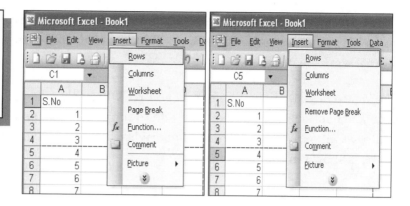

Figure 177

Toggle of Page Break and Remove Page Break in menu

As you can see in the above screenshots, the Insert menu item toggles between Page Break and Remove Page Break, depending on where the cursor is currently placed. If the active cell is just below a page break line, the menu item on the "Insert" menu becomes "Remove Page Break".

The following figure shows an example of Page Break Preview:

Chapter 8

Figure 178

A workbook viewed in Page Break Preview mode

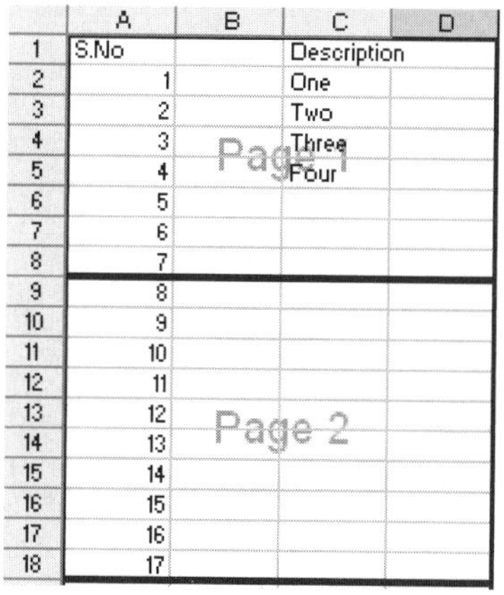

If you set the page breaks manually, the texts within the page break will be automatically adjusted in size so that the selection within two consecutive page breaks will print on one page, as intended.

To return to normal viewing mode, click on View → Normal from the Main menu bar. This closes the Page Break Preview mode and gets you back to the normal worksheet screen.

The right-click menu available in Page Break Preview mode gives you additional options to set, reset, and add to the print area, as well as to insert and reset all page breaks. This unique right-click menu, available only in this mode, is shown in the figure below.

Figure 179

Right-click menu available in Page preview mode

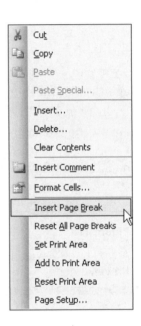

Print Area – Setting, Clearing

You can easily define and control which part of the worksheet area you want to print.

This control is available through File → Print Area on the Main menu bar, and is shown in the figure below.

Figure 180

Print Area settings under the Main menu

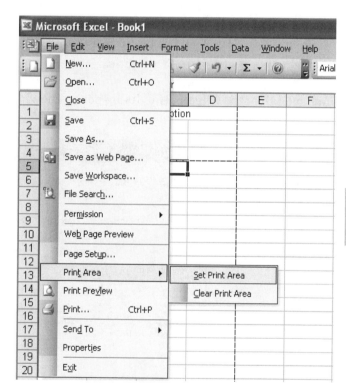

You can easily set or clear the print area in any worksheet by selecting the desired range and then selecting Set Print Area from File → Print Area as shown above or from the right click menu in Print Preview mode.

The Set Print Area option defines a print area; when selected from the right-click menu, it allows you to add an additional print area, apart from the one already defined. The Clear Print Area option resets the print area, whether selected under the File menu or the right-click menu.

Page Control – Orientation, Size, Scaling, Quality

We will now analyze the options available under File → Page Setup on the Main menu bar. The Page tab on the **Page Setup** dialog box lets you set or alter the paper and print size qualities.

The Page tab of the Page Setup dialog box is shown below:

Figure 181

Page settings tab of the Page Setup dialog box

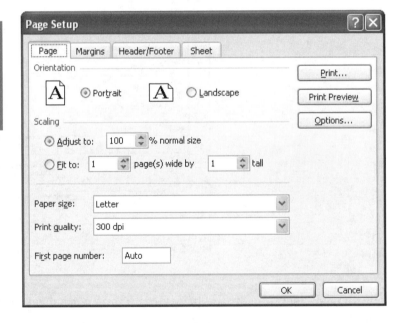

In this box, the Print and Print Preview buttons open the relevant dialog boxes, which we have already covered in detail. The Options button takes you to the **Options** dialog box, where you can fine tune the printer properties.

The other features available in this tab are:

> - **Orientation:** Can be set either as Portrait (Vertical view) or Landscape (Horizontal view)

> - **Scaling:** Print can be at 100% of original size, or anywhere between 10% to 400% of the original size. You can also choose to fit the entire worksheet / print area within one or a specified number of page(s) by selecting the "Fit to…" option.
>   Try your hand at different Fit to… options to better understand how to use this option.

> - **Paper Size:** Select the size of the paper currently in the printer tray, set or alter the margins, and preview more accurately.

> - **Print Quality:** Select between one of three levels – normal at 300 dpi, good at 600 dpi, or best at 1200 dpi.

Chapter 8

Alignment Control – Margins, Centering Report

The Margins tab of the **Page Setup** dialog box is shown below:

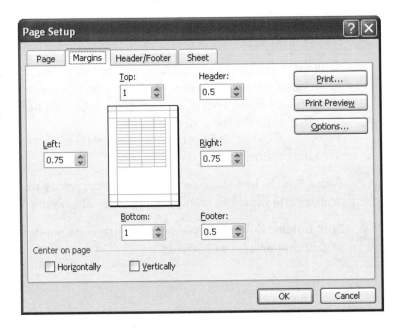

Figure 182

Margins tab of the Page Setup dialog box

You can adjust the Top, Bottom, Right, and Left margins in this tab as well as the gap for Header and Footer. The page graphic in the center of the screen previews the changes as you make adjustments. Use this graphic for a general idea of the results of your changes to the page layout; use Print Preview for an exact look at the page.

Use the two check boxes in the bottom pane of the Margins tab to center data on the printed page horizontally and / or vertically.

Headers and Footers, First Page Numbers

The Header/Footer tab of the **Page Setup** dialog box is shown below:

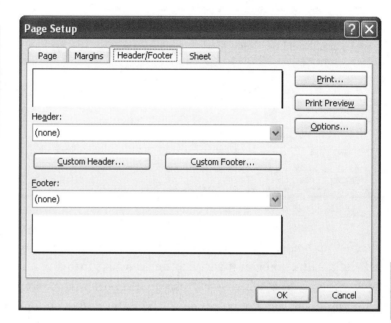

Figure 183

Header/Footer tab of the Page Setup dialog box

You can customize the header and footer of the printout to a great extent to suit your requirements; they can indicate the nature of the printout, location of the file, date and time of printout, and other such information.

The basic header and footer settings are available under the relevant fields as "Drop-down" lists. For detailed customization, click on the Custom Header / Custom Footer button. A screenshot of the **Custom Header** dialog box is shown below.

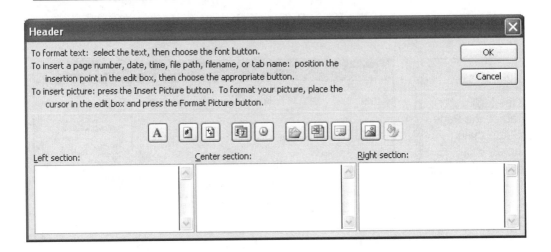

Figure 184   Setting up a Custom Header/ Footer

The custom header / footer is divided into three distinct sections – left, center, and right – and you can insert customized text into any one or in all three of these sections. You can really dress up a report with custom headers and footers by inserting a page number, the date, and even a picture. Experiment with the buttons shown above and detailed below to add a professional touch to your next stockholder report.

See the following figure for the detailed options of customization, shown as buttons in the dialog box:

Chapter 8

	Button	Description
Figure 185 Options for setting up a custom Header/Footer	A	Change the Font formatting options except Color
	#	Insert the current page number into the Header / Footer
		Insert the total number of pages into the Header / Footer
		Insert the current Date into the Header / Footer
		Insert the current Time into the Header / Footer
		Insert the current Path & Filename into the Header / Footer
		Insert the current Filename into the Header / Footer
		Insert the current Sheet name into the Header / Footer
		Insert a Picture into the Header / Footer
		Format the Picture (enabled only if picture is inserted)

Controlling Sheet Properties During Printing

The last tab on the **Page Setup** dialog box is the "Sheet" tab; it enables you to specify the Print Area as well as the Print Titles, which could be either row titles to repeat on each page at the top, or column titles to repeat on each page at the left side. This is a real blessing for reports that span several pages.

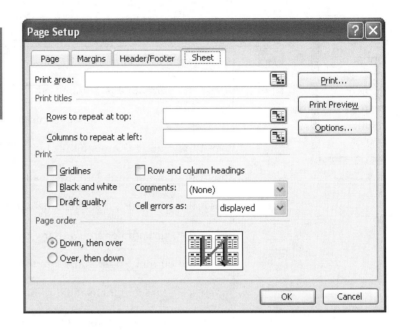

Figure 186

Sheet tab of the Page Setup dialog box

For example, let's say that you are printing a worksheet containing some titles in rows 1 to 3 and the worksheet runs on for fifty pages. It is essential that all fifty pages carry the titles contained in rows 1 to 3. To accomplish this, you need to enter "$1:$3" in the "Rows to repeat at top:" field, either by typing or by using the selector button.

You can also choose to print the worksheet with or without gridlines, and also to print it in Black and White as well as in Draft quality – all these options are available under the Print section of the Sheet tab.

The Row and Column Headings checkbox lets you print the worksheet along with the names / headings of rows and columns such as A,B,C and 1,2,3. This is very useful when you are making printouts of Formula views, because the user can better understand and relate to the formulas when he can view the cell references on each page.

Since the options available in printing cell errors and comments were covered in an earlier chapter on Auditing Tools starting on page 201, they are not explained in detail here.

The page order of printing can also be set here – the choices available are "Down, then over" and "Over, then down". Click between the two of them and watch the arrow to see how the page flow changes.

Printing Charts

When you are printing charts, the **Page Setup** dialog box has a Chart tab in the place of a Sheet tab (See screenshot below).

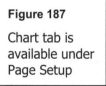

Figure 187

Chart tab is available under Page Setup

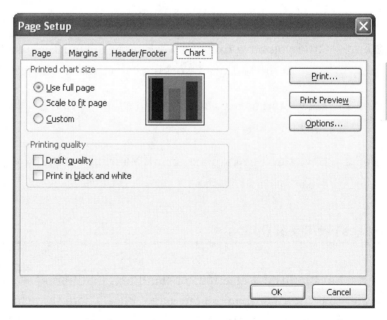

The Chart tab enables you to print the chart as a full page chart, to scale it to fit the selected page size, or in custom sizes. You can also choose to print the chart in draft or normal quality and in color or in black and white. Exercise your options carefully using the checkboxes to get the maximum benefit.

Four More Topics

Here are some additional important topics relevant to formatting and printing reports.

Massive Printing of Blank Pages

During a printing operation, you may notice that you continuously print blank pages. This is probably due to incorrect boundary markings or print borders. You can avoid this by doing the following.

Step 1 – After you have finished working with your file, use the Ctrl+End keys to go to the last used working cell of the worksheet.

Step 2 – Select and delete the rows and columns that are beyond your used working range.

Step 2 – Save the file again and print. Your file should now print with no blank pages.

Pages per Sheet Option

If you have multiple selections of small text in different worksheets, you may prefer to print all of them on one page. Please note that this ability is dependent on your printer properties and settings.

You can select this option from the Printer properties. Select Properties from the **Print** dialog box; in the resulting dialog box, click on the Layout tab and select Pages Per Sheet. You can modify the number to fit multiple pages on one printed sheet.

This option is illustrated in the figure that follows.

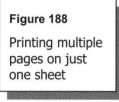

Figure 188

Printing multiple pages on just one sheet

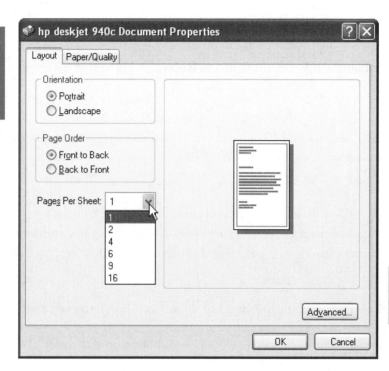

Printing to PDF

The best option to print any file to PDF is to use a free PDF converter such as Primo PDF, which comes with a routing printer, directed to activate the PDF application. Select the PDF driver from the list of printers, then just go ahead and print to get the PDF file.

If you don't have the necessary PDF printer drivers but you want to create a PS or PDF file, you can use VBA codes to print to PDF. We will cover this process in the chapter on VBA basics.

My favorite PDF creator is the Primo PDF, which is available for free download at www.primopdf.com

Copying Page Setup Options Between Different Sheets

One common problem that many senior managers face, particularly those in the Analysis and Reporting wing, is that of repeating the same Page Setup multiple times, over and over again, because there are so many different files and sheets to work with.

There is a little known secret, detailed below, that lets you copy the page setup options across different worksheets. Follow the instructions step-by-step and you will find it quite easy and much more appealing than doing the steps manually.

Chapter 8

Step 1 – Click on the sheet in which you have already made the page setup.

Step 2 – Hold down the Ctrl key and click on the sheet(s) that you want to format.

Step 3 – Select File → Page Setup from the Main menu and either press the Enter key or click the OK button.

That's all there is to it! Your page setup options are completely transferred to the target sheets.

For Further Study

Here are some nice links for further exploration and future reference.

http://www.busn.ucok.edu/jartmayer/excel/webpages/Printing.html

http://www.mvps.org/dmcritchie/excel/fitprint.htm

http://www.mvps.org/dmcritchie/excel/printing.htm

http://www.mvps.org/dmcritchie/excel/logoshd.htm

Chapter 8

Chapter 8

Adding Interactivity and Publishing Reports on the Web

In the last chapter, we covered quite a bit of valuable information about the various ways to format and print reports. Now let us see how to make the reports available to a large user base by publishing them onto an intranet or the internet.

A report that you publish on the web can be laced with some interactivity features that will enable the users not only to view the data but also to work on the data from their browsers, without needing to copy the data to Excel at all.

 Note:

Many of the features and facilities described in this chapter are available in Excel 2000 onwards, though the screenshots were done with Excel 2003.

You can publish one or all of the following elements of Excel to the web; we will review each one of these in detail.

Topics in this chapter:

Chapter 9

- Saving as a web page

- Publishing an entire workbook on a web page

- Publishing one worksheet / range / other items

- Publishing a chart on a web page

- Publishing a PivotTable report on a web page

- Further information...

Saving as a Web Page

This is probably the easiest of all options – to save an entire workbook or selected sheets as web page(s), as non-interactive reports.

Step 1 – From your open workbook, select File → Save as Web Page from the Main menu bar. The **Save As** dialog box opens.

Figure 189   Save as Web Page option

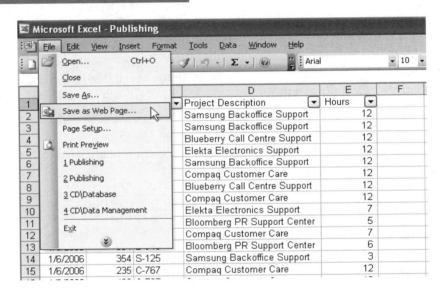

Step 2 – Specify the name of the HTML file . Click on the Change Title button to change the Title of the webpage. The optional **Set Page Title** dialog box opens, as shown below:

Chapter 9

Figure 190   Setting a different Page Title

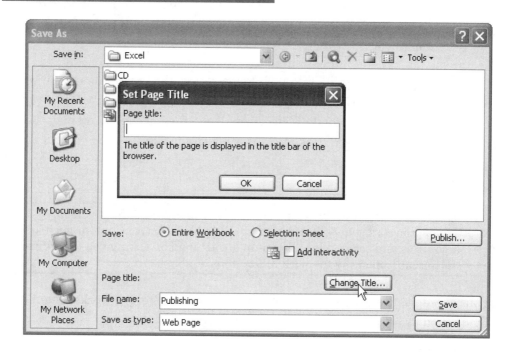

Step 3 –   Select the appropriate file path and make any changes to the file name or the title, then click on the Save button.

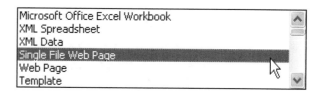 Note:

The two radio buttons titled "Entire Workbook" and "Selection:Sheet" let you to save the file appropriately.

Chapter 9

Step 4 –   In the "Save as type" option, choose either the Web Page or the Single File Web Page option.

Figure 191

Selecting from the list of "save as" file types

```
Microsoft Office Excel Workbook
XML Spreadsheet
XML Data
Single File Web Page
Web Page
Template
```

- Select Web Page (default option) to save the web page as an HTML file plus a folder with the same name that contains the files necessary to display the HTML file properly. You need to copy both the HTML file and the folder when you put the information onto your intranet.

- Save as a Single File Web Page to save the entire file in a single file (no extra folder) with an .MHT extension (.MHTML file). This facilitates uploading, because all the files needed to display the HTML file are packaged into this single file.

 Note:

You may need to alter your browser's security settings for the file to display correctly, as browsers generally are configured to block Active Content such as ActiveX controls and scripts. It will pop-up a warning box asking you to confirm if you want to really open the file with full options enabled.

In our example, the source workbook contains three different worksheets. When saved as a web page, the result looks like this:

Chapter 9

Figure 192

Web page with clickable tabs generated from Excel

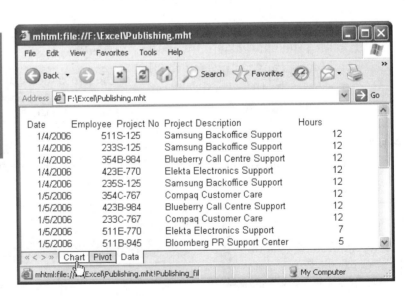

You may notice from the preceding result that the web page is clickable with different tabs, very much like the workbook; however, because the fields are not modifiable, it is more of a read-only workbook.

Saving an entire workbook as an HTML page like this is useful if you do not want to maintain a master copy of the Excel workbook, but want to be able to open the resulting HTML file directly in Excel and make and save changes using Excel features and functionality.

Now let's find out how to publish the workbook, which will allow you to play around with the contents online in the browser itself – without the need to open up Excel again.

Publishing an Entire Workbook on a Web Page

When you choose to publish an interactive workbook on a web page, your output is an HTML file blended with some special components that allow users to interact with the workbook from within their own browsers.

The special MS-Office components within the browser create an Excel atmosphere for the user to operate the HTML file as though it were an Excel workbook. Though the user can work interactively with and make changes to the file, it cannot be opened or modified in Excel.

 Note:

Always a maintain a master copy of the original source workbook so that you can make changes and republish it later.

Chapter 9

Step 1 – To publish a workbook with interactivity features, select the File → Save as webpage option. In the resulting window, ensure that you select the check box titled Add interactivity (circled).

Step 2 – Select the appropriate path to save the resulting HTML file and click on the Save button.

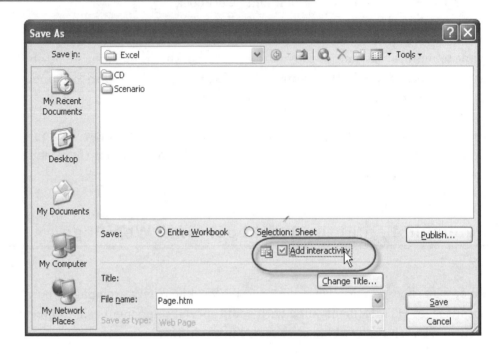

Figure 193   Publishing an interactive Excel workbook

Publishing One Worksheet / Range / Other Items

With very slight modifications to the above procedure, you can publish only one spreadsheet out of an entire workbook, or only a selected range of cells or items on a spreadsheet to a web page, with or without interactive functionality.

When you follow the correct procedure and publish a spreadsheet after using the Add Interactivity feature, the users of the HTML file will be able to enter and format new data, sort, filter, or analyze the data, and perform calculations.

 Note:

When you save without interactivity, the users can only view, but not manipulate, the data or formatting.

If you want to publish only one worksheet or a range of cells or items on a specific worksheet, use these steps.

Step 1 – With your required file open, select the File → Save as Web Page option, which opens the **Save As** dialog box.

Figure 194 Selecting the option to publish a workbook

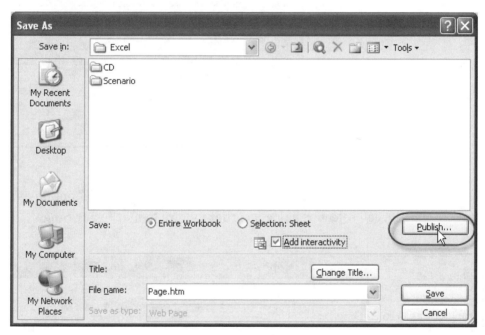

Step 2 – Ensure that you have selected the right path. Select the "Add interactivity" checkbox and then click on the Publish button. The Publish as **Web Page** dialog box opens (see following page).

Step 3 – Select which item(s), from any available worksheet(s), you want to publish. This example includes the Data, Pivot, and Chart sheets.

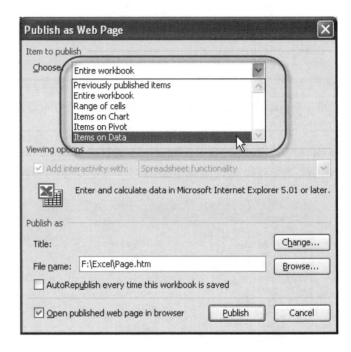

Figure 195

Selecting the items
to publish

Step 4 – To select only a range of cells, select the "Range of cells" option and
use the cell selector dialog box that follows to mark your range.

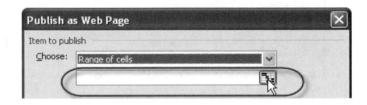

Figure 196

Selecting the
range of cells to
be published

Step 5 – To select some items on only one of the sheets, select the "Items on
Data" drop down menu, which is followed by the relevant sheet name.
This will present you with a small list box that details the items
available within the selected sheet. (see below).

Figure 197

Selecting a set of items to publish on a worksheet

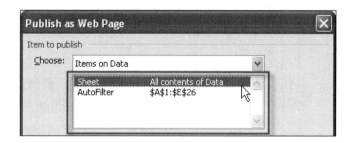

Step 6 – To change the Page title, use the Change button. To change the file location, use the Browse button.

Step 7 – To ensure that every time you make any changes to the source file the information will be automatically republished to the Web page, select the "AutoRepublish every time this workbook is saved" checkbox.

Step 8 – To automatically open the page when the HTML file is created, select the "Open published web page in browser" checkbox.

Step 9 – Click on Publish button to create the HTML file.

Figure 198

Final Steps in publishing a workbook

Chapter 9

Publishing a Chart on a Web page

Publishing a chart is similar to the procedure above, except for some minor modifications. Let us now go through the steps to publish a chart.

Step 1 – Select "Items on Chart" from the **Publish** dialog box.

The menu item under "Add interactivity with:" changes to "Chart functionality" under the Viewing Options in the middle section of the dialog box (see figure below)

Figure 199

Selecting a chart to be published with interactivity

Step 2 – Select the "Add interactivity with" check box and "Chart functionality" from the drop-down list to add to interactivity your web page. If desired, use the other buttons to change the file name or title and then click on Publish.

The resulting window, which embeds the PivotChart functionality, is shown below:

Figure 200   A published Chart, with the PivotTable functionality

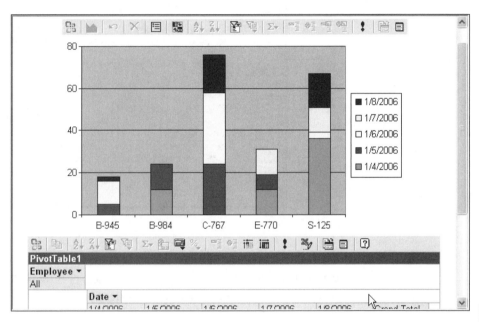

Publishing a PivotTable Report on a Web Page

Publishing a PivotTable report is just as simple as publishing a chart. Using the example above, let us publish PivotTable report on a web page using the **Publish** dialog box.

Step 1 – Select "Items on Pivot" from the drop down list; you will have two sub items in the listbox. Select PivotTable.

Figure 201

Selecting a
PivotTable report
to publish

Step 2 – Under the "Viewing Options", ensure that the check box next to the item "Add interactivity with:" is ticked; in the drop down next to it, select "PivotTable functionality" (see above figure).

Step 3 – If desired, change the title or the file name as well as the location and then click on Publish to create the HTML file with embedded PivotTable features.

The final output of the above exercise provides a wonderful HTML file with many amazing PivotTables features. A sample report is shown below.

 Note:

You might lose some formatting and features
when you save with interactive functionality.

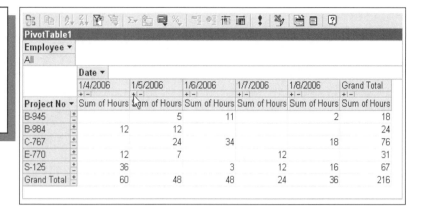

Figure 202

A published PivotTable Report, as viewed in a browser

Notice in the above report that the PivotTable drill down features are available in the form of +/- indicators. The fields are also capable of being dragged and dropped to make it truly an interactive report.

Further Information...

Take a look at the following information sources for further clarity on this topic.

http://www.database2net.com/

http://www.accountingsoftwareadvisor.com/excel/web-webpage.xls

http://www.abdn.ac.uk/diss/webpack/factsheet17.shtml

http://ict.cas.psu.edu/training/howto/excel/excweb_interactive.html

http://www.trinity.edu/rjensen/dhtml/excel01.htm

http://freud.franklin.edu/freudaccess/excel/index.htm

Chapter 9

Chapter 9

An Introduction to VBA

Most of us treat Excel as a standalone application, and do not think of going beyond the worksheet grid. But just give it a thought – if you could control the way the worksheet behaves by modifying some of its core program components to make them work for you – how great would that be?

Fortunately, you are not day dreaming – you can make Excel work for you with the help of VBA, which stands for "Visual Basic for Applications". This is a very extensive and voluminous topic by itself, and there are many books on this subject by industry experts such as John Walkenbach, Bill Jelen, and others.

It is essential for power users of Excel to be aware of the features and capabilities of VBA so that they can implement a VBA-based solution in situations that truly demand it. Unless you know what is available with VBA, you will not be able to decide when and where to utilize it.

That is the purpose of this brief chapter – to give you a quick understanding of the potential of VBA and to give you some insight into its basic programming structures.

Topics in this chapter:

Chapter 10

- What is a Macro and what is it used for?

- Recording a Macro – the toolkit

- Writing a Macro – the VBE window

- Running a Macro

- Other advanced topics and links

What Is a Macro and What Is It Used for?

A macro is a series of commands and/or functions that are stored in a Visual Basic module so that you can run it whenever you want to perform the full series of commands.

Macros are essentially time savers – they record commands and their sequencing and can replay that with another selection, thus automating your task and saving time and costs.

In other words, you can automate a task that you perform repeatedly in Excel with a macro to save time and effort. For example, you might create a macro to apply a specific custom date format to your selection.

Macros from untrustworthy sources can be dangerous to execute; before you enable macros in any workbook, confirm the authenticity and reliability of the source of the workbook.

 Caution!

Dangerous macros can take over complete control of your computer, and can create unimaginable harm to your entire system.

To ensure that you retain control over selecting macros and allowing them to run, go to Tools → Macros → Security on the Main menu.

From the **Security** dialog box (see below), select the Medium option and click on OK. This will ensure that every time a workbook with Macros is opened, you have the option to decide whether to allow the Macros to run or not.

If you choose the High option, any unsigned macros will be automatically disabled.

Figure 203

Security Settings affecting Macro operation

Recording a Macro – the Toolkit

Excel makes it very simple for any user to work with Macros by enabling you to record any activity you are doing in Excel and to review it later. The complete set of tools for this is available under the Tools → Macros in the Main menu.

Chapter 10

Figure 204   Invoking the Macro menu from the menu bar

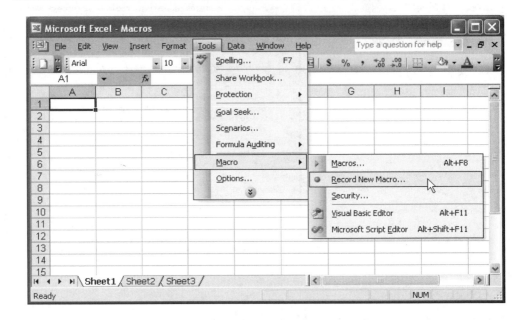

Step 1 –   To record a new macro, click on the Record New Macro menu item, as shown above. This brings up the **Record Macro** dialog box, where you can assign a name to the macro, define its shortcut key, and attach comments to it.

Figure 205

Record Macro dialog box

Excel for the CEO

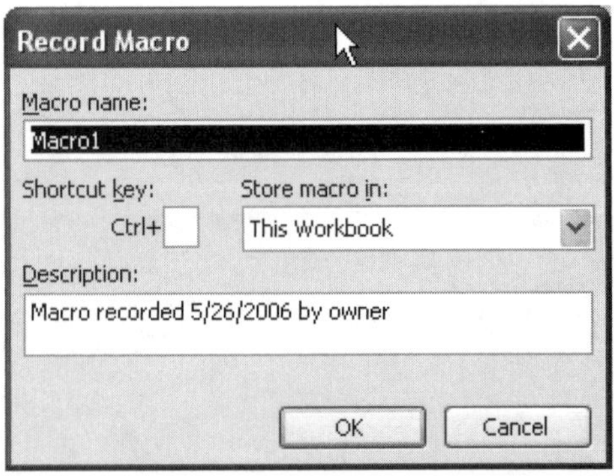

Step 2 – To modify the name of the macro, type a new name under the "Macro name:" field.

Step 3 – Define a shortcut key combination by first clicking on the field, then pressing the desired key combination – for example, Shift+M.

 Note:

It is a good idea to associate a shortcut key with the Shift key, because there are already so many default shortcut keys that use the Control key.

 Note:

It is even easier to record the macro with the default name and with no shortcut key. In that case, just press the OK button to start recording. You will see a floating toolbar that carries two buttons in it – one for stopping the recording, and another to capture the action in R1C1 mode, rather than associating it with the cell address such as A1, B1, etc.

Figure 206	Macro Recording Control floating tool bar

Step 4 – Perform the shortcut actions. In this case, we'll do some formatting in cell A1 to make the cell alignment be Wrap text mode.

- Keep your cursor in cell A1 and press Ctrl+1 to bring up the **Format Cells** dialog box.

- Go to Alignment tab and select the checkbox for Wrap text.

- Click on the first button (looks like a Square button – see above) to stop the recording.

Step 5 – Press the Alt+F11 keys together to open up Visual Basic Editor (VBE), where you can review the macro that you just recorded. In VBE, you

Chapter 10

will see a small pane to the left side with your file name, followed by a tree structure of Microsoft Excel Objects and Modules.

Step 6 – Click on the plus (+) sign next to the Modules; expand it and double-click on Module1 to open it up. This will open up and display your macro.

Figure 207   Visual Basic Editor (VBE) environment

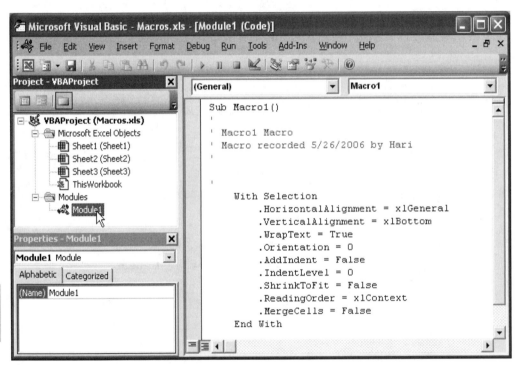

The macro has captured all the elements of formatting within the Alignment tab, even though you only modified the WrapText portion.

Step 7 – To have the macro perform only the WrapText operation, delete all the other line items that lie within the loop, starting with the dot (.).

Chapter 10

Writing a Macro - the VBE Window

Writing a macro is an option for advanced users who know the VBA language and syntax quite well. However, even beginners can try their hand with the VBE window, because of the support provided to auto-fill the syntax.

There is a type-ahead feature in VBE, much as there is when you enter a formula within Excel, that shows any additional arguments that are required for the current line or syntax to function properly.

We will now write a small, simple macro that pops up a message box announcing your first macro.

Step 1 – Go to the VBE window, using the procedure previously mentioned (Remember? – Alt+F11).

Step 2 – Go to Insert → Module; enter the code given below in the module window.

```
Sub firstmacro()
    MsgBox ("This is my first Macro!")
End Sub
```

Step 3 – Press F5 or select Run → Run Sub/User Form in the VBE window.

Step 4 – Excel will show a list of macros available in the workbook. Choose your macro (firstmacro) and click on Run.

Step 5 – Your macro will now produce a message box like this one.

Figure 208

Your first dialog box in VBA

Running a Macro

You can run a macro by pressing F5 from the VBE window or by selecting Run → Run Sub/UserForm from the VBE Main menu.

Step 1 – To execute a macro from inside Excel, press the Alt+F8 keys to bring up a list of macros available to execute within the workbook.

You can also bring up this dialog box by selecting Tools → Macro → Macros from the Main menu bar of Excel.

Figure 209

Selecting Macros to run or edit.

Step 2 – Click on Run to apply the macro. You can also click on Options button to modify the macro by adding a shortcut key or a description.

Other Advanced Topics and Links

- To undo an unwanted action in a macro, open the macro in the VBE and remove any unwanted steps.
  Alternatively, you can also record the macro again without performing the unwanted action.

- To stop a macro that is currently running, press ESC, and click End in the **Visual Basic** dialog box that ensues.
  You can also press Ctrl+Break to stop a VB macro while it is running.

- To prevent a macro from running automatically when you start Microsoft Excel, hold down the Shift key during startup.

- To delete a macro, press Alt+F8 keys to bring up the list of macros. Select the unwanted macro and then press the Delete button.

- A module is a container for procedures.
  A procedure is a unit of code enclosed either between the Sub and End Sub statements or between the Function and End Function statements.

- Procedures in Visual Basic can have either private or public scope. By default, procedures have public scope.

- A private scope procedure is only accessible to the other procedures in the same module.

- A public procedure is accessible to all procedures in every module in the workbook in which the procedure is declared, and in all workbooks that contain a reference to that workbook.

 Note:

Add the word Private as the first word in the first line to make it a Private procedure. For example, a procedure that starts like "Sub test()" is a public procedure named Test. "Private Sub test()"indicates that Test is a private procedure.

Chapter 10

- VBA is a powerful tool with provisions for including variety of decision-making and conditional tools such as If-Then statements, Logical Checks, Boolean Operators, Loops, and Select Case statements.

- With a simple sub statement, you can even alter the title of your Excel Application – instead being "Microsoft Excel", it can say something like "Hari's Excel" or be called by your name.

This trick was mentioned in an earlier chapter; the Sub() for this is below:

```
Sub title()
Application.Caption = "My Own Excel"
End Sub
```

Understanding the complete power of VBA can go a long way in fine tuning Excel to meet your requirements. For further information on this subject, check out Excel's built-in Help system.

Here are some websites that provide good information, tutorials, and examples on VBA:

http://www.functionx.com/vbaexcel/Lesson01.htm

http://www.anthony-vba.kefra.com/

http://www.vbaexpress.com/

http://j-walk.com/ss/excel/tips/index.htm

http://www.mindspring.com/~tflynn/excelvba.html

http://www.xl-logic.com/pages/vba.html

http://www33.brinkster.com/rbad/default.aspx?section=utilities&page=home

Chapter 10

Case Studies

You have progressed far enough that you are ready for a deep dive into some case studies that will expose you to real-life situations and practical applications that use the advanced powers of Excel.

Topics in this chapter:

- 🪙   Peter F. Drucker's advice for CEOs

- 🪙   Reviewing projects and their profitability

- 🪙   Checking delivery schedules using Gantt charts

- 🪙   Comparing Excel worksheets / workbooks

- 🪙   Financial analysis models – creation and automation

- 🪙   Having your own menu bar

- 🪙   Controlling reports using PivotTables

- 🪙   Using conditional statements for reporting

- 🪙   Controlling entry of dates – the dating problem!

- 🪙   Some interesting examples

Chapter 11

Peter F. Drucker's Advice to CEOs

Peter F. Drucker, the Guru of Modern Management, wrote about his view of the concept and duties of the American CEO. The full article is available on the web at this location:

http://www.opinionjournal.com/editorial/?id=110006100

In his article, Drucker points out that CEOs have a work of their own to perform, besides having a responsibility for the work of everybody else in the organization. And it is not only work that *only* CEOs can do, but also work that CEOs *must* do.

The CEO, Drucker said, is the link between the Inside and the Outside. In the article, Drucker's review of the work that only CEOs can and must do drives us to the conclusion that most of these tasks are ones that only Excel users can accomplish.

Duties of the CEO

To prove the point of how Excel can ably assist the CEOs in performing their unique duties, we need to study those duties, as detailed by Drucker. These include:

➢ **Define the meaningful Outside of the organization.**
For example, is the meaningful Outside for a bank the local market for commercial loans? Is it the national market for mutual funds? Or is it major industrial companies and their short-term credit needs? Only the CEO can make this decision. But also the CEO *must* make it.

➢ **Determine what information regarding the Outside is meaningful and necessary for the organization, and then work on getting it into a usable form.**
Organized information has grown tremendously in the last hundred years. But the growth has been mainly in Inside information, e.g., in accounting. As regards the Outside, there has been an enormous growth in data – beginning with Herbert Hoover in the 1920s.

Chapter 11

But few CEOs, whether in business, in nonprofits, or in government agencies, have as yet organized this data into systematic information to help them in performing their own work.

Key Decision Making Points

The definition of the institution's meaningful Outside, and of the information it needs, makes it possible to answer the key questions: "What is our business? What should it be? What should it not be?" The answers to these questions establish the boundaries within which an institution operates. And they are the foundation for the specific work of the CEO. Particularly:

➤ The answers enable the CEO to decide what results are meaningful for the institution. To decide what results a given bottom line represents is a major job of the executive. It is not based on facts – there are no facts about the future. It is not made very well by intuition. Instead, it is a judgment. Only the CEO can, and must, make this judgment.

➤ The answers to the questions "What is our business? And what should it be?" enable CEOs to decide what information is meaningful for the business and for themselves. It is information about the Outside that needs the most work.

➤ The CEO has to decide the priorities, because in any organization, there are always far more tasks than there are available resources to accomplish these tasks. The CEO's most critical job – also the CEO's most difficult job – is to say "No.", which should not be said arbitrarily, but out of an inordinate amount of study and work.

➤ The CEO places people into key positions. This, in the last analysis, determines the performance capacity of the institution. Nothing requires as much hard work as "people decisions". The only thing that requires even more time (and even more work) than putting people into jobs is unmaking wrong people decisions. And again, only the CEO can make critical people decisions.

Chapter 11

OK, But Where Does Excel Come in?

Now you have the gist of what Drucker has to say about the CEO's basic duties. Much of it revolves around making informed decisions about "the Outside" and about "what information is useful and relevant" to be collated, organized, studied, and analyzed in greater detail.

We also know that, in deciding what exactly is "the Outside", a CEO is making a choice from many alternatives, and he most likely does so with the help of analyses prepared in Excel.

Excel proves to be a wise choice, over many other market applications, to achieve this objective. It can take data from many sources and summarize, evaluate, and represent them across a standardized bench mark, as required by the user. With such wonderful tools as Web Query, Database Query, Goal Seek, Scenario Builder, PivotTable and PivotChart, Filters, Validations, Error Checking, and Formula Auditing in its armory and the all-powerful VBA by its side, Excel is well-positioned to provide the complete solution base for you, the CEO, to perform your own duties in the best possible way.

However, a lot of planning at the initial stage of database design is definitely required before starting out to capture "Outside information". A knowledgeable Excel user can guide this project to a resounding success using Excel-friendly OLAP databases, which can quickly retrieve the requisite data using the concept of data cubes.

On-Line Analytical Processing (OLAP) is a way to organize large databases for optimum performance. OLAP databases are organized to fit the way you retrieve and analyze data so that it is easier to create the reports you need. OLAP databases are designed to speed up the retrieval of data. A set of levels that encompass one aspect of the data, such as geographic locations, is called a dimension.

Chapter 11

OLAP databases are called cubes because they combine several dimensions, such as time, geography, and product lines, with summarized data, such as sales or inventory figures.

When you create an OLAP cube from a query, you turn the flat set of records into a structured hierarchy that allows reports to focus on the desired level of detail. You also predefine the summary values for the reports, which speeds up report calculation.

With a data cube, you can work with more data in your reports than you could otherwise return to Excel without running out of system resources, and you can create and update reports faster than if you based them on the individual records from the database

Reviewing Projects and Their Profitability

Excel can be effectively used by companies to keep a finger on the pulse of their profitability for ongoing projects. For instance, there is a plethora of new-age services and BPO companies where manpower is the crux, and every single minute really counts, casting a huge shadow on the bottom line.

Such companies need to keep a regular review of the manpower spent as it happens. There is no point in reviewing the issue after the end of the project – only to understand that a huge loss has been suffered. Real-time review and timely corrective action will significantly help the company in avoiding possible loss situations.

Chapter 11

Let us take an example of a case where the time spent by each employee is captured live (or on an "end of the day" basis) in a separate database. The forms of databases supported by Excel are: dBase, Excel, Access, Visio, OLAP Cubes, and Queries.

Let's say that the CEO of the company has a very simple file in his desktop showing the list of projects, their estimated billing value/ceiling of costs for the manpower, and the actual manpower spent so far on each such project. An example is given below:

Figure 210   Basic Profitability Review report

S.No	Project No	Project Description	Est Billing Value ($)	Allocated Manhours	Manhours spent so far
1	S-125	Samsung Backoffice Support	200000	6,655	
2	B-984	Blueberry Call Centre Support	150000	4,991	
3	C-767	Compaq Customer Care	750000	24,955	
4	E-770	Elekta Electronics Support	50000	1,664	
5	B-945	Bloomberg PR Support Center	360000	11,978	

Profitability Review & Control Module - status report as on: 4/20/2006 21:51
E1 = =NOW()

In this report, all the data in Columns A to E are static and are key inputs for the top line. The data to come in Column F will be updated real-time – it is dynamic, not static like the other data.

The data in column F has to come from the database, and can be pulled into Excel through any of the query models – including PivotTables, which were discussed in an earlier chapter at length (see Introducing PivotTables on page 166).

For the sake of simplicity, let us assume that the data in Column F has to come in from an Excel database. This data file will look like this:

Figure 211 Datasheet for the profitability review report

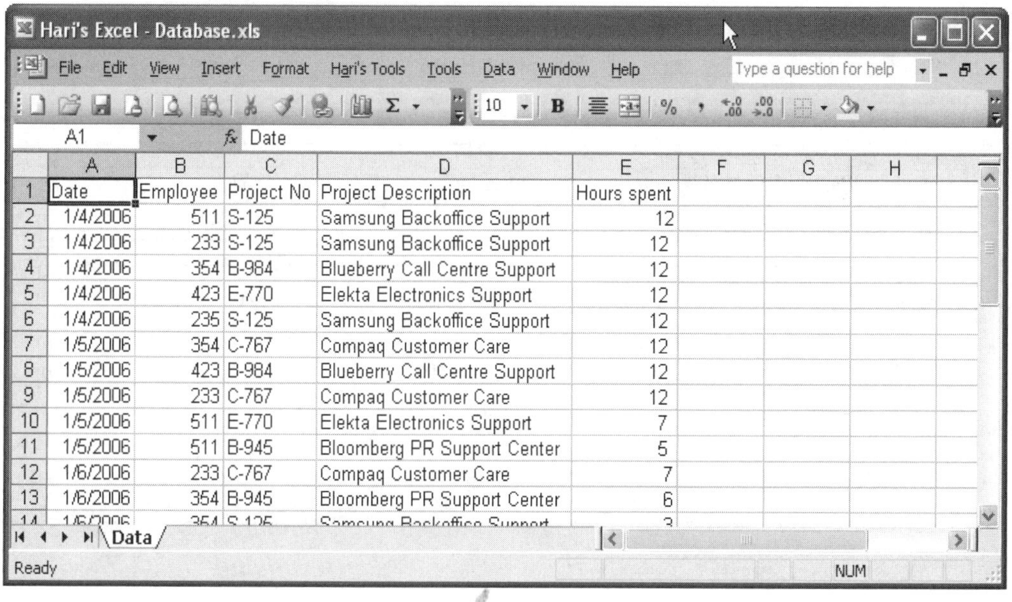

	A	B	C	D	E
1	Date	Employee	Project No	Project Description	Hours spent
2	1/4/2006	511	S-125	Samsung Backoffice Support	12
3	1/4/2006	233	S-125	Samsung Backoffice Support	12
4	1/4/2006	354	B-984	Blueberry Call Centre Support	12
5	1/4/2006	423	E-770	Elekta Electronics Support	12
6	1/4/2006	235	S-125	Samsung Backoffice Support	12
7	1/5/2006	354	C-767	Compaq Customer Care	12
8	1/5/2006	423	B-984	Blueberry Call Centre Support	12
9	1/5/2006	233	C-767	Compaq Customer Care	12
10	1/5/2006	511	E-770	Elekta Electronics Support	7
11	1/5/2006	511	B-945	Bloomberg PR Support Center	5
12	1/6/2006	233	C-767	Compaq Customer Care	7
13	1/6/2006	354	B-945	Bloomberg PR Support Center	6

Having examined the data structure, it becomes a simple matter to get the live update into the Final Report file using a simple formula in Column F. This formula ensures that any time the report is opened, it will provide a live feedback of the bottom line movement on each project.

For example, the formula in cell F5 would be:

=SUMIF([Database.xls]Data!D:D,Report!C5,[Database.xls]Data!E:E)

This formula runs through column D in the sheet named Data in the file named Database.xls, and looks for any field matching the cell C5. If it finds matches, it then sums up the value found against that row in column E of the Data sheet.

The resulting window is shown here:

Figure 212   Profitability Review Report with actual figures

S.No	Project No	Project Description	Est Billing Value ($)	Allocated Manhours	Manhours spent so far
		Profitability Review & Control Module - status report as on:		4/20/2006 23:09	
1	S-125	Samsung Backoffice Support	200000	6,655	105
2	B-984	Blueberry Call Centre Support	150000	4,991	2400
3	C-767	Compaq Customer Care	750000	24,955	12500
4	E-770	Elekta Electronics Support	50000	1,664	430
5	B-945	Bloomberg PR Support Center	360000	11,978	8150

You can that this one step further if there is another file maintained by a different department that shows the percentage of work completed against each project. In that case, you can pull the percentage up from the relevant file using the VLOOKUP function; with that available, you can determine if the man-hours spent are well within the limits or not.

In the example above, for the first project, S-125, it is OK to have spent only 66.55 hours if only 1% of the project is complete. However, if the time spent so far is 105 hours, this will require raising an Alert flag.

An Alert flag can be simply programmed using an IF function triggered by the percentage completion as compared against the actual hours spent.

See cell H5 in the following figure.

Chapter 11

Figure 213   Adding an Alert flag to facilitate quick review

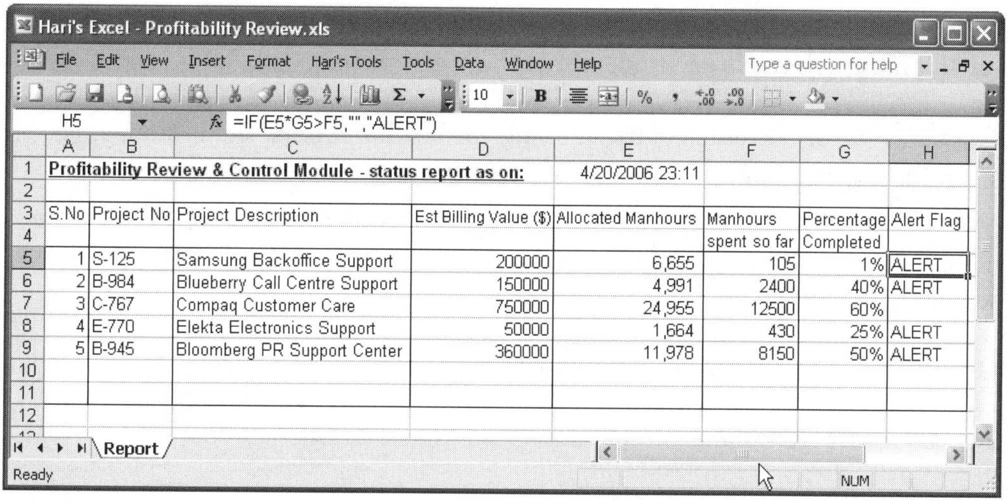

As you may notice, the Alert flag is a just simple formula, but it achieves the purpose. We can even program it to show in Red color if the difference is too far out of bounds by using Conditional Formatting.

A simple report structure such as the one created above will help you to review the bottom line effect throughout the life of a project. Also, it will require entering the project details just once – all other data will be grabbed from the sources and presented automatically.

Chapter 11

Checking Delivery Schedules Using Gantt Charts

Gantt charts are a special kind of bar charts used in scheduling and program management. These are useful to show graphically when tasks must start and finish and which tasks are underway at any given time.

A set of tasks or activities is listed along the left hand axis; the bottom axis shows dates. The bars indicate when each task begins and ends and which tasks are in progress at any given time. Gantt charts help in scheduling the many tasks in a program and in identifying potential resource issues in the schedule.

Let us make a Gantt chart in a step-by-step procedure.

Step 1 – Start with some sample data – see figure below:

Figure 214

Data Sheet for building a Gantt Chart

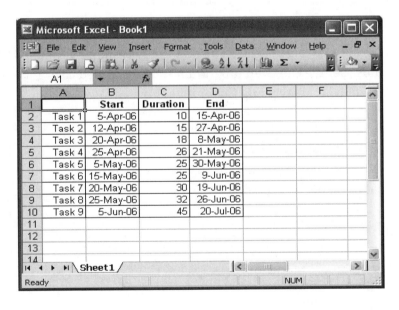

Chapter 11

Step 2 – Select the data in range A1:C10 and then select Insert → Chart from the Menu bar. In the resulting window, select Bar under the Chart type; in the right side window, select Stacked Bar under the Chart sub-types and click on Finish.

Now you will have a chart in your worksheet as shown below:

Figure 215   Steps to building a Gantt Chart – the Stacked Bar

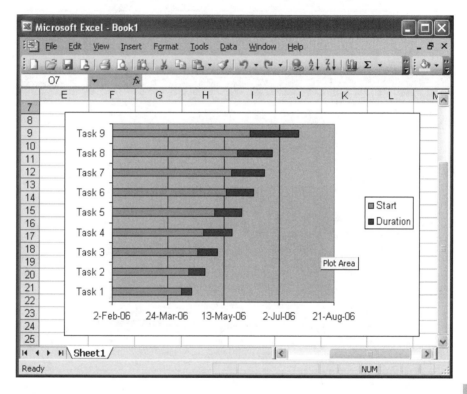

Step 3 – Double-click on the Category Axis (Task name). In the options box that comes up, place a tick against "Categories in reverse order" and also against "Value (Y) axis crosses at maximum category".

Step 4 – Double-click on the Value Axis (Dates). In the resulting options, enter the earliest date appearing in column D (the first of the task finish deadlines). Also, against the value box "Major units:", you can enter the number of days you want to have grouped together and displayed in the chart – let us say, 10 days. Please note that the earliest date can be entered in date format (01-Apr-06), and Excel will convert it into a number format (38808). And when you enter the major units, just enter the number there (10); no text is allowed.

Now you will see a chart modified as follows:

Figure 216   Steps to building a Gantt Chart –Stacked Bar (reverse order)

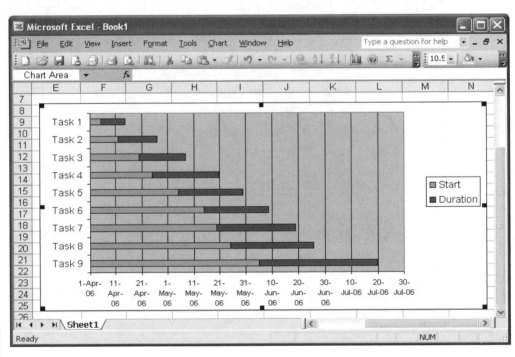

Step 5 – Select the Start series by double-clicking anywhere on the blue color data area. In the resulting options box, select None under both the Border and Area options.

Step 6 – Click on the legend box, and delete it.

This will leave you with a Gantt chart that will truly reflect your data in a meaningful, professional way. The chart that will look like this:

Figure 217   Gantt Chart – The Final Result

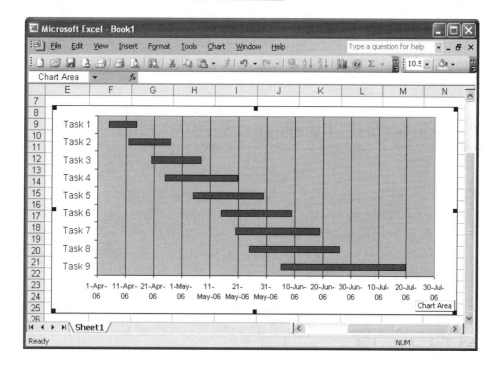

That's it – you have just created a professional looking Gantt chart.

To get some ideas on how to create an advanced Gantt chart that shows deadlines and delays with different color codes, visit this link:

http://peltiertech.com/Excel/Charts/GanttChart.html

Chapter 11

The above hyperlink takes you to the website of Jon Peltier, one of the most respected Excel gurus, and to whom I owe much of the credit for the countless techniques I have learned in Excel charting.

Jon continues to inspire every aspirant of Excel with his amazing collection of tools and techniques, and by spreading his rich knowledge and experience through his wonderful website.

 Note:

I am sure you will add this site to your Favorites list, once you visit there and realize what it has to offer.

Comparing Excel Worksheets/Workbooks

Ever ended up in a situation where you have two nearly identical worksheets that contain slightly different data in some obscure spots on the worksheets? Although you could use the Track Changes option to protect such situations from occurring in the future, you cannot do much about files that already have some discrepancies.

A classical example is the Trial Balance for a particular date that goes through multiple rounds of revisions until no one is certain any longer which one is the final version. At this point, you may long for something on the lines of the Compare Documents option available in MS-Word. Unfortunately, there is no standard function available in Excel to meet this demand.

Below we have two very similar sample worksheets:

Figure 218

Source worksheet for comparison

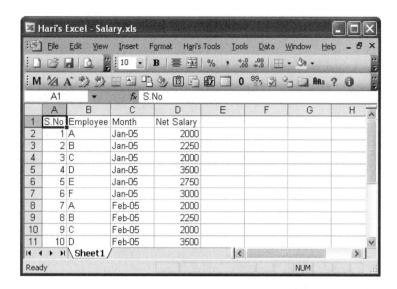

Figure 219

Target worksheet for comparison

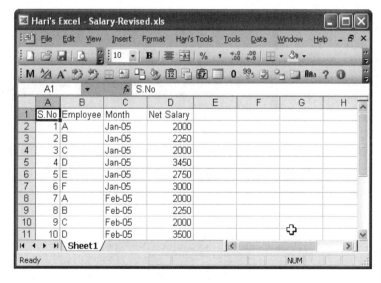

Although both files look identical at first glance, there is a difference somewhere that needs to be identified.

To accomplish this, we can use one of the very popular Excel add-in made available by Rob, an Excel guru. You can download this wonderful add-in here:

http://www33.brinkster.com/rbad/default.aspx?section=utilities&page=compare sheets

The best part of Rob's add-in is that he allows us to read through the VBA code to learn what he did. The password to open the VBA project is mentioned on the website.

Once you install the add-in and activate it from the Tools menu, you will be able to compare the two sheets and produce the result in just one click.

Comparison Process

Figure 220

Process of worksheet comparison

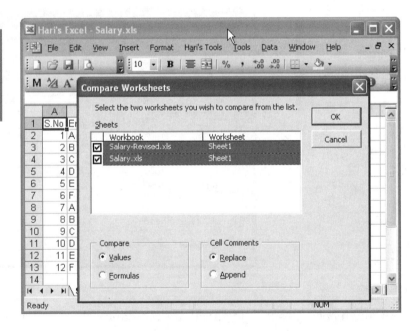

Chapter 11

Once this process is activated, the cells containing the different elements will be tagged with a comment, which makes it very easy to identify and attend to them. The result window is shown below.

Figure 221   Results of doing the worksheet comparison

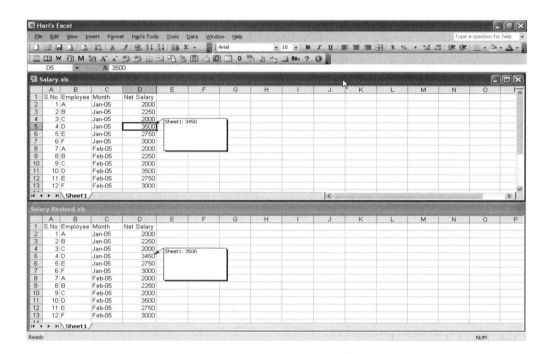

There are a couple more compare functions available on the internet that you can find at the links below:

Chapter 11

http://www.mvps.org/dmcritchie/excel/comparexl.htm

There is also some wonderful freeware for identifying and managing duplicates – a creation of Dave, another Excel expert. This tool can be had from his webpage:

http://members.iinet.net.au/~brettdj/

Financial Analysis Models – Creation and Automation

A major chunk of the topic of financial analysis revolves around the computation of ratios, comparing them against the industry standards and benchmarks, and arriving at conclusions.

With Excel at hand, it is easy to standardize a data input form that can take in the basic data from a company's balance sheet and income statements and work out the ratios and analysis automatically.

In my profession as an auditor, I have had to perform many financial analyses, so I created a tool for myself to simplify the tasks. I named it the FinRatio tool – meaning Financial Ratios Tool.

This tool takes in the standardized data in a sheet and provides options to generate a set of ratios. Another option allows you to generate a completely automated analytical report based on the ratios, as compared against the general benchmarks.

A glance at the tool makes it clear that its programming structure is very simple; however, its functionality is very powerful, thanks to the programmable features of Excel. The tool build is incredibly simple – looking at it from the standpoint of programming – but the output of functionality and reporting is extremely powerful. Such power is achieved by the customizable features of Excel combined with the functional know-how of the user. This tool will inspire fellow auditors and professional management accountants to design and develop similar tools that can greatly facilitate their jobs.

Chapter 11

A screenshot of the FinRatio follows:

Figure 222 FinRatio Package

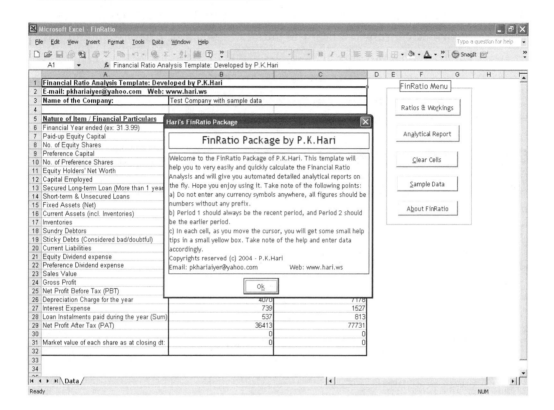

Steps involved in building this tool:

Step 1 – Design a standard Data sheet with enough comments to enable any user to easily capture and provide the correct data.

Step 2 – Allow only the required fields to be editable; locking and protecting the descriptive cells and comments.

Step 3 – Prepare a worksheet containing formulas and routines to calculate and output a report of Ratios.

Step 4 – Ensure that the report is fully protected and hidden, except in so far as it draws on data entered in the main data sheet.

Step 5 – Provide data validation functions to ensure that if the data is incorrectly formatted or if the data field is blank where it should not be, an appropriate result will be output in the report.

Figure 223   Sample of the Ratios & Workings report

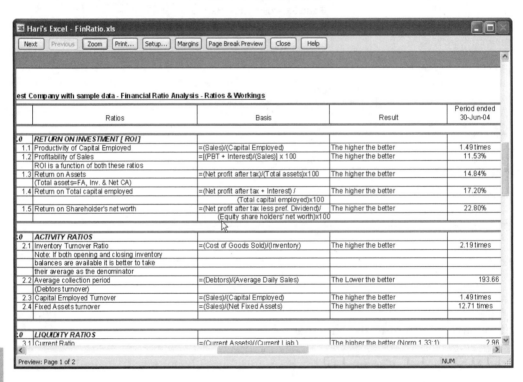

Step 6 – Another sheet containing the text portion of the analytical report is prepared with necessary protections and data validations.

Step 7 – Once the user clicks on the Analytical Report button, this particular sheet is activated, and outputs the report only through a printable

Chapter 11

window –not as an editable window. This way, the integrity of the report is protected and we can be sure that the report remains the way it was originally designed.

A snapshot of the analytical report available in the FinRatio tool is below:

Figure 224   Sample of the Analytical Report inside the FinRatio

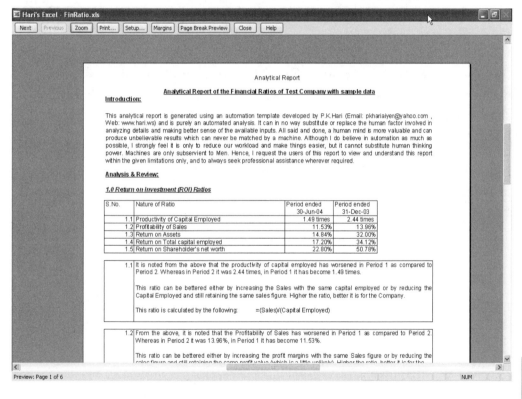

Chapter 11

The FinRatio tool is available for free download at the following link in my website:

http://www.hari.ws/Excel/finratio.zip

I have provided a couple of buttons in my tool to clear out the data entered and to put in some sample data so that the user can make a sample report to understand the working style of the tool.

This can be customized and used easily by anyone having sound functional knowledge.

Having Your Own Menu Bar

For the sake of convenience, it is common for advanced users of Excel to create their own set of tools in Excel. Having all your commonly used tools in one place is a great time-saver. Your subordinates and colleagues who happen to see your new customized tool menu in your Excel, personalized with your name, will be impressed with your level of Excel knowledge.

Now let us see how to create your own menu bar. To get an idea of how it will look, see the screen shot below that contains my personal menu bar, named Hari's Tools:

Chapter 11

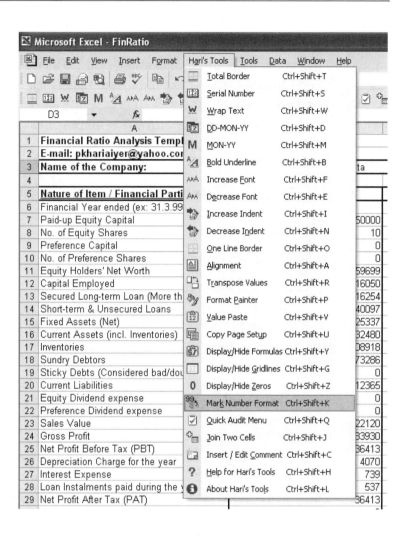

Figure 225

Hari's Tools list

As you can see in the above tools list, I made Help one of the items so that a new user can easily become familiar with the set of tools. Actually, explaining in detail about how to create a fully customized toolbar and menu bar would take a lot of pages and figures.

Chapter 11

 Tip:

You can download my toolbar from www.hari.ws/Excel/haristools.zip.

So, I will make this very short and sweet to learn – we will make your toolbar and menu bar in a reasonably simple style – not too advanced. We are talking the fast food route rather than the time consuming gourmet cooking method. As you follow this procedure, you will automatically learn how to make more customizations and modifications with the resource links given here.

Steps to create your own toolset:

Step 1 – Download the Menumaker.xls file from John Walkenbach's Excel Portal:

http://www.j-walk.com/ss/excel/tips/tip53.htm

Step 2 – To identify and select the different icons available, check out this link:

This file contains some basic VBA code and a worksheet that will help you create your own MenuSheet. You can customize both the text part of the menu, as well as the icon shown next to it.

http://www.j-walk.com/ss/excel/tips/tip40.htm

Step 3 – Create a copy of the workbook and do all your changes in that, just to be safe – of course, if something goes wrong, you can always download it again from John's site, but working from a copy is a good idea any time you are making significant structural changes.

Step 4 – Before you start modifying the MenuSheet, decide in advance what effects or tools you want to have in your toolset. It is a good practice to write down a list of tools and the relevant FaceIDs that you plan to use.

Step 5 – Identify which functions help you most and create a macro for them.

The simplest way to capture a macro for your favorite activity, and to make it one of the tools on the customized menu bar, is to use the

Macro Recorder for each activity that you want, and then to copy the Macro that Excel creates in the background.

For example, let's assume that you want to create a menu item which, on clicking, will put a double bottom border on the selected cells.

a. Open a new worksheet and select some cells.

b. Select Tools → Macro → Record New Macro from the menu, and click OK on the dialog box.

c. Go the borders tool and select the double border from the drop down. Then, click on the Stop recording button in the Macro floating toolbar.

d. Your macro is now ready to copy. To find it, press Alt+F11 to open the VBA editor, look for your file name in the left window, and under that look out for Modules, within which you will find a Module1 (may be Module2 or Module3 if there are others as well) containing your code.

There is quite a lot of content on the web explaining how to create and customize your own menu bar. Some links are given below to worthwhile sites where you can browse and learn more.

http://msdn.microsoft.com/library/en-us/odc_vsto2003_ta/html/odc_VSTCommBar.asp

http://www.cpearson.com/excel/menus.htm

http://www.ozgrid.com/FreeDownloads/AddingCustomMenus.zip

http://www.vbaexpress.com/kb/getarticle.php?kb_id=427

http://www.mvps.org/dmcritchie/excel/toolbars.htm

Chapter 11

Creating your own toolbar (the ones carrying just the icons appearing below the menu bar) is a little more complex, and is not touched upon in this chapter.

However, if you are interested in learning about this, you can see these links for further details:

http://office.microsoft.com/en-gb/assistance/ha010548161033.aspx

http://www.ozgrid.com/News/excel-custom-toolbars.htm

http://office.microsoft.com/training/training.aspx?AssetID=RC010036361033

Distributing your toolbar to others involves an additional step of converting it into an XL Addin. Further details on this can be had from here:

http://msdn.microsoft.com/archive/en-us/dnarexcel9/html/xlcraddns.asp

Another interesting freeware toolset is available at the following location:

http://www.asap-utilities.com

Control Reports Using PivotTables

PivotTables lend themselves to innumerable varieties of reporting and charting, without harming the data in any way. Now let us see how CEOs can exercise practical control on project schedules with a simple PivotTable-based report.

The following case study assumes a BPO back office accounting environment, where the CEO refers to just a single page PivotTable report that will draw data from a database of jobs maintained by the Operations Manager.

Chapter 11

A sample snapshot of the Pivot Report is shown below:

Figure 226 Control Report using PivotTable Features

	Customer	Process	Sub-Activity	Scheduled Start Dt	Actual Start Dt	Delay At Start	Scheduled End Dt	Actual End Dt	Delay At End
8	Microsoft	BRS	Preparation	19-Aug-05	19-Aug-05	0	19-Aug-05	19-Aug-05	0
9		Fixed Assets	Depreciation	12-Aug-05	12-Aug-05	0	12-Aug-05	12-Aug-05	0
10		Inventory	Cost Updation	8-Aug-05	9-Aug-05	(1)	9-Aug-05	10-Aug-05	(1)
11			Reports	10-Aug-05	11-Aug-05	(1)	11-Aug-05	12-Aug-05	(1)
12			Update records	7-Aug-05	7-Aug-05	0	7-Aug-05	7-Aug-05	0
13			Variance analysis	9-Aug-05	10-Aug-05	(1)	9-Aug-05	10-Aug-05	(1)
14		Payroll	Bank transfers	26-Jul-05	28-Jul-05	(2)	28-Jul-05	29-Jul-05	(1)
15			Benefits	15-Jul-05	15-Jul-05	0	15-Jul-05	15-Jul-05	0
16			Payslips	29-Jul-05	29-Jul-05	0	29-Jul-05	29-Jul-05	0
17			Reports	25-Jul-05	25-Jul-05	0	25-Jul-05	25-Jul-05	0
18			Salaries	6-Jul-05	8-Jul-05	(2)	13-Jul-05	15-Jul-05	(2)
19			Statutory records	17-Jul-05	18-Jul-05	(1)	17-Jul-05	17-Jul-05	0
20			Tax calculations	30-Jul-05	30-Jul-05	0	30-Jul-05	30-Jul-05	0
21			Tax returns	31-Jul-05	31-Jul-05	0	31-Jul-05	1-Aug-05	(1)
22		Procurement	Expenses	11-Jul-05	12-Jul-05	(1)	13-Jul-05	14-Jul-05	(1)
23			Purchases	6-Jul-05	6-Jul-05	0	10-Jul-05	12-Jul-05	(2)
24			Services	14-Jul-05	14-Jul-05	0	14-Jul-05	14-Jul-05	0
25		Sales	Order Processing	1-Jul-05	2-Jul-05	(1)	3-Jul-05	5-Jul-05	(2)
26			Quotations	4-Jul-05	4-Jul-05	0	6-Jul-05	6-Jul-05	0
27			Receivables	4-Jul-05	4-Jul-05	0	5-Jul-05	6-Jul-05	(1)
28	Samsung	BRS	ABN - Acct 3	7-Aug-05	7-Aug-05	0	7-Aug-05	7-Aug-05	0
29			BOA - Acct 1	30-Jul-05	28-Jul-05	2	30-Jul-05	29-Jul-05	1

At a click, the report will be able to provide the following information:

> **Status of projects** – for each manager, for specific clients, for company as a whole, and only unfinished projects, etc. – the options are virtually unlimited.

> **Delayed projects** – can be separately filtered, with an option to see the data for each manager.

> **Delays** – at one glance, the CEO can decide on the status of the projects, and can focus on any alarming delays by looking at the delay triggers and the days delayed.

Chapter 11

The database from which the report draws information captures each process and subactivity as separate row items; the scheduled start and end dates, the team manager, and estimated hours for completion are also listed. The data sheet snapshot follows:

Figure 227 Datasheet for the PivotTable-based Control Report

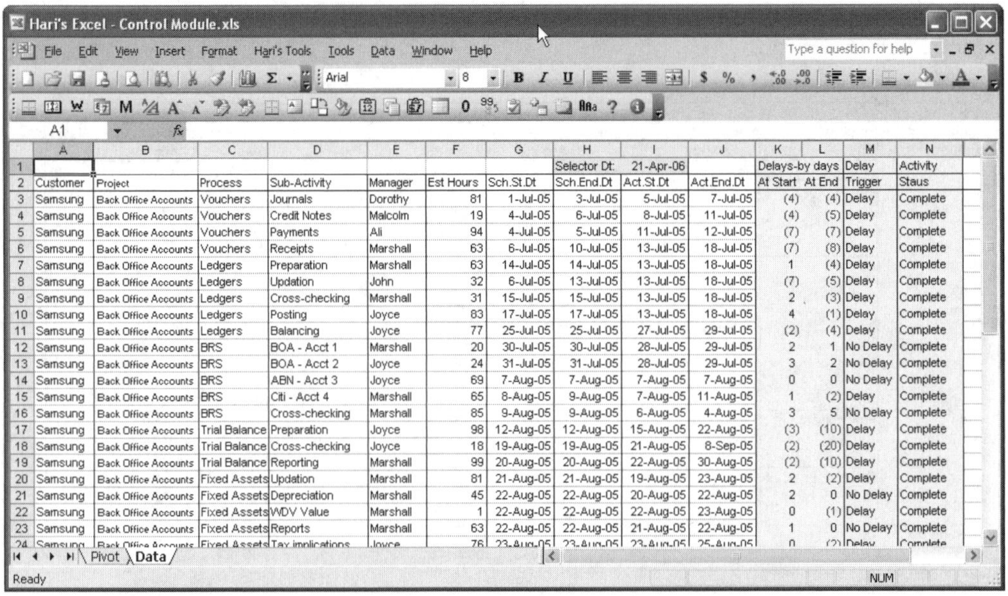

	A	B	C	D	E	F	G	H	I	J	K	L	M	N
1								Selector Dt:	21-Apr-06		Delays-by days		Delay	Activity
2	Customer	Project	Process	Sub-Activity	Manager	Est Hours	Sch.St.Dt	Sch.End.Dt	Act.St.Dt	Act.End.Dt	At Start	At End	Trigger	Staus
3	Samsung	Back Office Accounts	Vouchers	Journals	Dorothy	81	1-Jul-05	3-Jul-05	5-Jul-05	7-Jul-05	(4)	(4)	Delay	Complete
4	Samsung	Back Office Accounts	Vouchers	Credit Notes	Malcolm	19	4-Jul-05	6-Jul-05	8-Jul-05	11-Jul-05	(4)	(5)	Delay	Complete
5	Samsung	Back Office Accounts	Vouchers	Payments	Ali	94	4-Jul-05	5-Jul-05	11-Jul-05	12-Jul-05	(7)	(7)	Delay	Complete
6	Samsung	Back Office Accounts	Vouchers	Receipts	Marshall	63	6-Jul-05	10-Jul-05	13-Jul-05	18-Jul-05	(7)	(8)	Delay	Complete
7	Samsung	Back Office Accounts	Ledgers	Preparation	Marshall	63	14-Jul-05	14-Jul-05	13-Jul-05	18-Jul-05	1	(4)	Delay	Complete
8	Samsung	Back Office Accounts	Ledgers	Updation	John	32	6-Jul-05	13-Jul-05	13-Jul-05	18-Jul-05	(7)	(5)	Delay	Complete
9	Samsung	Back Office Accounts	Ledgers	Cross-checking	Marshall	31	15-Jul-05	15-Jul-05	13-Jul-05	18-Jul-05	2	(3)	Delay	Complete
10	Samsung	Back Office Accounts	Ledgers	Posting	Joyce	83	17-Jul-05	17-Jul-05	13-Jul-05	18-Jul-05	4	(1)	Delay	Complete
11	Samsung	Back Office Accounts	Ledgers	Balancing	Joyce	77	25-Jul-05	25-Jul-05	27-Jul-05	29-Jul-05	(2)	(4)	Delay	Complete
12	Samsung	Back Office Accounts	BRS	BOA - Acct 1	Marshall	20	30-Jul-05	30-Jul-05	28-Jul-05	29-Jul-05	2	1	No Delay	Complete
13	Samsung	Back Office Accounts	BRS	BOA - Acct 2	Joyce	24	31-Jul-05	31-Jul-05	28-Jul-05	29-Jul-05	3	2	No Delay	Complete
14	Samsung	Back Office Accounts	BRS	ABN - Acct 3	Joyce	69	7-Aug-05	7-Aug-05	7-Aug-05	7-Aug-05	0	0	No Delay	Complete
15	Samsung	Back Office Accounts	BRS	Citi - Acct 4	Marshall	65	8-Aug-05	9-Aug-05	7-Aug-05	11-Aug-05	1	(2)	Delay	Complete
16	Samsung	Back Office Accounts	BRS	Cross-checking	Marshall	85	9-Aug-05	9-Aug-05	6-Aug-05	4-Aug-05	3	5	No Delay	Complete
17	Samsung	Back Office Accounts	Trial Balance	Preparation	Joyce	98	12-Aug-05	12-Aug-05	15-Aug-05	22-Aug-05	(3)	(10)	Delay	Complete
18	Samsung	Back Office Accounts	Trial Balance	Cross-checking	Joyce	18	19-Aug-05	19-Aug-05	21-Aug-05	8-Sep-05	(2)	(20)	Delay	Complete
19	Samsung	Back Office Accounts	Trial Balance	Reporting	Marshall	99	20-Aug-05	20-Aug-05	22-Aug-05	30-Aug-05	(2)	(10)	Delay	Complete
20	Samsung	Back Office Accounts	Fixed Assets	Updation	Marshall	81	21-Aug-05	21-Aug-05	19-Aug-05	23-Aug-05	2	(2)	Delay	Complete
21	Samsung	Back Office Accounts	Fixed Assets	Depreciation	Marshall	45	22-Aug-05	22-Aug-05	20-Aug-05	22-Aug-05	2	0	No Delay	Complete
22	Samsung	Back Office Accounts	Fixed Assets	WDV Value	Marshall	1	22-Aug-05	22-Aug-05	22-Aug-05	23-Aug-05	0	(1)	Delay	Complete
23	Samsung	Back Office Accounts	Fixed Assets	Reports	Marshall	63	22-Aug-05	22-Aug-05	21-Aug-05	22-Aug-05	1	0	No Delay	Complete
24	Samsung	Back Office Accounts	Fixed Assets	Tax implications	Joyce	76	23-Aug-05	23-Aug-05	23-Aug-05	25-Aug-05	0	(2)	Delay	Complete

In the above snapshot, you will notice four columns (K-N) that are separately colored – these contain formulas that keep the report live and up-to-date for the Pivoting. There is also a Selector Dt field on top to indicate the date of reporting for the Pivot.

The formulas entered in the columns K to N are as shown below:

Figure 228

Formulas keeping data up-to-date

Cell Ref	Formula
K3	=IF($I$1>=G3,(IF(I3="",-($I$1-G3),-(I3-G3))),0)
L3	=IF($I$1>=H3,(IF(J3="",-($I$1-H3),-(J3-H3))),0)
M3	=IF(K3<0,"Delay",(IF(L3<0,"Delay","No Delay")))
N3	=IF($I$1>=J3,(IF(J3<>"","Complete", "Incomplete")),"Incomplete")

These formulas are copied and pasted down to all rows.

Let's examine how the PivotTable is constructed, step-by-step.

Step-by-Step Construction of the Control PivotTable

Step 1 – Invoke the PivotTable construction by going to Data → PivotTable & PivotChart Report, selecting the data range and clicking on Finish to open the Pivot in a new worksheet.

Step 2 – Once you are in the Pivot worksheet with the field list open, drag the Manager, Project, Trigger, and Status fields to the Page Fields area on top.

Step 3 – Similarly, on the Row Fields area to the left side, drag and drop the Customer, Process, and Sub Activity fields.

Step 4 – In the Data Items area, drop the fields Sch. Start Date, Act. Start Date, Sch. End Date, Act. End Date, Delays At Start, and Delays At End fields.

Your PivotTable will now look like this:

Chapter 11

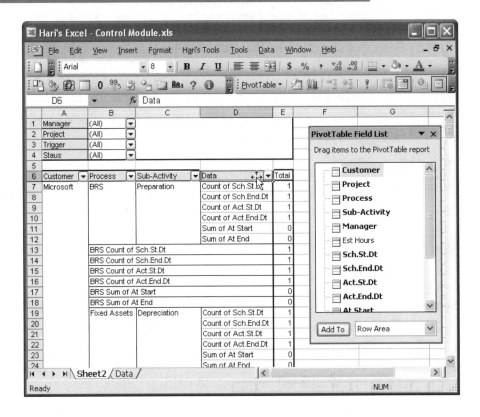

Figure 229 Constructing the PivotTable for the Control Report

Step 5 – Click on the title called "Data" appearing after the "Sub-Activity", and drag it onto the word "Total", which will make the entire data spread across columns. This operation will result in the following:

Figure 230   Setting the Columnar data format

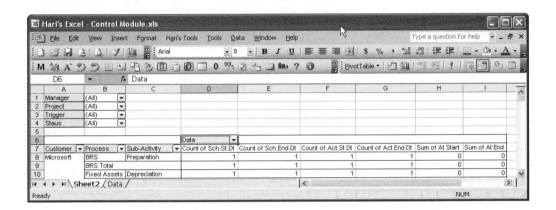

Step 6 –   For both Customer and Process fields, right-click and go to Field Settings; and select None under Subtotals and click OK.

Step 7 –   Right-click anywhere in the Pivot and select Table Options. Disable the checkboxes for "Grandtotals for Rows" and "Grandtotals for Columns".

Step 8 –   To display the dates properly, you need to format all four date fields (this does not include the delay at start and delay at end fields, which are numbers only). Right-click on each field, and select Field Settings.

- Under the Summarize by option, select Sum instead of the default, Count, and then click on the Number button. Select the Date format to be applied in the Format Cells menu and click OK to accept the settings.

- Repeat these steps for all four dates. For the delays at start and end fields, do the same except that in the formatting screen, select the formatting option that shows numbers in red as (1234) and set the number of decimals to 0 on top.

Chapter 11

Excel for the CEO

- While you are doing field settings, you can rename the fields in the same dialog box. This will give you a different display on the report without affecting the original field name in the database.

Step 9 – Now, go to cell D2 or any open cell and type the words "Date of Report". In the next immediate cell, enter a formula linking the "Selector Date" field in the database – for instance, =Data!I1, as per our example screen above.

The PivotTable report is all set, and any one of these fields can be moved here and there, from the Page area to the Row area and vice versa. This gives you tremendous flexibility to select and view specific information either at the company level, at the customer level, at the project manager level, from the viewpoint of completion, from the viewpoint of delays, and on and on.

The report will now look exactly the same as that shown in the beginning of this topic. You can download the example file to experiment with the PivotTable from here:

www.hari.ws/Excel/controlmodule.zip

Using Conditional Statements for Reporting

Conditional statements, such as the all-famous IF functions, are powerful tools – if used in the right way. We can see an example of this by analyzing one portion of my FinRatio package (the Financial Ratio analysis – automated Excel file).

Chapter 11

Let us look at part of the automatically generated "Analytical Report" – Section 3.0 – Liquidity Ratios, and examine how it is generated.

In this section we compare the results of the formulas that calculate the Current Ratio and the Quick Ratio. By comparing the results of the formulas for the two different periods, we can determine whether there has been an improvement or a deterioration in the financial status of the company.

We will start with a sample screenshot of this part of the report and then we will step in to analyze how the commentary was programmed. Please note that the ratio figures are picked up from the data provided by the user and are calculated using the standard formula for these ratios. We will analyze only the commentary programming now.

Figure 231   Working parts of the Liquidity Ratios inside FinRatio

	A	B	C	D	E	F	G	H	I	J
121	3.0 Liquidity Ratios									
122										
123	S.No.	Nature of Ratio					Period ended	Period ended		
124							30-Jun-04	31-Dec-03		
125	3.1	Current Ratio					2.96	2.46		
126	3.2	Quick Ratio or Acid Test Ratio					0.45	0.39		
127										
128	3.1	The current ratio shows an improving trend, which is a good sign for the Company as liquidity gets better. Whereas								
129		in Period 2 Current Ratio was 2.46, in Period 1 it has become 2.96.								
130										
131		This ratio can be bettered either by increasing the current asset base without reducing the current liabilities figure, or								
132		by ensuring that the current liabilities are reduced without impacting the current asset base. Higher the ratio, better it								
133		is for the Company. Ideal norm is 1.33 minimum.								
134										
135		This ratio is calculated by the following:				=(Current Assets)/(Current Liab.)				
136										
137										
138	3.2	The Quick ratio shows an improving trend, which is a good sign for the Company as immediate liquidity gets much								
139		better. Whereas in Period 2 Quick Ratio was 0.39, in Period 1 it has become 0.45.								
140										
141		Quick assets are Current assets less inventories and debts which cannot be quickly converted into cash. This ratio								
142		can be bettered either by increasing the quick assets like cash, bank balance, short term deposits or quickly								
143		maturing debts without disturbing the current liabilities figure, or by ensuring that the current liabilities are reduced								
144		without impacting the quick assets. Higher the ratio, better it is for the Company. An ATR (Acid Test Ratio) of 1.00								
145		minimum is considered as good.								
146										
147		This ratio is calculated by the following:				=(Quick Assets)/(Current Liab.)				
148										

Chapter 11

As you can see in the above figure, there is a commentary for both the ratios, namely 3.1-Current Ratio and 3.2-Quick Ratio. We will start with the programming of 3.1-Current Ratio. The current ratios of the two periods are captured and presented in the fields H125 and G125, representing Period 1 and Period 2, respectively.

Cell B128 has been set up with the following formula:

> =IF(G125<=H125,("The Current Ratio shows a deterioration trend, which is not a good sign as the Company will get stuck more with tighter cash flows. Whereas in Period 2 Current Ratio was "&ROUND(H125,2)&", in Period 1 it has become "&ROUND(G125,2)&"."),("The current ratio shows an improving trend, which is a good sign for the Company as liquidity gets better. Whereas in Period 2 Current Ratio was "&ROUND(H125,2)&", in Period 1 it has become "&ROUND(G125,2)&"."))

The range of cells B128:J129 has been merged, left-aligned, and wrap-text-enabled to ensure that the reporting commentary displays in two lines with proper formatting.

Although the formula seems to be slightly big and lengthy, it is actually not. When we analyze it in its the core detail, this is all it is:

> IF(G125<=H125,"Deteriorating trend","Improving trend")

What I have done is to expand the Deteriorating trend into a more detailed reporting statement and to show the statement with the figures blended in after rounding them off to two digits. I have used the concatenation operator (&) to merge the texts and formula and have achieved an output that does not seem to be auto-generated. The report will indicate whether the trend is good or bad, depending on the results, and a commentary that is auto generated like this is sure to capture the interest of the knowledgeable reader.

The content in cells B131:J133 and B135:J135 is standard text only, formatted and presented in a reporting style. This is only for reference and clarity for the user, so no formula is involved.

Chapter 11

Let us also look at the formula used in the range B138:J139 to present the analytical statement for Quick Ratio.

> =IF(G126<=H126,("The Quick Ratio shows a deteriorating trend, which is not a good sign as the Company will get into real problem with very tight cash flows. Whereas in Period 2 Quick Ratio was "&ROUND(H126,2)&", in Period 1 it has become "&ROUND(G126,2)&"."),("The Quick ratio shows an improving trend, which is a good sign for the Company as immediate liquidity gets much better. Whereas in Period 2 Quick Ratio was "&ROUND(H126,2)&", in Period 1 it has become "&ROUND(G126,2)&"."))

This works on a principle similar to the earlier one, with only minor variations in the reporting statements. Essentially it is the same, with texts and formulas concatenated and the results presented in a proper format.

There is one more scenario to be covered in these reports: where data is zero or completely absent. If such a possibility exists, we need to provide for this situation and account for it in the report. Such a situation is handled in the Dividends analysis part of my FinRatio package, and is reviewed here.

Figure 232   Working parts of the Coverage Ratios inside FinRatio

	A	B	C	D	E	F	G	H	I	J
223	*6.0 Coverage Ratios*									
224										
225	S.No.	Nature of Ratio					Period ended	Period ended		
226							30-Jun-04	31-Dec-03		
227	6.1	Interest coverage ratio					50.26 times	51.89 times		
228	6.2	Dividend coverage ratio					No Dividends	No Dividends		
229	6.3	Debt service coverage ratio					76.75	106.38		
230										
231	6.1	The above working shows that the number of times interest payment is covered has worsened in Period 1 as								
232		compared to Period 2. Whereas in Period 2 it was 51.89 times, in Period 1 it has become 50.26 times.								
233										
234		Interest Coverage Ratio gives the level of comfort or discomfort to the the Creditors / Financiers. With this ratio, they								
235		determine whether the net profits made by the Company would be enough to cover the interest payments regularly								
236		and whether the Company can service the interest payments in time. This ratio can be bettered only by improving the								
237		net profit margins. Higher the ratio, better it is weighed by Creditors and other financiers.								
238										
239		This ratio is calculated by the following:			=(Net profit before interest & Tax)/(Interest charges)					
240										
241										
242	6.2	No Dividends have been paid during one of these periods and hence no comparative analysis is possible.								
243										
244		Dividend Coverage Ratio just proves how many times the amount of equity dividend is covered by the net profits								
245		made by the Company. A higher ratio gives more comfort to the equity shareholders, but it cannot be at the cost of								
246		having a reduced dividend figure. A reduced dividend figure can show this as a higher ratio, but the equity								
247		shareholders would be obviously upset about the same. Higher the ratio, better it is weighed by the equity								
248		shareholders.								
249										
250		This ratio is calculated by the following:			=(Net profit after Tax & Pref. dividend)/(Equity dividend)					
251										

Chapter 11

Now let us see the formula used in cells G228 and H228, where it reports "No Dividends" instead of any figures. The formula used is this:

=IF(Data!B21<=0,"No Dividends",(Data!B29+Data!B22)/Data!B21)

This formula checks the data entry sheet; if the value of Dividends field is blank or zero, it reports "No Dividends". However, if there is some value, it adds the Net Profit after Tax field (cell B29) to the Preference Dividend field (cell B22) and then divides it by the Equity dividend (cell B21), to produce the final resulting ratio of Dividend Coverage.

At the next stage, in the commentary part, we analyze the result and handle three possible situations.

> ➤ There are no dividends

> ➤ Dividend coverage is higher in Period 2 than in Period 1

> ➤ Dividend coverage is lower in Period 2 than in Period 1

This requires a compound IF formula, one that nests two IF formulas within one formula. In essence, it is like this:

> =IF(Dividends is Zero,"No Dividends", IF(Dividend is Lower in period 2,"Report Statement X"," Report Statement Y"))

The actual formula used here is as follows:

> =IF(Data!B21<=0,"No Dividends have been paid during one of these periods and hence no comparative analysis is possible.",IF(((Data!B29+Data!B22)/ Data!B21)<=((Data!C29+Data!C22)/Data!C21),"As seen above, times dividend is covered has worsened in the Period 1 as compared to Period 2","As seen above, times dividend is covered has bettered in the Period 1 as compared to Period 2"))

The full fledged, multi-page report of my FinRatio package has been designed in a similar way, using the same idea. What has been actually achieved is to convert the functional knowledge into an automated body of knowledge using the powers of Excel.

 Note:

The FinRatio tool is available for free download at the following link in my website:

http://www.hari.ws/Excel/finratio.zip

It goes without saying that similar effects can be achieved across many other industries, if the user is sufficiently strong enough in his/her own domain and reasonably proficient with the capabilities and potential of Excel.

Controlling Entry of Dates – the Dating Problem!

There are numerous occasions when we face trouble with the capturing of dates. I refer to this jocularly as the "dating problem".

Each machine's regional settings are different; thus, when the user enters data in his own style as "6/3/06", the system may take in the data either as 6th March 2006 or as 3rd June 2006, depending on the system's regional settings.

When multiple users work on one single file for updating data, they often run into hot water because of this problem – one person enters data as "6/3/06" assuming that he is entering it as 6th March, whereas it might actually be recorded as 3rd June. And the exact opposite can happen with another user, depending on his system settings.

This becomes more complicated because, with the default view of dates in Excel, the data displays as "6/3/2006", and each user is justified in assuming he or she has entered the correct date.

To address this issue, especially in structured databases where capturing of accurate data is vital, what I normally do is to put in a worksheet function that automatically converts the date into a standard format that displays the date as 06-Mar-2006.

Chapter 11

By this function, the user will immediately know, as soon as he types the data in the cell, whether he has entered the date of 6th March or 3rd June. This function proves to be extremely helpful and I make sure that, wherever capturing of dates is involved, this function is put in place to avoid possible problems.

This is how to make this function work.

Step 1 – Open the Excel file in which you want to have this function.

Step 2 – Right-click on the sheet name (assume "Sheet1") and select View Code from the shortcut menu.

Step 3 – Once you are in the VBA window, in the right side blank window, type in the following text:

```
Private Sub Worksheet_Change(ByVal Target As Range)
Application.EnableEvents = False
If Not Application.Intersect(Target, Range("A:A")) Is Nothing Then
    Target(1) .NumberFormat = "[$–409]d–mmm–yy;@"
End If
Application.EnableEvents = True
End Sub
```

Step 4 – In the coding above, it is assumed that the date is captured in the column A, so the range is specified as Range("A:A") – you can change it to some other column or to a specific area of cells such as Range("A12:C25"), as necessary.

Step 5 – Press Ctrl+S to save the code, and Alt+Q to come back to the Excel window, exiting the VBA window.

Step 6 – Now, every time any date is entered in any of the cells in column A (or in whatever range you specify), it will automatically be pre-formatted as dd-mon-yy.

Step 7 – By this simple utility, you can avoid any confusion arising out of the capturing of dates (the Dating Problem!).

Chapter 11

Some Interesting Examples

You will find some very interesting and practical macros and procedures in this section – many of these are creations of some stalwarts like John Walkenach, Brad, Dave, Bill, Pearson, and others, but have become public property by common usage.

I am taking the liberty of reproducing some such interesting nuggets here, which will be useful to you as well as kindling your interests in furthering your use of Excel.

Using Word Count in Excel

```
Sub CountWords()
    Dim WordCount As Long
    Dim Rng As Range
    Dim S As String
    Dim N As Long
    For Each Rng In  ActiveSheet.UsedRange.Cells
        S = Application.WorksheetFunction.Trim(Rng.Text)
        N = 0
        If S <> "" Then
            N = Len(S) – Len(Replace(S, " ", "")) + 1
        End If
        WordCount = WordCount + N
    Next Rng
    MsgBox WordCount
End Sub
```

Showing Formulas in Different Color

```
Sub ColorFormulas()         'x197 up use xcelltypeformulas
    Cells.Font.ColorIndex = xlAutomatic
    Selection.SpecialCells(xlFormulas).Font.ColorIndex = 5
End Sub
```

Deleting Empty Worksheets

```
Sub delempty()
For Each myXLSheet In ActiveWorkbook.Worksheets
    If WorksheetFunction.CountA(Cells) = 0 Then
        Application.DisplayAlerts = False
        myXLSheet.Delete
        Application.DisplayAlerts = True
    End If
Next
End Sub
```

Sorting All Sheets by Name

```
Sub SortALLSheets()
    'modification of coded example by Bill Manville
    Dim isheet As Long, iBefore As Long
    For iSheet = 1 To ActiveWorkbook.Sheets.Count
        Sheets(iSheet).Visible = True
        For iBefore = 1 To iSheet – 1
            If UCase(Sheets(iBefore).Name) > UCase(Sheets(iSheet).Name) Then
                ActiveWorkbook.Sheets(iSheet).Move Before:=ActiveWorkbook.Sheets(iBefore)
                Exit For
            End If
        Next iBefore
    Next iSheet
End Sub     '—SortALLSheets()
```

Forcing Caps on Entry

Note: In code below, change Range("C:C") as needed.

```
Private Sub Worksheet_Change(ByVal Target As Range)
Application.EnableEvents = False
If Not Application.Intersect(Target, Range("C:C")) Is Nothing Then
    Target(1).Value = UCase(Target(1).Value)
End If
Application.EnableEvents = True
End Sub
```

Chapter 11

Deleting Every nth Row

```
Public Sub DeleteEveryNthRow(Optional N As Long = 2)
'The default is to delete every 2nd row
Dim rDelete As Range
Dim i As Long
With ActiveSheet
    Set rDelete = .Rows(N)
    For i = 2 * N To .UsedRange.Rows.Count Step N
        Set delRange = Union(rDelete, .Rows(i))
    Next i
End With
rDelete.Delete
End Sub
```

Merging Data of Multiple Columns into One Column

```
Public Sub ColumnsToText(Optional rRng As Range, _
Optional sDelim As String = "")
'Purpose:Merge values in a multi-column array into the first column
'Returns:Merged values in column 1 of rRng
'J.E. McGimpsey http://www.mcgimpsey.com/excel/mergedata.html
Dim vtxtArr As Variant
Dim nTop As Long
Dim i As Long
Dim j As Integer
If rRng Is Nothing Then Set rRng = Selection
Set rRng = Intersect(rRng, rRng.Parent.UsedRange)
vTxtArr = rRng.Value
nTop = UBound(vTxtArr, 1)
    For i = 1 To nTop
        For j = 2 To UBound(vTxtArr, 2)
            vTxtArr(i, 1) = vTxtArr(i, 1) & sDelim & vTxtArr(i, j)
        Next j
    Next i
ReDim Preserve vTxtArr(1 To nTop, 1 To 1)
rRng.Resize(, 1).Value = vTxtArr
End Sub
```

Chapter 11

Merging the Selection into One Cell

```
Public Sub MergeToOneCell(Optional rRng As Range, _
Optional sDelim As String = "")
'Purpose: Merge cells, retaining all data
'Returns: Merged values in the first cell of rRng
'J.E. McGimpsey http://www.mcgimpsey.com/excel/mergedata.html
Dim rCell As Range
Dim sMergeStr As String
If rRng Is Nothing Then Set rRng = Selection
    With rRng
        For Each rCell In .Cells
            sMergeStr = sMergeStr & sDelim & rCell.Text
        Next rCell
        Application.DisplayAlerts = False
        .Merge Across:=False
        Application.DisplayAlerts = True
        .Item(1).Value = Mid(sMergeStr, 1 – (sDelim <> ""))
    End With
End Sub
```

Inserting a Blank Row Between Every Row of Data

```
Sub Insert_Blank_Rows()
'Select last row in worksheet.
Selection.End(xlDown).Select
Do Until ActiveCell.Row = 1
'Insert blank row.
    ActiveCell.EntireRow.Insert shift:=xlDown
    'Move up one row.
    ActiveCell.Offset(–1, 0).Select
Loop
End Sub
```

Coloring Alternate Rows with a Distinct Shade

```
Public Sub ApplyConditionalFormatting()
    Application.ScreenUpdating = False
    Cells.Select
    Selection.FormatConditions.Delete
    Selection.FormatConditions.Add Type:=xlExpression, Formula1:= _
        "=MOD(ROW(),2)=0"
    Selection.FormatConditions(1).Interior.ColorIndex = 35
    Cells(1, 1).Select
    Application.ScreenUpdating = True
End Sub
```

Using VBA to Print Your File to PDF

```
Sub print2pdf()
ActiveWorksheet.PrintOut , , 1, False, "Acrobat Distiller"
End Sub
```

Note that in the above code, "Acrobat Distiller" is assumed as the name of the printer driver – you can substitute it with whatever other drivers you have in your system – could be a "Bluebean PDF" or may be a "Primo PDF", etc.

Chapter 11

Chapter 11

Goal Seek and Scenario Builder

It has been quite a journey, hasn't it? Well, now the end is in sight and we have saved two of the most rewarding stops for last.

On the last leg of the journey, we will explore a couple of topics you will find immeasurably valuable, Goal Seek and Scenario Builder, and we will end our adventure with Excel by taking note of some exciting developments and their related websites.

Topics covered in this chapter:

🍶   Using Goal Seek

🍶   Using Scenario Builder

🍶   Other new techniques and developments

Using Goal Seek

Goal-seeking is a method of searching for a way to attain a goal – determining a specific value for one cell by adjusting the value of another cell. Goal Seek is part of a suite of "What-If" functions available in Excel.

We use the Goal Seek function when we know the desired result of a formula but do not know the input value required to get that result.

Chapter 12

With the Goal Seek function, Excel varies the value in a cell that you specify until a formula that is dependent on that cell returns the result you want.

Let us look at the following example see how Goal Seek works. This example is aimed at identifying the interest rate that results in a monthly payment of $625.

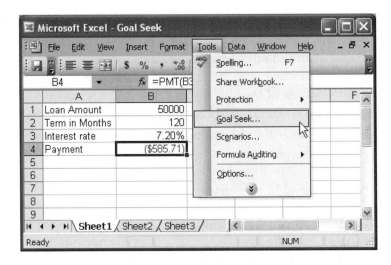

Figure 233

Activating the Goal Seek function

You can see that the monthly payment figure is $585.71 with the interest rate at 7.20%. The monthly payment field is derived as a result of the following formula: =PMT(B3/12,B2,B1), which clearly indicates that it is dependent on the interest rate (B3 field), among others.

You can invoke the Goal Seek function by selecting Tools → Goal Seek, which displays the easy-to-use **Goal Seek** dialog box shown below.

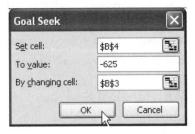

Figure 234

Setting up the Goal Seek parameters

Notice that "Set cell:" is filled with $B$4, indicating that this is the field where we want the desired result. The "To value:" field is the actual desired result ($625). In "By changing cell:", we have marked $B$3, thereby instructing Excel to vary the interest rate until it finds an appropriate match of ($625) in cell $B$4, knowing that B4 is dependent on the value of B3.

Once we click OK with these settings in place, Excel starts its background process of seeking a value for B3 that ensures that a final result of $625 in B4. After a few seconds of processing, Excel notifies you whether or not it found a match.

You can choose not to apply the match into the workbook by pressing the "Cancel" button. To apply the matching result, just click on OK.

The screenshot of a match-found scenario is presented in the figure below:

Figure 235 Solution found – using the Goal Seek function

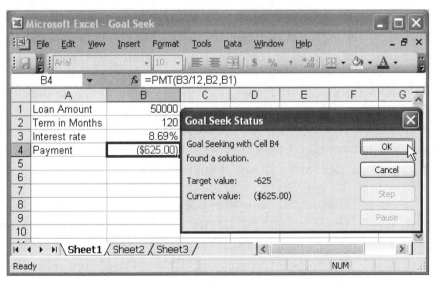

If you click on Cancel button, cell B3 will revert to its original state of 7.20% and B4 will revert to its original state of ($585.71).

The Goal Seek function is a very simple but capable work engine, which can be utilized in appropriate circumstances to save a lot of time and iterative processes.

Using Scenario Builder

Scenario Builder is another tool within Excel's "What-If" suite of commands. A scenario is a set of values that Excel saves and can substitute automatically in your worksheet.

Scenarios are generally used to forecast the outcome of a model, wherein you can create and save different groups of values on a worksheet and switch to any of these new scenarios to view different results.

Many companies do their sales forecast by averaging the three different scenarios – best, worst, and moderate. You can easily create all three of these scenarios and view their summaries from within Excel, without much trouble.

The following procedure shows you how to use the Scenario Builder tool.

Step 1 – Create a "Base Scenario" that uses the original cell values. Doing this before you create any other scenarios allows a quick restoration to the original values for the changing cells.

   a. Use the following example as the base scenario worksheet. You will vary cells B2, B3, B4, and B6 for different scenarios, and should name them appropriately. For example, name cell B2 "Units_Sold", name cell B3 "Sale_Price", and so forth.

Figure 236

Setting up a Base Scenario data table

Tip:

Give a name to each changing cell using Insert → Name → Define to make the process easier to keep track of and to understand when you change the cell values.

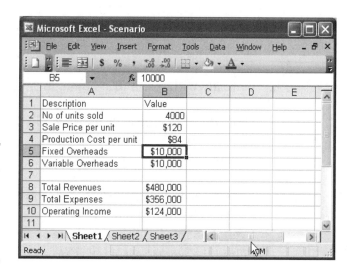

b. In the sheet above, Total Revenues, Total Expenses, and Operating Income are formulas that derive results from the cell values in the range B2:B6.

Step 2 – Select Tools → Scenario to open the Scenario Manager window.

Figure 237

Scenario Manager Dialog box

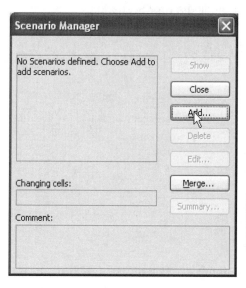

Chapter 12

a. Click Add. The **Add Scenario** dialog box opens, allowing you to add a new scenario.

b. Be ready with a scenario name, in this case, "Base".

c. Mark the changing cells as shown in the following figure.

d. Add any desired comments.

e. Protect the scenario data from accidental changes by selecting Prevent changes and/or Hide.
Even if enabled, neither of these options will have any impact unless the worksheet itself is protected using Tools → Protect → Protect Sheet. Once you check "Prevent changes", you cannot edit or delete the scenario unless you clear the checkbox again. Select "Hide" to completely remove the scenario data from view; reveal it again by un-checking the tick mark.

Figure 238

Adding a new Scenario

Step 3 – Click on the OK button in the **Add Scenario** dialog box. The **Scenario Values** dialog box displays, allowing you to key in new substitution values for the scenario just created. In creating the base scenario, we will not alter the values, but for the best, worst and moderate cases, we will modify the values to suit each scenario.

Figure 239

Setting up the scenario substitution values

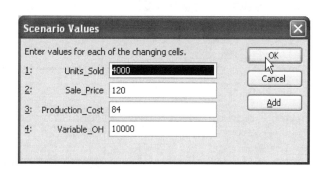

 Note:

The descriptions appearing on the left, such as Units_Sold and Sale_Price, are the result of naming the cells – otherwise the labels would only show as $B$2, $B$3, etc.

Step 4 – Add the Best case scenarios as shown below.

Figure 240

Setting up the values for the Best Case scenario

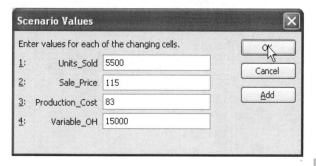

Step 5 – Add the Worst case scenario with the following values:

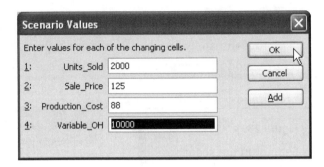

Figure 241

Setting up the values for the Worst Case scenario

Step 6 – Add the Moderate case scenario by entering the following values:

Figure 242

Setting up the values for the Mid (Moderate) Case scenario

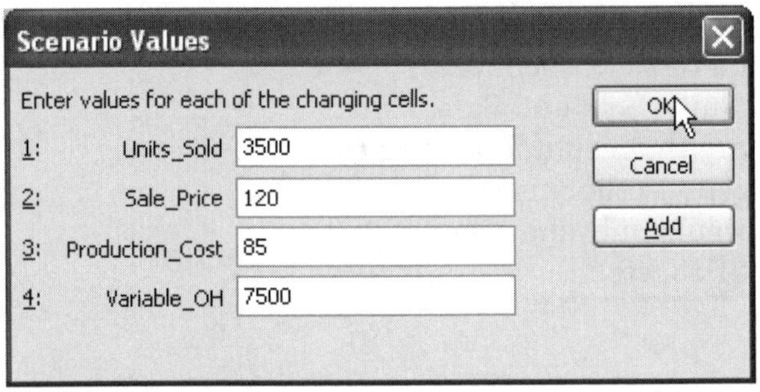

Now the **Scenario Manager** dialog box shows the four scenarios you just created: Base, Best, Worst, and Moderate:

Figure 243

Scenario Manager with various Case Scenarios

Step 7 – Click on any one of the Scenario names; then, click on the Show button. You will see the results of that scenario in the worksheet. Note that you can Add, Edit, or Delete any of the available scenarios, and can also Merge scenarios from different worksheets.

Step 8 – Generate and view a Summary result of the different Scenarios.

    a. Click on the "Summary" button and select "Scenario Summary".

    b. Under the "Result Cells" section, select the resulting cells, which in this case is in the B8:B10 range.

Figure 244

Scenario Summary Selector box

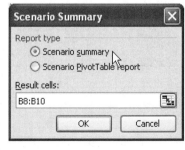

Chapter 12

Step 9 – Click on the OK button to see the result sheet.

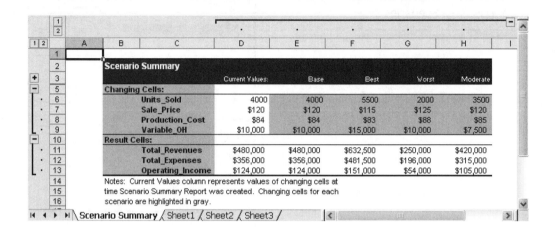

Figure 245   Scenario Summary Report, with Grouped/Outlined data

Step 10 – To review the scenario summary as a PivotTable report, select the radio button "Scenario PivotTable report" under the "Report type" in the "Scenario Summary" and click on OK. This will provide the following result.

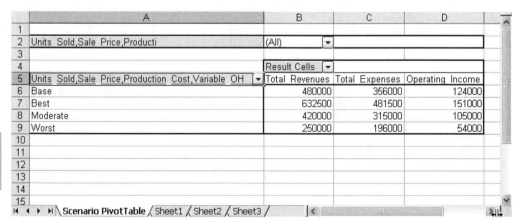

Figure 246   Scenario Summary PivotTable Report

Excel for the CEO

Other New Techniques and Developments

There are a lot of other new techniques that are worthwhile studying. A few of them are included below:

Dashboard Charting Techniques

http://peltiertech.com/Excel/Charts/Speedometer.html

http://www.exceluser.com/dash/index.htm

http://www.mrexcel.com/sunshop/index.php?action=item&substart=0&id=42

http://www.andypope.info/charts/gauge.htm

New Techniques with PivotTables

http://www.contextures.com/xlPivot01.html

New Techniques with Charting

http://peltiertech.com

http://www.andypope.info/charts.htm

Resources and Examples for the Finance People

http://www.lacher.com

Other Interesting Developments

Keep an eye on the following forums:

http://www.experts-exchange.com/Applications/MS_Office/Excel/

http://www.mrexcel.com/board2/

http://www.ozgrid.com/forum/

http://www.excelforum.com

Chapter 12

One Journey Ends – Another Begins

We started this journey by covering the basics. We took steps to understand Functions and Formulas and then moved on to Data Management and Advanced Data Management Functions.

Continuing on our trip, we took note of the powerful auditing features available in Excel, as well as its various reporting, printing, and publishing features.

We took a brief side trip to look at VBA and its capabilities, and reviewed some practical, real-life case studies as well as some interesting examples of applications using Excel and VBA.

As we neared the end of this journey, we looked at Goal Seek and Scenario Builder, adding these powerful "What-If" tools to our bag of tricks.

Have you been impressed by the power and potential of Excel? Have you discovered faster ways to make informed business decisions? Do you suspect that Excel may have still more hidden treasure waiting for you to discover?

I hope you answered "yes" to all of the above. Let this book support you as you master the topics it covers. Visit the Web sites it mentions. Experiment with the techniques it teaches. Discover that buried treasure!

I sincerely hope that this book has and will continue to help you master the key concepts, tips, tricks, and techniques that will give you an advantage over other general users. You can walk proud, knowing that you are one of the best in Excel, having learned not just theories, but very practical, application-oriented concepts as well.

So, this concluding chapter actually marks the beginning of a new chapter in your working experience with MS-Excel. Enjoy!

Chapter 13

A Word of Conclusion

I have sincerely tried to pick and present the most relevant content for the top people of an organization in this book. By fully reviewing and understanding the contents of this book, I am sure your confidence level in using Excel will increase dramatically.

Though I have done my best to explain the chosen topics in a simple and lucid way, there might be some areas that needed further explanation or examples. If there are areas that left you confused and frustrated, or that you wish had been included but were not, please send in your feedback, and I will try to shed light on those areas in the next release.

I also plan to pen a couple of other titles on specific topics in Excel, which will depend on the feedback and response I get from satisfied users of this book. So, please send in your valuable feedback to me at: pkhariaiyer@gmail.com

Wishing you all the Very Best to excel with Excel®,

P.K.Hari

Chapter 13

Appendix A – Finding and Launching Excel

Topic in this section:

    Where to find Excel

Where to Find Excel

Excel is installed as part of the Microsoft Office Suite, and can be found in the Start menu along with a host of other Microsoft programs. If it is not visible on the Startup Menu, you can generally find it in the following path:

C:\Program Files\Microsoft Office\OFFICE11\excel.exe

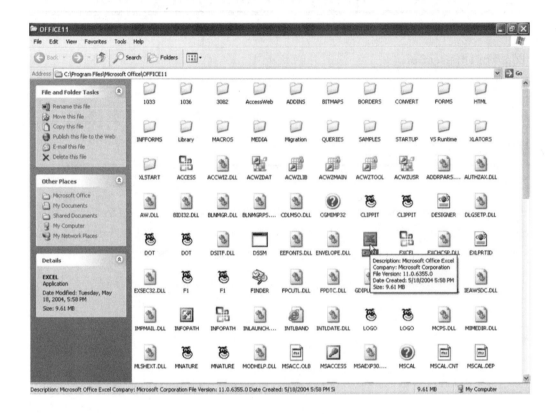

Figure 247   Where to find Excel – the directory path and the Exe file

As shown in the path above (also reflected in Figure 247), the program files will lie in the C:\ root directory path unless you chose a different path while installing. One other thing to note about the program name (Office11), is that it reflects that particular version of Office – it might be something else on your computer. You should recognize it when you browse through the Microsoft Office folder. In case you are not sure you have the right program, just use the windows search facility to look for "excel.exe" and – yes – you have arrived!

Appendix B – Excel's Roots

Topic in this section:

  How did it all start – Weaving the Excel magic

How Did It All Start – Weaving the Excel Magic

It is interesting to trace the history and growth of spreadsheets – from the "olden" days of a modern calculator to the today's powerful spreadsheets that can accomplish almost anything for the knowledgeable user.

In fact, I personally know of some users who are so fond of their favorite application that they even use Excel to type all their letters and reports, while others use the Table and Sum features in Word instead of using the OLE features to accommodate a small spreadsheet inside their documents. The fact that these users want to do everything with a single application shows their level of comfort and the power of each application.

Excel is, no doubt, one of the most powerful applications available today and is revered by people across different fields and professions. This is basically due to the fact that it is so flexible and can easily be adjusted for use in so many unprecedented and previously unthought-of ways.

Although it is touted as primarily a bean counter's tool (aka, an accountant's tool), Excel is used extensively by scientists, businessmen, researchers, teachers, marketing people, students, and people from almost every other walk of life.

Appendix

The present-day Excel took almost four decades to evolve. It all started with a Berkeley Professor, Richard Mattessich, who proposed electronic spreadsheets for solving budgetary what-if analyses.

The real growth of spreadsheets started with the efforts of Bricklin (MIT student) and Frankston, who introduced VisiCalc in 1979. In 1983, Lotus 1-2-3 was introduced, and Excel for the Mac followed in 1985. Q-pro was launched in 1987 and between 1989-93, all three companies were in a heated race for leadership. In the Office 97 suite, Excel took a leap forward with the 65,536 rows concept and a host of other improvements. By 2004, MS Excel held 90% of the market share of spreadsheets.

There is a lot more to know about the background of Excel's evolution and all this is available for an interesting read in a full color book, "The Spreadsheet at 25", published by Bill Jelen of Holy Macro! Books. It is certainly worth a read, and, with the special Pop-Up page they have, it is a real treasure.

Index

A

A1 Style. *See also* R1C1 Style, 80, 81, 267

Absolute References. *See also* Relative and Mixed References, 56, 80, 147

Abstract, 123

Action, Repeat, 33

Active Cell, 1- 7, 13-17, 34, 35, 37, 42, 207, 208, 210, 215, 233
   Comments, 211

Addition, 84, 140, 143, 144

Advanced Filter Dialog, 116

Aggregation Functions, 8, 120, 156, 174, 175
   Average, 8, 120, 174
   Count, 8, 120, 174
   Count Nums, 174
   Max, 8, 120, 174
   Min, 8, 120
   Product, 120
   StdDev, 174
   StdDevp, 174
   Sum, 8, 14, 120, 174
   Var, 120, 174
   Varp, 174

Alert Flag, 280, 281

Alert, Error, 126, 129, 130, 212

Alignment Control, 227, 238

Analysis ToolPak, 61

Analytical Report, 292, 293, 304-309

Annuities, 64, 318

Annuity Functions, 64-67

Arguments, 62-100, 138, 140, 219
   A1, 80
   Abs_num, 80
   Array, 80
   Array1, 74

Col_index_num, 80

Cols, 80, 82

Column_num, 80

Cost, 62, 63, 65, 69, 74, 80, 84, 87, 90, 93

Criteria, 74, 84, 138, 140, 143-145
   Single or Multiple, 138, 143-145

Data_field, 84, 141

Database, 84, 138, 140

Date_text, 68, 69

Day, 50, 68, 69

Decimals, 87

Divisor, 74

End_date, 68

End_Period, 62, 63

Error_val, 93

Factor, 63

Field, 84, 140

Field1,item1, 85, 141

Finance_rate, 64, 65

Find_text, 87

Format_text, 87

Friendly_name, 80

Function_num, 74

Functions, 60

Fv, 65

Guess, 65

Height, 80

Hour, 68, 69

Index_num, 81

Info_type, 93

Insert, 32

Instance_num, 87

Life, 62, 63

Link_location, 81

Logical, 90

Logical_test, 90

Logical1, 90

Lookup_array, 81

Lookup_value, 81

Lookup_vector, 81

Match_type, 81

Method, 68, 69

Minute, 68, 69
Month, 50, 63, 68, 69
Multiple Cell Reference (Range), 60
New_text, 87
No_commas, 87
No_switch, 62, 63
Nper, 64, 65
Num_chars, 87
Num_digits, 74
Number, 74, 87
Number_times, 88
Number1,, 74
Numeric Constant, 60
Old_text, 88
Per, 65
Period, 62, 63
Pivot_table, 85, 141
Pmt, 64, 65, 66
Pv, 65, 66
Range, 74
Range_lookup, 81
Rate, 64, 65, 66
Ref_text, 81
Ref1, 74
Reference, 81, 93
Reinvest_rate, 64, 65
Result_vector, 81
Return_type, 69, 71
Row_index_num, 81
Row_num, 81
Rows, 80, 81
Salvage, 62, 63
Second, 68, 69
Serial_number, 50, 68, 69, 71
Sheet_text, 81
Significance, 74
Single Cell Reference, 60
Start_date, 68
Start_num, 88
Start_Period, 62, 63
Sum_range, 74
Table_array, 81
Text, 88
Text Constant, 60
Text1,text2, 88
Time_text, 68, 70
Type, 65
Type_text, 93
Value, 64, 65, 88, 93

Value_if_false, 90
Value_if_true, 90
Value1, 81
Width, 82
Within_text, 88
Year, 50, 68, 70
Arithmetic Mean, 21, 74, 76
Array Formulas, 53, 57, 58
    Create, 57
Arrows
    Dependents, 46, 203, 208, 209
    Errors, 210
    Precedents, 46, 203, 207, 208, 210
    Remove, 201, 209
Auditing Tools, 201-203, 211, 217- 221, 226
AutoComplete, 30
AutoFill, 17
AutoFilter, 103, 106, 112-114
AutoFormat, 188
AutoScroll, 15
AutoSum, 21
Average, 8, 21, 74, 76, 83, 120, 139, 174

B

Baht Currency Format, 85
Balance Sheet, 290
Benchmarks, 290
Black and White Prints, 242, 244
Blank Pages Print, Troubleshooting, 244
Borders, 34
Boundary Markings, 244
Business Analysis, 202
Buttons
    ƒx, 6, 97
    Tick Mark, 6
    X, 6

C

Calculated Fields. *See also* Data Fields, 165, 183-187
    Create, 185
    Delete, 187
    Modify, 183, 187

Calculations, 54

Capitalization, 312

Categories. *See also* Segmentation, 60, 71
    Functions, 60, 71

Cells, 1, 5, 13, 19
    Blank, Insert, 29, 35
    Copy, 30, 32, 33, 35, 41
    Cut, 33
    Delete, 34, 47
    Delete Contents, 41, 42
    Edit Contents, 44
    Entry, Cancel, 40
    Fill, 30, 32, 41
    Format, 1, 19, 30-34, 47, 50, 87, 303
        Currency, 34, 47
        Dates, 34, 303
        Exponential, 34, 55
        Numbers, 19, 34, 47, 55, 148, 152, 192
        Percentage, 34, 148, 152
        Time, 34
    Line Breaks, 41, 50
    Merge Selection into One, 314
    Replicate Copy, 45
    Select, 1, 13, 31, 38, 40-44

CEOs, 274, 275
    Decide Priorities, 275
    Define the Meaningful Outside, 274, 275
    Determine Meaningful Outside Information, 274-276
    Link between Inside and the Outside, 274
    Make People Decisions, 275

Changes, Track, 201, 219-221, 286

Chart Wizard, 24, 25

Charts, 1, 24, 25
    Create, 1, 24, 25, 30, 40, 44
    Data Source, 24
    Interactive, 259
    Legends, 284
    Location, 24
    Print, 228, 243
        Custom Size, 243

        Full Page, 243
        Scale to Fit, 243
    Publish on Web, 249, 258, 259
    Type, 24

Clipboard, 32, 33

Collated Copies, 231

Color Prints, 242, 244

Column Area, Pivot Tables, 172, 173

Column Headings, 1, 2, 5, 13, 242

Column-oriented Data Tables, 145, 150

Columns, 1, 13, 84, 104, 106, 138, 140
    Hide and Unhide, 30, 31, 34
    Merge Multiple, 313
    Select, 1, 13, 41

Comma Separated Values. *See* CSV Files, 130

Commands
    Repeat, 33
    Reverse, 33
    Undo, 33

Comments
    Clear, 18
    Edit, 37, 201, 211
    Insert, 37, 201, 210
    Print, 202, 223-225
    View, 202, 223

Concatenation, 55, 86, 88, 306, 307

Conditional Statements, 304-309

Consecutive Numbering, 47

Consolidation of Data, 85, 103, 135, 137, 156-158
    3D Formulas, 156-158, 252

Control Reports, 298-304

Count, 8, 174

Criteria for Formula, 22

CSV Files, 130

Currency Format, 85, 86

Current Ratio, 304

Cursor, Move, 36, 37, 40, 42, 43

Custom Filters, 103, 112-120

Custom Functions, 23

Custom Headers and Footers, 240, 241

Custom Number Format, 50

Customized Menu Bar, 294-298

D

Data, 1, 16-19, 109
   Analyze, 54
   Consolidation of, 85, 103, 135, 137, 156-158
      3D Formulas, 156-158, 252
   Copy, 16, 17
   Cut, 17
   Delete, 1, 16-18, 41
   Delimited, 132-134
   Edit, 1, 16
   Filter, 103, 104, 106, 112-120
   Find, 30, 32, 37
   Fixed Width, 132-134
   Format, 1, 19, 20, 50
   Group and Ungroup, 50, 103, 104, 120-125
   Import, 85, 103, 104, 130-135, 137, 159-161
   Insert, 18
   Invalid, 201, 211, 213, 214
   Merge Multiple Columns, 313
   Move, 1, 16, 17
   Outline, 103, 104, 120, 123-125
   Paste, 16, 17
   Replace, 1, 16, 17
   Select, 51
   Sort, 103, 104, 109-112, 120-123, 165, 176-179
   Subtotals, 103, 104, 120-123, 303
   Text to Columns, 104, 130-134
   Update, 1, 16, 17
   Validation, 104-106, 125-130, 201, 211-214, 292
      Error Alert, 126, 129, 130, 212
   XML, 85, 103, 135, 137, 162, 163
Data Analysis, 103
   PivotTables, 166, 167
Data Area, PivotTables, 172-174
Data Capture
   Form, 107-109
   Manual, 106, 107
Data Cubes, 276, 277
Data Fields. *See also* Calculated Fields, 172
Data Management, 85, 103-106, 135, 137, 140, 142, 165

Data Menu, Activate, 39
Data Range, 161
Data Region, 42
Data Source, PivotTables, 170
Data Sources, 24, 196
Data Tables, 85, 103, 135, 137, 145-152
   Column-oriented, 145, 150
   Delete, 149
   One- or Two-Variable Type, 145-148, 150-152
   Row-oriented, 145, 146, 150
Database
   Arguments, 84, 138, 140
   Functions, 53, 58, 83-85, 103, 135-144
   Management, 140, 142
Databases, 103, 104, 109-112, 120-123, 137-142, 165, 176-179
   Create, 106-109
   Fields, 84, 104, 106, 107, 138, 140
   Records, 84, 104, 106, 107, 138, 140
   Sort, 109-112, 120-123, 176-179
Date Functions, 48, 50, 68-71
Dates, 273, 309, 310
   Enter, 35, 273, 309, 310
   Format, 34, 303
   Insert Current, 48
   Join with Text, 55, 86, 88, 306, 307
Days in a Month, 50
Delayed Projects, 299
   Delay Triggers, 299
Delimited Data, 132-134
Dependents
   Remove Tracing Arrows, 201, 209
   Trace, 46, 203, 208, 209
Depreciation Functions, 62, 63
Depreciation of an Asset, 62, 63, 66
Details, Drill Down to See, 165, 166, 180, 194
Deviation, Standard, 83, 120, 139, 140
Dialog Boxes
   Close, 40
   Options, 40, 42
   Tab, Switch to Next, 40
Dividends, 307, 308
Drill Down, 165, 166, 180, 194

E

Edit Menu, Activate, 39

Empty Worksheets, Delete, 312

Entries, Cancel, 40

Equals Sign, 54, 207

Equity, 308

Error Alert, 126, 129, 130, 212

Error Checking, 201, 203-206, 211-213, 224, 276
  Arrows, 210
  Edit Formulas, 206
  Report, 203
  Reset Errors, 205
  Rules, 206
  View and Print Errors, 202, 223-225

Error Messages, 59
  #DIV/0, 59
  #NAME!, 59
  #VALUE!, 59

Errors, Trace, 210

Evaluate Formula Option, 201, 206, 218, 219

Excel
  History, 334
  Program Path, 331, 332
  Quit, 40

External Data Toolbar, 159, 161

External Data, Import, 159, 160

F

Feedback, Live, 279-281

Field Settings, PivotTables, 174, 190-192, 303

Fields, 84, 104, 106, 107, 138, 140
  Add to PivotTable, 175
  Filter PivotTable, 174
  Remove from PivotTables, 175
  Sort PivotTable, 176-179

File Menu, Activate, 39

Files
  Delimited, 132-134
  Find, 33
  Fixed Width, 132-134
  New, 33
  Open, 33, 36
  Print to PDF, 315
  Protected, Open, 50
  Save, 33

Fill, 30, 32, 41

Filtered Data, 103-106, 112-120
  Copy, 103, 112, 116-120

Filtered Records, 103, 112, 114-120
  Copy, 103, 112, 116-120

Filters, Custom, 103, 112, 114-120

Financial Analysis, 290-293, 304-309
  Balance Sheet, 290
  Benchmarks, 290
  Income Statements, 290
  Ratios, 290-293

Financial Functions, 61-67
  Annuity and Investment, 64, 65
  Depreciation, 62, 63, 66
  Interest Computation, 66

Financial Ratios Tool. *See* FinRatio Tool, 290, 293

Find, 30, 32, 37

FinRatio Tool, 290-293
  Analytical Report, 292, 293

Fixed Width Data, 132-134

Footers, 227, 239-241
  Custom, 240, 241

Format
  Cells, 1, 18, 19, 30-33, 47, 50, 87, 303
  Currency, 19, 34, 47, 86
  Data, 1, 19, 20, 50
  Date, 34, 303
  Exponential, 34, 55
  General Number, 34
  Number, 19, 34, 47, 48, 55, 86, 87, 148, 152, 192
  Percentage, 34, 148, 152
  PivotTables, 194
  Ranges, 32, 33
  Text, 19, 48, 86, 87
  Times, 34
  XML, 163

Format Menu, Activate, 39

Formats, Clear, 18

Formatting Toolbar, 1, 2

Formula Bar, 1, 2, 5, 6, 35, 40, 41, 97, 206

Formulas, 1, 51-54, 59, 101
    Addition, 54
    Auditing Tools, 201-203, 211, 217-221, 226
    Color, 311
    Copy, 35
    Create, 23, 97
    Criteria, 22
    Division, 54
    Edit, 206
    Enter, 1, 23, 59, 97
    Entry, Cancel, 40
    Error Messages, 59
    Evaluate, 6, 55, 97-100, 201, 206, 218, 219
    Multiplication, 54
    Named, 96
    Names, 44
    Nested, 94, 95
        Multi-level, 96
    Operands, 54
        Absolute Values, 54
        Cell References, 54
        Functions, 54
        Labels, 54
        Ranges, 54
    Operators, 54, 55, 56
        Addition, 55
        Division, 55
        Exponentiation, 55
        Multiplication, 55
        Percentage, 55
        Precedence, 55, 56
        Subtraction, 55
    Print, 201, 221-223
    Protect, 49
    See All, 35
    Starting Tag, 54, 60
    Subtraction, 54
    Troubleshoot, 6, 97-100, 201, 206, 219
    View, 201, 221-223

Function
    ABS, 72, 75
    ADDRESS, 78, 82
    AND, 90, 91, 94, 95
    AREAS, 78, 82
    AVERAGE, 21, 74, 76, 78, 138
    AVERAGEA, 76, 78
    BAHTTEXT, 85, 89
    CEILING, 72, 75

CELL, 91, 94
CHAR, 85, 89
CHOOSE, 79, 82
CLEAN, 85, 89
CODE, 85, 89
COLUMN, 79, 82
COLUMNS, 79, 82
CONCATENATE, 86, 88, 89
COUNT, 21, 74, 76, 78, 138
COUNTA, 47, 74, 76, 78
COUNTBLANK, 76, 78
COUNTIF, 76, 78
DATE, 50, 68, 70, 71
DATEVALUE, 68, 70, 71
DAVERAGE, 83, 138, 139, 145
DAY, 50, 68, 70, 71
DAYS360, 68, 70, 71
DB, 62, 67
DCOUNT, 83, 138, 139, 144
DCOUNTA, 83, 139, 144, 145
DDB, 62, 67
DGET, 83, 139, 145
DMAX, 83, 138, 139, 144, 145
DMIN, 83, 138, 139, 144, 145
DOLLAR, 86, 89
DPRODUCT, 83, 139, 145
DSTDEV, 83, 139, 145
DSTDEVP, 83, 140, 145
DSUM, 84, 138, 140, 143-145
DVAR, 84, 140, 145
DVARP, 84, 140, 145
ERROR_TYPE, 94
EVEN, 72, 75
EXACT, 86, 89
FALSE, 63, 81, 90, 91, 96
FIND, 86, 89
FIXED, 86, 89
FLOOR, 72, 75
FV, 64, 67
GETPIVOTDATA, 84, 140
HLOOKUP, 79, 82
HOUR, 68, 70
HYPERLINK, 79, 82
IF, 21, 47, 90, 91, 93-96, 280, 304, 306, 308
INDEX, 79, 82
INDIRECT, 79, 82
INFO, 91, 94
INT, 72, 75
IPMT, 66, 67

IRR, 64, 65, 67
ISBLANK, 91, 94
ISERROR, 92, 94
ISEVEN, 92
ISLOGICAL, 92, 94
ISNA, 92, 94
ISNONTEXT, 92, 94
ISNUMBER, 92, 94
ISODD, 92
ISPMT, 66, 67
ISREF, 92, 94
ISTEXT, 92, 94
LARGE, 76, 78
LEFT, 86, 89
LEN, 86, 89
LOOKUP, 79, 82
LOWER, 86, 89
MATCH, 79, 82
MAX, 21, 74, 76, 78, 138
MAXA, 78
MID, 86, 89
MIN, 21, 74, 77, 78, 138
MINA, 77, 78
MINUTE, 68, 70
MIRR, 64, 65, 67
MOD, 49, 72, 75, 315
MONTH, 50, 68, 71
N, 92, 94, 224, 300, 311, 313
NA, 92, 94
NOT, 90, 91
NOW, 48, 68, 70
NPER, 66, 67
NPV, 64, 67
ODD, 72, 75
OFFSET, 79
OR, 90, 91, 95
PERCENTILE, 77, 78
PERCENTRANK, 77, 78
PMT, 64, 318
PMTB, 67
PPMT, 64, 67
PRODUCT, 73-75
PROPER, 86, 89
PV, 64, 67
RAND, 21, 73, 75
RANK, 77, 78
RATE, 66, 67, 146, 150
REPLACE, 86, 89
REPT, 86, 89

RIGHT, 86, 89
ROUND, 21, 75, 306
ROUNDDOWN, 73, 75
ROUNDUP, 73, 75
ROW, 49, 79, 82, 315
ROWS, 79, 82
SEARCH, 86, 89
SECOND, 68, 70
SIGN, 73, 75
SLN, 62, 67
SMALL, 77, 78
SQRT, 73, 75
STDEV, 74, 77, 78
SUBSTITUTE, 87, 89
SUBTOTAL, 73-75
SUM, 8, 21, 54, 73-75, 138, 158
SUMIF, 73- 75, 279
SUMPRODUCT, 73-75
SUMSQ, 73, 75
SYD, 62, 67
T, 87, 89
TEXT, 48, 87, 89
TIME, 68, 70
TIMEVALUE, 68, 70
TODAY, 69, 70
TRANSPOSE, 79, 82
TREND, 58, 77, 78
TRIM, 87, 89
TRUE, 63, 81, 87, 90-92
TRUNC, 73, 75
TYPE, 91, 92, 94
UPPER, 87, 89
VALUE, 87, 89
VAR, 74, 77, 78
VDB, 62, 67
VLOOKUP, 80, 82, 280
WEEKDAY, 69, 70, 71
YEAR, 50, 69, 71

Function Wizard, 6, 21, 22, 60, 97

Functions, 1, 21, 51, 53, 59, 60, 101
    Arguments, 60, 63, 65, 69, 74, 80, 84, 87,
        90, 93, 138
    Categories, 53, 58, 60-94, 137
        Database, 53, 58, 83-85, 137
        Date and Time, 68, 69, 70
        Financial, 61-67
            Annuity and Investment, 64, 65
            Depreciation, 62, 63, 66
            Interest Computation, 66

Information, 91-94
Logical, 90, 91
Lookup and Reference, 78-82
Math and Trig, 71-75
Statistical, 76-78
Text, 85-89
Create, 23
Custom, 23
Enter, 1, 6, 21, 22, 37, 60
Evaluate, 6, 97
Names, 60
Nested, 94, 95
Paste, 37
Syntax, 61-66, 69, 74, 80, 84, 87, 90, 93
Troubleshoot, 6, 97
Future Value, 65

G

Gantt Charts, 273, 282-284

Go To, 30, 32, 44

Goal Seek, 276, 317-320

Grammar, 44

Gridlines, 242

Group and Ungroup, 50, 103, 104, 120, 123-125, 181, 182
Manually, 123
Fields by Months, 181

Guess, 65

H

Headers, 227, 239-241

Help Bar, 1, 2, 4

Help Menu, Activate, 39, 44

History of Excel and Spreadsheets, 333, 334

Hot Key, 28

HTML Files, 252-254, 257, 260

Hyperlinks, 32

I

Imported Data, 85, 103, 104, 130-137, 159-161

Income Statements, 290

Industry Standards, 290

Information Functions, 91-94, 224, 300, 311, 313

Insert Menu, Activate, 39

Inside, 274

Interactive Charts, 259

Interactive PivotTable Reports, 260, 261

Interactive Reports, 249, 253-256, 261

Interest Computation Functions, 65-67, 146, 150

Interest Rate, 65, 318, 319

Invalid Data, 201, 211, 213, 214

Investment Functions, 64-67

L

LARGE Function, 76

Line Breaks, 41, 50

Lists, 32, 85, 103, 135, 137, 152-156
Create, 32, 154, 155
Creating and Managing, 85, 103, 135, 137
Data Range, 154
Edit, 152, 153
Tool Bar, 155
Total Row, 153, 156
Update, 152, 153
View, 152, 153

Live Feedback, 279-281

Location of Charts, 24

Logical Functions, 21, 47, 63, 81, 87, 90-96, 280, 304, 306, 308

Lookup and Reference Functions, 49, 78-82, 280, 315

M

Macro Sheets, 36

Macros, 40, 263-272, 296
Capture, 296

Create, 40
Delete, 271
Procedures, 271
Record, 263, 265-268
Run, 40, 263, 270
Security, 264
Select, 40
Shortcut Keys, 266-268
Stop, 271
Write, 263, 269, 270

Margin Control, 229, 238

Margins
Hide, 229

Math and Trig Functions, 8, 21, 49, 54, 71-75,
158, 279, 315

Max, 8, 120, 174

Menu Bar, 1, 2, 3, 28, 37, 294-298
Activate, 28
Customized, 294-298
Distribute, 298

Menus
Activate Data Menu, 39
Activate Edit Menu, 39
Activate File Menu, 39
Activate Format Menu, 39
Activate Help Menu, 39
Activate Insert Menu, 39
Activate Tools Menu, 39
Activate View Menu, 40
Activate Window Menu, 40
Close, 40
Select, 42

Message Window, Close, 40

MHT Extensions, 252

Min, 8, 120

Minus Sign, Trailing, 134

Mixed References. *See also* Absolute and Relative
References, 57

Modules, 271

Monthly Payment, Determine, 318, 319

Multi-level Nested Formulas / Functions, 96

Multiple Copies, Collated, 231

Multiplication, 83, 139

Multiply by Percentage, 47

N

Name Box, 1, 2, 6, 7

Names
Defined, 35, 44
Formulas, 44
Functions, 60

Nested Formulas / Functions, 94, 95
Multi-level, 96

New Line, 50
Start, 41

Non-interactive Reports, Web Page, 251-254

Number Format, 19, 34, 48, 86, 87, 148, 152

Numbering, Consecutive, 47

Numbers
Display in Millions, 47
Display in Thousands, 47
Format, 47
Join with Text, 55, 86, 88, 306, 307

O

Objects
Display, 31
Copy, 33
Hide, 31
Placeholders, 31
Select, 41

OLAP, 85, 141, 276, 277

OLAP Databases, 276, 277
Dimensions, 276

OLAP PivotTables, 85, 141

On-Line Analytical Processing . *See* OLAP, 276

Operands, 54
Absolute Values, 54
Cell References, 54
Functions, 54
Labels, 54
Ranges, 54

Operators, 54-56
Addition, 55, 56
Comparison, 55, 56
Concatenation, 55, 56
Division, 55, 56

Exponentiation, 55, 56
Multiplication, 55, 56
Negation, 55, 56
Percentage, 55, 56
Precedence, 55, 56
Reference, 55, 56
Subtraction, 55, 56

Orientation, 19, 236, 237

Outline, 103, 104, 120, 123-125
Automatically, 124
Manually, 124, 125

Outline Symbols, 31, 125

Outside, 274
Define, 274, 275
Meaningful Information, 274-276

P

Page Area, PivotTables, 172, 173, 192, 304
Show Individual Pages, 195

Page Break Preview, 229, 232-234

Page Breaks, 191, 227, 229, 232-234
Insert, 232, 233
Remove, 227, 232, 233

Page Setup, 48, 224, 227, 229, 236, 237, 241, 243, 246
Copy, 246
Settings, 48

Paper Size, 237

Passwords, 50

Paste Special, 47

Payment Periods in Annuity, 65

Payments, 64-66, 318

PDF, Print to, 245, 246, 315

Percentage Format, 34, 148, 152

Peter F. Drucker, 273, 274

PivotChart Wizard, 196, 197

PivotCharts, 196-198
Create, 196-198
Field Names, Hide, 199
Modify, 199
Reports, 196
Source Data, 196

PivotTable Report, 326
Interactive, 260, 261
Publish on Web, 249, 259-261

PivotTable Wizard, 167-173, 193

PivotTables, 84, 140, 156, 165-173, 200
Add Fields, 175
Calculated Fields. *See also* Data Fields, 165, 183-187
Create, 185
Delete, 187
Modify, 183, 187
Column Area, 172, 173
Control Reports, 298-304
Create, 156, 165, 167-173
Data Analysis, 166, 167
Data Area, 172-174
Data Fields. *See also* Calculated Fields, 172
Data Source, 170
Change, 193
Drill Down, 165, 180
Field List, 171
Field Settings, 174, 190-192, 303
External Data, 191
Field Layout, 191
Hide Field/Items, 190, 192
Numeric Data, 192
Subtotals, 190
Format, 194
Page Area, 172, 173, 192, 304
Show Individual Pages, 195
Refresh Data, 192, 194
Remove Fields, 175
Reports, 153, 165, 166, 173, 183, 185, 188-195, 259, 298, 304, 326
Format, 188-190
Row Area, 172, 173, 186, 304
Sort Data, 165
Sort Fields, 176-179
Source Data, Summarize, 166

PivotTables, OLAP, 85, 141

Precedents
Remove Tracing Arrows, 201, 209
Trace, 46, 203, 207, 208, 210

Present Value, 65

Print
Settings, 33, 230, 231, 244

Print Area, 227, 228, 234-237, 241
Clear, 236

Set, 235, 236

Print
Borders, 244
Options, 229
Quality, 237, 242, 244
Selection, 227, 230, 231
Titles, 241, 242

Print Previews, 29, 46, 227-229, 232, 235-238

Print to File, 232

Printing Time, Insert Current, 48

Private Procedures, 271

Procedures, Public or Private, 271

Product, 120

Profitability, 277-281

Project Status, 299-304

Projects, Profitability, 277-281

Public Procedures, 271

Q

Queries, 159-162, 170, 278

Quick Ratio, 304

R

R1C1 Style. *See also* A1 Style, 80, 81, 267

Random Numbers, 21, 73

Range, Replicate Copy, 45

Ranges
Add Cells, 38
Named, 95
Select, 13, 34

Rank, 77

Rate of Return, 64, 65

Ratios, 290-293, 304-309

Records, 84, 104, 107, 138, 140

Reference Functions, 49, 78-82, 280, 315

References
Absolute, 56, 147
Mixed, 57
Relative, 56

Regions, Select, 41

Relative References. *See also* Absolute and Mixed References, 56, 80

Replicate Copy, 45

Report of Errors, 203

Reporting, 304-309

Reports, 227, 249
Format, 49, 227, 244-246, 249
Interactive, 249, 253-256, 261
Non-interactive, 251, 252
PivotTable, 153, 165, 166, 173, 183, 185, 188-195, 259, 261, 298, 304, 326
Print, 29, 46, 48, 224, 227-246, 249
Blank Pages, 244
Center on Page, 238
Headers and Footers, 238-241
Page Order, 243
Pages Per Sheet, 244, 245
PDF, 245, 246
Publish on Web, 249, 254, 259-261
Scenario Summary, 326

Reports, Control, 298-304

Right-click Menus, 15, 18, 19, 38, 174, 193, 196, 210, 234, 236

Row Area, PivotTables, 172, 173, 186, 304

Row Headings, 1, 2, 5, 13, 242

Row-oriented Data Tables, 145, 146, 150

Rows, 1, 13, 84, 104, 106, 138, 140
Delete, 313
Hide, 30, 31
Insert Blank, 314
Select, 1, 13, 41
Shade Alternate, 49, 315
Unhide, 30, 34

S

Sales Forecast, 320, 322, 323, 325, 326

Save As, 10, 38, 40, 44, 250, 255

Scaling, 236, 237

Scenario Builder, 276, 317, 320-323
Add Scenario, 322
Base Scenario, 320, 323
Best Case Scenario, 323
Data, Protect, 322

Scenario Summary, 325, 326

Scroll Bars, 1, 2, 7

Scroll Lock, 13, 15

Selection, Merge into One Cell, 314

Serial Numbers, 48, 50, 68, 69, 71

Shared Workbooks, 153, 220

SharePoint, 152, 155

Sheet Properties, 228, 241-243

Sheet Tabs, 1, 2

Shortcut Keys, 28-32, 34, 36, 39, 40, 51
    Alt+1, 39
    Alt+2, 39
    Alt+3, 39
    Alt+4, 39
    Alt+5, 39
    Alt+6, 39
    Alt+7, 39
    Alt+8, 39
    Alt+9, 39
    Alt+D, 39
    Alt+Down Arrow, 30, 42
    Alt+E, 39
    Alt+Enter, 41, 50
    Alt+F, 39
    Alt+F1, 30, 40
    Alt+F11, 40, 48, 267, 269, 297
    Alt+F2, 40
    Alt+F4, 4, 40
    Alt+F8, 40
    Alt+H, 39
    Alt+I, 39
    Alt+O, 39
    Alt+PgDn, 15, 43
    Alt+PgUp, 15, 43
    Alt+Shift+F1, 29
    Alt+Shift+Left Arrow, 50
    Alt+Shift+Right Arrow, 50
    Alt+Spacebar, 41
    Alt+T, 39
    Alt+V, 40
    Alt+W, 40
    Arrow, Left or Right, 42
    Arrow, Up or Down, 42
    Backspace, 41
    Crtl+N, 9
    Crtl+O, 11, 12

Crtl+S, 10, 57, 310
Ctrl+−, 18, 34
Ctrl+', 35
Ctrl+!, 34
Ctrl+#, 34
Ctrl+$, 34
Ctrl+%, 34
Ctrl+&, 34
Ctrl+(, 34
Ctrl+), 34
Ctrl+*, 34
Ctrl+:, 35
Ctrl+;, 30, 35
Ctrl+@, 34
Ctrl+^, 34
Ctrl+_, 34
Ctrl+`, 35
Ctrl+~, 34
Ctrl++(Plus Key), 19, 35
Ctrl+0, 30, 31
Ctrl+1, 30, 31, 47, 50, 267
Ctrl+2, 31
Ctrl+3, 31
Ctrl+4, 31
Ctrl+5, 31
Ctrl+6, 31
Ctrl+7, 31
Ctrl+8, 31
Ctrl+9, 30, 31
Ctrl+A, 32
Ctrl+Arrow, 42
Ctrl+B, 32
Ctrl+Backspace, 13, 15
Ctrl+C, 16, 32
Ctrl+D, 30, 32
Ctrl+End, 43
Ctrl+Enter, 30, 41
Ctrl+F, 32
Ctrl+F1, 5, 11, 35
Ctrl+F10, 4, 36
Ctrl+F11, 36
Ctrl+F12, 11, 12, 36
Ctrl+F3, 35
Ctrl+F4, 35
Ctrl+F5, 35
Ctrl+F6, 35
Ctrl+F7, 35
Ctrl+F8, 35
Ctrl+F9, 4, 36

Ctrl+G, 32
Ctrl+H, 32
Ctrl+Home, 43
Ctrl+I, 32
Ctrl+K, 32
Ctrl+L, 32
Ctrl+N, 33
Ctrl+O, 33
Ctrl+P, 33
Ctrl+PgDn, 43
Ctrl+PgUp, 43
Ctrl+R, 17, 30, 33
Ctrl+S, 33
Ctrl+Shift+:, 30
Ctrl+Shift+0, 30
Ctrl+Shift+9, 30
Ctrl+Shift+A, 32
Ctrl+Shift+Arrow, 42
Ctrl+Shift+End, 43
Ctrl+Shift+Enter, 57, 58
Ctrl+Shift+Home, 43
Ctrl+Shift+PgDn, 43
Ctrl+Shift+PgUp, 43
Ctrl+Shift+Plus Sign, 29
Ctrl+Shift+Spacebar, 41
Ctrl+Shift+Tab, 40
Ctrl+Shift+Z, 33
Ctrl+Spacebar, 13, 41, 126
Ctrl+Tab, 29, 40
Ctrl+U, 33
Ctrl+V, 16, 17, 33
Ctrl+W, 33
Ctrl+X, 17, 33
Ctrl+Y, 33
Ctrl+Z, 6, 18, 23, 33
Delete, 42
End, 43
Enter, 41
ESC, 35, 40, 271
F1, 4, 44
F10, 28, 29, 41, 44
F11, 30, 40, 44
F12, 10, 44
F2, 6, 18, 23, 44, 202
F3, 44
F4, 44, 48
F5, 12, 30, 32, 44, 47, 49, 269, 270, 279
F7, 44
F8, 14, 37, 44, 270, 271

F9, 44
Home, 43
Page Down, 43
Page Up, 43
Shift+-, 37
Shift+., 37
Shift+/, 37
Shift+1, 36
Shift+2, 36
Shift+3, 36
Shift+4, 36
Shift+6, 36
Shift+7, 37
Shift+8, 37
Shift+9, 37
Shift+Alt+F1, 37
Shift+Arrow, 42
Shift+Enter, 37, 41
Shift+F10, 38
Shift+F11, 29, 38
Shift+F12, 38
Shift+F2, 37
Shift+F3, 22, 37, 60
Shift+F4, 30, 32
Shift+F5, 30, 32, 37
Shift+F6, 37
Shift+F8, 14, 38
Shift+F9, 38
Shift+Spacebar, 13, 37, 41
Shift+Tab, 37, 40
Spacebar, 41
Tab, 40

Shortcut Menus, 15, 18, 38, 310

Sort Order, 109-112, 120-123, 176-179

Sorted Data, 103, 104, 109-112, 120-123, 165, 176-179

Source Data, PivotCharts, 196
    Summary, 166

Spelling, 44

Split Panes. *See also* Task Pane and Work Pane, 37

Spreadsheet, Publish Single, 254

Spreadsheets, History of, 333, 334

Standard Deviation, 83, 120, 139, 140

Standard Toolbar, 1, 2, 4
    Hide, 31

Starting Tag, 54, 60

Statistical Functions, 21, 47, 58, 71-78

Status Bar, 1, 2, 8, 14, 15, 44

Subtotals, 103, 104, 120-123, 303

Sum, 8, 14, 84, 120, 140, 143, 144, 174

Syntax, 61, 63, 65, 66, 69, 74, 80, 84, 87, 90,
    93, 97-100, 219

T

Tab Scroll Buttons, 1, 2, 7, 12

Task Pane, 1, 2, 5, 35, 37

Terminology, 1, 2

Text
    Copy, 33
    Join with Dates or Numbers, 55, 86, 88, 306,
        307
    Format, 19, 31, 33, 48, 86, 87
        Capitalize, 86
        Lowercase, 86
        Uppercase, 87
        Underline, 31, 33

Text Functions, 48, 85-89

Text to Columns, 104, 130-134

Time
    Enter, 30, 35
    Insert Current, 48

Time Functions, 48, 50, 68-71

Times, Format, 34

Tips on Excel, 27

Title Bar, 1, 2, 3

Today's Date, Enter, 48

Tools Menu, Activate, 39

Toolset, Customized, 294-298

Top 10, Numeric Sort/Filter, 113, 114, 177, 178,
    191

Total Expenses, 321

Total Revenues, 321

Tracing Arrows
    Dependents, 46, 203, 208, 209
    Errors, 210
    Precedents, 46, 203, 207, 208, 210

Remove, 201, 209

Track Changes, 201, 219-221, 286

Trailing Minus Sign, 134

Transposition (Turn on Side), 79

Trend, Linear, 58, 77

Trends, 306

Triggers, Delay, 299

Type of Chart, 24

U

Undo Command, 33

Ungroup, 50

V

Validation, 104, 106, 125-130, 201, 211-214, 292
    Circles, 201, 211, 213, 214
        Clear, 201, 214
    Data, 104, 106, 125-130, 211, 212, 292
        Error Alert, 126, 129, 130, 212

Values, 65
    See All, 35

Variables, Data Tables, 145-152

Variance, 74, 77, 84, 95, 120, 140, 174

VBA, 22, 23, 263, 272

VBA Editor, 40

VBE, 263, 267, 269-271
    Auto-Fill Syntax, 269, 270

Vertical Lookup. *See* Functions, VLOOKUP, 80,
    280

View Menu, Activate, 40

Visual Basic Editor. *See* VBE, 267

Visual Basic for Applications. *See* VBA, 263

Visual Basic Modules, 264

W

Watch Windows, 201, 215, 216

Web Page, 249-261
  AutoRepublish, 257
  Interactive Reports, 253-256
  Non-interactive Reports, 251, 252, 254

Web, Publish on, 249

What-If Analysis, 145, 146, 149, 150, 317, 320

Window Menu, Activate, 40

Word Count, 311

Work Area. *See also* Task Pane, 37

Workbooks, 1, 2, 9, 13
  Close, 1, 9, 33, 35, 40
  Create, 1, 9
  Macro Sheets, 36
  Navigate Between, 13, 51
  Open, 1, 9
  Protect, 20
  Save, 1, 9
  Shared, 220
  Terminology, 1, 2
  Track Changes, 219-221
  Window
    Maximize, 36
    Minimize, 36
    Move, 35
    Size, 35
    Switch to Next, 35

Worksheets, 1, 5, 9, 12, 13
  Background, 21
  Calculate, 38, 44
  Close, 1, 9, 12, 45
  Color, 21
  Compare, 286-289
  Copy as Screenshot, 45
  Create, 1, 9

Default Number to Open, 1, 9, 46
Delete Empty, 312
Format, 1
Hide and Unhide, 1, 21, 48
Name, 1, 21
Navigate Between, 12, 46
New, Insert, 29, 37, 38
Open, 1, 9, 11
  Default Location, 11
  Files by Default, 9
Protect, 49
Publish on Web, 249, 251-257
  Single Item, 254-256
Save, 1, 9, 10
Save As, 10, 38, 40, 44, 250, 255
Select, 32, 41, 43
Sort, 312

X

XML Data, 85, 103, 135, 137, 162, 163
  Format, 163
  Import or Export, 162
  Map, 162
  Query, 162

Y

Year Functions, 50, 69

Z

Zoom Control, 29, 46, 227-229, 232, 235, 237, 238
Zoom Level, 15

HOLY MACRO! BOOKS QUICK ORDER FORM

Fax Orders: (707)-220-4510. Send this form.
E-Mail Orders: store@MrExcel.com – Online: http://www.MrExcel.com
Postal Orders: MrExcel, 13386 Judy Ave NW, PO Box 82, Uniontown OH 44685, USA

Quantity	Title	Price	Total
	Learn Excel from Mr Excel By Bill Jelen ISBN 1-932802-12-6 (853 pages – 2005)	$39.95	
	Excel for Teachers By Conmy, Hazlett, Jelen, Soucy ISBN 1-932802-11-8 (236 pages – 2006)	$24.95	
	Excel for Marketing Managers By Bill Jelen and Ivana Taylor ISBN 1-932802-13-4 (172 Pages – 2006)	$24.95	
	Excel for the CEO (CD-ROM) By P.K. Hari Hara Subramanian ISBN 1-932802-17-7 (351 pages – 2006)	$24.95	
	Office VBA Macros You Can Use Today By Gonzales et al ISBN 1-932802-06-1 (433 Pages – 2006)	$39.95	
	Holy Macro! It's 2,200 Excel VBA Examples (CD-ROM) By Hans Herber Bill Jelen and Tom Urtis ISBN 1-932802-08-8 (2200 pages – 2004)	$89.00	
	Slide Your Way Through Excel VBA (CD-ROM) By Dr. Gerard Verschuuren ISBN 0-9724258-6-1 (734 pages – 2003)	$99.00	
	Join the Excellers League (CD-ROM) By Dr. Gerard Verschuuren ISBN 1-932802-00-2 (1477 pages – 2004)	$99.00	
	Excel for Scientists (CD-ROM) By Dr. Gerard Verschuuren ISBN 0-9724258-8-8 (589 pages – 2004)	$75.00	
	Guerilla Data Analysis Using Microsoft Excel By Bill Jelen ISBN 0-9724258-0-2 (138 pages – 2002)	$19.95	
	The Spreadsheet at 25 By Bill Jelen ISBN 1-932802-04-5 (120 color pages – 2005)	$19.95	
	Grover Park George On Access By George Hepworth ISBN 0-9724258-9-6 (480 pages – 2004)	$29.95	
	Your Access to the World (CD-ROM) By Dr. Gerard Verschuuren ISBN 1-932802-03-7 (1450 pages – 2004)	$99.00	
	Access VBA Made Accessible (CD-ROM) By Dr. Gerard Verschuuren (1323 pages – 2004)	$99.00	
	DreamBoat On Word By Anne Troy ISBN 0-9724258-4-5 (220 pages – 2004)	$19.95	
	Kathy Jacobs On PowerPoint By Kathy Jacobs ISBN 0-9724258-6-1 (380 pages – 2004)	$29.95	
	Unleash the Power of Outlook 2003 By Steve Link ISBN 1-932802-01-0 (250 pages – 2004)	$19.95	
	Unleash the Power of OneNote By Kathy Jacobs & Bill Jelen (320 pages – 2004)	$19.95	
	VBA and Macros for Microsoft Excel By Bill Jelen and Tracy Syrstad ISBN 0789731290 (576 Pages – 2004)	$39.95	
	Pivot Table Data Crunching By Bill Jelen and Michael Alexander ISBN 0789734354 (275 Pages – 2005)	$29.95	

Name: _____

Address: _____

City, State, Zip: _____

E-Mail: _____

Sales Tax: Ohio residents add 6% sales tax

Shipping by Air: **US:** $4 for first book, $2 per additional book. $1 per CD.
       International: $9 for first book, $5 per additional book. $2 per CD
       FedEx available on request at actual shipping cost.

Payment: Check or Money order to "MrExcel" or pay with VISA/MC/Discover/AmEx:
      Card #:_____ Exp.:_____
      Name on Card: _____

Bulk Orders: Ordering enough for the entire staff? Save 40% when you order six or more of any one title.